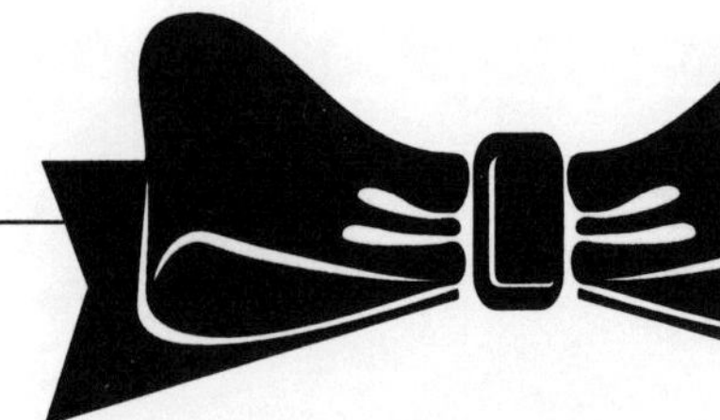

PATRI
& Her

Eastern Kentucky Soldi

A Gift to

---

from

GREENUP COUNTY PU
614 MAIN ST
GREENUP, KY

PATRIOTS & Heroes

Eastern Kentucky Soldiers of WWII

PATRIOTS & Heroes

Eastern Kentucky Soldiers of WWII

by

Jack D. Ellis

with a Foreword by

James M. Gifford

Jesse Stuart Foundation
Ashland, Kentucky
2003

First Edition

Library of Congress Cataloging-in-Publication Data

Ellis, Jack D., 1927-
Patriots & heroes : eastern Kentucky soldiers of WWII / by Jack Ellis.
p. cm.
Includes bibliographical references and index.
ISBN 1-931672-12-1
1. World War, 1939-1945--Kentucky. 2. Soldiers--United States--Biography. 3. Marines--United States--Biography. 4. Airmen--United States--Biography. 5. Kentucky--History--1865- 6. Kentucky--Biography. I. Title: Patriots and heroes. II. Title

D769.85.K4 E44 2002
940.54'1273'0922769--dc21

2002034134

Published by:
Jesse Stuart Foundation
P.O. Box 669 • Ashland, Ky 41105

DEDICATION

Over 258,000 young men did not return from WW II, including sixty from my hometown of Morehead, Kentucky. Many of those sixty were childhood friends and will always remain young in my memory. This book, written by one who thankfully returned safely from WW II, is tearfully and respectfully dedicated to those who did not return. **THEY ARE THE TRUE HEROES!**

Using a blanket as a stretcher, Marines carry a wounded comrade down Mt. Suribachi. (Yank).

ACKNOWLEDGMENTS

There are so many who helped in preparing this book that it is impossible to name them all. However, at the risk of missing some, I want to gratefully acknowledge many of those who have significantly contributed to this book. First, my deep appreciation goes to Mrs. Ruth (Crisp) Robinson, my former secretary, who patiently typed and re-typed the manuscript and stored it on a computer disk. Without her professional assistance this book could never have been written. Also, a very special thanks to Mrs. Helen Williams, a former colleague at Morehead State University's Camden-Carroll Library, for her valuable assistance in editing this book.

My deepest appreciation goes to those "old soldiers" of WW II included in this publication who unselfishly shared their stories with me. I'm sure many times they did not feel like talking, yet they were always gracious on the phone or in person. Sadly, J.T. Daugherty, who shared his story with this writer, died before his story could be published. My deep appreciation to his widow and to all of the wives, widows, and family members who helped in preparing this publication. Their assistance was invaluable.

This book is the result of five years of interviews, research, and writing. Because it was written for a general public audience, I chose not to use formal footnotes. However, I have included an extensive bibliography of sources used for this publication including interviews, memoirs, letters, periodicals, and books. It is my intention to present realistic accounts as seen through the eyes of those men who experienced WW II.

Members of American Legion Post 126 in Morehead, Kentucky, were especially helpful in sharing their records. Also, a special thanks goes to Tim Holbrook for his expertise in preparing the photographs for this book and Tim Sloan for scanning those photographs on to a computer disk.

Among others who helped in the preparation of this book are the staff members of the Morehead State University Library, Rowan County Public Library, and the Fleming County Public Library. Their help is gratefully acknowledged. Also, I want to thank Dr. James Gifford and Brett Nance for their expert advice in putting this book together, as well as John M. Trowbridge, Kentucky Military Historian, for his many valuable suggestions.

Lastly, I want to publicly thank Janis Ruth, my wife of over fifty years, for her valuable assistance, patience, and understanding during the writing of this book.

Jack D. Ellis

TABLE OF CONTENTS

PART III

Iwo Jima: The Flag, Fight, and Photo

PART IV

Kentucky's Flying Leatherneck: In War and Peace

PART V

"Roaring Bull": 35 Missions Over Germany

PART VI

Pearl Harbour Survivor

PART VII

PART VIII

PART IX

★★★★★

"They were patriots for what they did and heroes for what they were willing to do"

James M. Gifford

★★★★★

PUBLISHER'S FOREWORD

Historically, the people of Appalachia have played a major role in fighting for and defending America's freedom. From Colonial times to our current war against terrorism, Appalachian men (and to some extent women)[1] have been at the forefront of battle.

Soldiering was easy for mountain boys because their life experiences often provided the skills necessary for survival and success. They came from a rugged, agrarian background that prepared them for the hardships of military life. Most were able marksmen. They could outmarch and outride their urban counterparts. They were comfortable out of doors and accustomed to living off the land. In many respects, soldiering was easier than the life of grinding work and economic privation they returned to at the end of every war.

In the Revolutionary War, "the over mountain men" from the Watauga settlement helped to defeat the British at Kings Mountain. The Colonists won their independence on fields of battle, and Appalachian marksmen contributed to every American victory. Four decades later, America fought another war for independence. Although history books often present the War of 1812 as the military version of a comic opera, the fact remains: we were fighting the British again, and, if they had won, we would have lost our hard-earned freedoms and probably returned to a colonial status. Andrew Jackson, the hero of the War of 1812, was a prototypical backwoodsman who symbolized a new age in American history and rode the wave of his popularity as the hero of the Battle of New Orleans to the White House in 1828.

As the antebellum period continued, men from Appalachia continued to play a major role in our military efforts. In 1836, the heroes of the Texas War for Independence were men like Jim Bowie and Davy Crockett. Ten years later, Uncle Sam beat the drums of war, and a new generation of mountain boys marched forth to help us win the Mexican War. Tennessee is called the Volunteer State because of the high incidence of volunteerism that began with the Mexican War and continued into the twentieth century. Many mountain counties met their draft quotas in World War I and World War II entirely through volunteers.

The Colonial wars, the American War for Independence, and the continuing military conflicts of the antebellum period paled to insignificance compared to the Civil War, which was often fought in the heart of Appalachia. Mountain boys served with bravery and distinction on both sides. When the war ended, no section of America had suffered more than Appalachia.

Before the Civil War, the people of Appalachia had been prosperous, independent, prideful, and literate. The Civil War and the post-reconstruction discriminations of home rule greatly undermined the quality of life in Appalachia. By the turn of the century, Appalachia was an island of poverty in a national sea of plenty.

Historical circumstances worked against our region in the nineteenth century, but historical events of the twentieth century would help Appalachia rebuild its quality of life. For example, World War I provided gainful employment for tens of thousands. As was often the case, an Appalachian soldier became the hero who captured the popular imagination. Alvin York, a mountain boy from Tennessee's Cumberland plateau, went out on patrol in 1918 and singlehandedly killed twenty-five Germans with twenty-five shots and returned with 132 German soldiers whom he had captured. The men who surrendered to York had twenty-five machine guns among them. When York marched his captives to division headquarters, his commander remarked, "Well, York, I hear you have captured the whole damn Germany army." York saluted and modestly asserted,

"No sir, I just got 132 of them."

Kentucky produced a number of heroic soldiers like Alvin York. Sergeant Willie Sandlin of Leslie County assaulted three entrenched German machine gun nests. Armed only with grenades and a rifle, Sandlin fought and killed all the occupants, captured a battalion headquarters, and created a hole in the German lines. Like Alvin York, Sandlin was awarded the Congressional Medal of Honor.

Another Eastern Kentuckian, Peter McCoy of Pike County, fought his way into a German trench, killed seven enemy soldiers, and captured seventeen more. At the end of the battle, his uniform and the pack on his back bore 177 bullet holes. McCoy was one of eight men from his company who survived this battle. For his valor, McCoy was awarded our country's second highest military honor, the Distinguished Service Cross.

Three decades later Appalachian men and women helped America fight a two-front war that spanned the entire globe. Franklin Sousley, from Fleming County, was one of the six men who raised the flag on Mount Suribachi at Iwo Jima. Sousley was killed in action three weeks later, but many of his Appalachian brothers and sisters returned to a hero's welcome. More importantly, they derived the educational benefits of the G.I. Bill, and used their education and training to revitalize the quality of life in their Appalachian homeland.

Another famous—albeit indirectly—Eastern Kentucky soldier of the World War II era was Robert Lee Stewart of Letcher County.[2] Stewart served in "F" Company, 27th Infantry regiment of the 25th Infantry Division. Soldiering with him was James Jones, a young man from Robinson, Illinois, who later wrote a trilogy of WWII novels: *From Here to Eternity, The Thin Red Line*, and *Whistle*. In each novel, a principal character is a heroic rifleman from Appalachia. Although Jones gives him a different name in each novel, all three were modeled after Stewart. In a letter to editor Maxwell Perkins, Jones saluted Stewart's alter ego, Robert E. Lee Prewitt, as a man of "intense personal pride." Later, he described the Stewart/Prewitt character as an example of Appalachian men as great combat soldiers and observed, "I have seen such men do absolutely unbelievable things in combat." Through his fictional persona, Robert Lee Stewart became a symbol for the Appalachian soldiers of World War II, just as Alvin York and Willie Sandlin represented mountain soldiers of World War I.

Sadly, the war to make the world safe for democracy and the war to end all wars did not eliminate international warfare, and throughout the rest of the twentieth century Appalachian men continued to march forth in service to their country in Korea, Vietnam, and the Middle East. Research by East Tennessee State University's Pat Arnow and Bert Allen, a professor of Psychology at Milligan College, indicates that Appalachian soldiers in the Korean War comprised eight percent of the fighting force and received eighteen percent of the Medals of Honor. In the Vietnam War, Appalachian soldiers were awarded thirteen percent of the Medals of Honor, although only seven percent of the fighting forces were from the Appalachian region.

John M. Trowbridge, a freelance military historian, has compiled a list of ninety-two men with ties to Kentucky who have been awarded the Congressional Medal of Honor; twenty are from the Appalachian counties. In the Korean War, all five of Kentucky's Medal of Honor winners were from Appalachia: Captain William E. Barber of Morgan County; Corporal John Walton Collier of Greenup County; First Lieutenant Carl H. Dodd from Harlan County; Private David M. Smith from Rockcastle County, and Private First Class Ernest Edison West from Greenup County. These statistics testify to the significant role that Appalachian people have played in America's military history, but statistics alone can never completely capture the enormous contribution these men have made.

We begin another century of American life with many of the same sad themes of our past. Americans continue to fight for the freedoms that we won on the field of battle in 1776, and the people of Appalachia continue to play a major role in our military efforts.

Ask any old soldier about heroes, and he will tell you that the real heroes are the men and women who did not return. They were young people in an enemy's land, far from home and the people they loved. They wanted to live. They wanted to come back home, marry, build a home and a life. But they paid the ultimate price for the freedoms and privileges that we Americans enjoy today.

All of us owe a great debt to America's soldiers. Every one of us should sit down and make a list of the freedoms we love and the comforts we enjoy. Look at your list. It's a copy written in ink. The original was written in the bright red blood of an American soldier.

This book does not—and could not—provide the story of each of our region's patriots and heroes. The men described in this book are from a five county area of Eastern Kentucky: Rowan, Bath, Morgan, Elliott and Fleming. But they march across these pages as representatives of every Eastern Kentucky patriot and hero, just as every Eastern Kentucky soldier represents Appalachian soldiers from many other states.

Looking back on Appalachia's role in American military history, we can easily overemphasize the popular heroes like Andrew Jackson, Davy Crockett, and Alvin York and not provide enough praise for the thousands and thousands of other men and women who served their country quietly and bravely. The book that you hold in your hands is a testimony to unrecognized heroes. It honors every man and woman from Appalachia who served our country. They were patriots for what they did, and heroes for what they were willing to do. Patriots and heroes, I salute you.

James M. Gifford
Ashland, Kentucky
June 25, 2002

[1] The Jesse Stuart Foundation is preparing to publish *Women In War: Appalachian Profiles*, a book that focuses on the role that Appalachian women have played in America's war efforts.

[2] See Loyal Jones' fine essay "James Jones' Appalachian Soldier in His World War II Trilogy" in the *Journal of the Appalachian Studies Association*, 1991. Jones is retired from his long-time position as Director of Berea College's Appalachian Center. He has published numerous articles and books, and he is a popular speaker on Appalachian topics. Loyal Jones has been a good friend to me and to the Jesse Stuart Foundation, and, like people throughout the region, I am grateful for all that he has done.

Jack Ellis, Cpl., Army Air Corps, 1944-1947.

INTRODUCTION

News Anchor Tom Brokaw, in his two national best-selling books, called the veterans of WW II the "Greatest Generation." Some have called them the "noble generation," while others have referred to them as the "heroic generation." But this writer thinks of them as the "unselfish generation." They were men and women who grew up during a devastating depression and knew what it was to sacrifice and do without. They were the citizen soldiers who unselfishly answered the call of their country and became the unheralded freedom fighters of their generation.

They knew what it was to say goodbye tearfully to those they dearly loved. They knew what it was to board a train and wave a red-eyed goodbye out the window as the train slowly pulled away—never knowing if you would ever see each other again. They knew what it meant to be separated from family for months and years. They knew what it was to prepare rigorously for the physical and emotional strain of being taught to kill.

The WW II generation knew what it was to be placed in a kill or be killed arena. They knew what it was to see their comrades blown to pieces in battle, shot out of the skies, or sunk at sea. But they never wavered in their resolve. They believed their country needed them and that they were called upon to do a job, and they were determined to do that job to the best of their ability. Certainly they never thought of themselves as heroes. Most thought of themselves as being at the right place at the right time, or at the wrong place at the wrong time, depending on your point of view. But looking at the WW II generation through the telescope of time, they were an extraordinary and an unselfish generation. Their goal was to win the war and come home.

This book recalls the suffering and sacrifice of a representative group of that extraordinary generation. It profiles personal experiences of combat veterans who were prisoners of war, missing in action, killed in action and those that returned safely. Because of their experiences, they shared unbreakable bonds of brotherhood that have lasted a lifetime.

Of the 15,000,000 men in WW II, there were millions of heroes by today's definition of "hero." Yet few of those men would ever classify themselves as heroes. But they stood tall at a time in their nation's history when freedom was threatened. They should never be forgotten. This book is an attempt to preserve their memory by profiling a few of those men from the Appalachian region of Kentucky. Their stories are representative of the heartache, horror, sacrifice, suffering, and separation endured by many of those citizen soldiers during WW II. Those brave, peace-loving men answered the call of their country and sacrificed years out of the most productive periods of their lives. They gave up some of their personal freedom in order to preserve this nation's freedom. They did so without complaint because they recognized the reality that this nation's freedom and liberty hung in the balance. Over 268,000 men were listed as "KIA," killed in action, or "MIA," missing in action, or "POW," prisoners of war. Those KIAs and MIAs would never come home after a hard day's work to a wife and family, or grow old together with the love of their life.

Vague memories dimmed by time are about all that remains of those MIAs and KIAs. Their names are included in the more than 268,000 men who died in defense of freedom during WW II. The only evidence that some of those KIAs and MIAs ever existed is a cross or head stone in a foreign land, or a foot stone at a cemetery in their hometown, or their name on a plaque on a memorial wall in a public square in their hometown.

Many of those surviving POWs suffered unbelievable hardships or inhuman treatment as prisoners of war. Their life was a living hell for many months or years, and half of them died in enemy prison camps. Those surviving prisoners of war continued to suffer post-traumatic stress syndrome for the remainder of their lives.

Vast numbers of America's citizen soldiers returned to their homes and families following WW II. Although they had survived, their lives were forever changed. Many subconsciously felt guilty because they had survived and their comrades had not. Many suffered physical wounds that were clearly visible, but their psychological and emotional scars were hidden from view. Perhaps their immediate family were the only ones to know about those hidden scars. Many times no one but God knew of the mental and emotional anguish because they suffered in silence. One veteran this writer interviewed, now deceased, confessed to me that he didn't think God would ever forgive him because he was a sniper in WW II and had killed many men. After some prayer and counseling, I was able to help him to realize that God would forgive him. Emotional scars run deep and are usually more difficult to treat than physical wounds.

The psychiatrists, sociologists, educators, and clergy in the post WW II era theorized that those men trained to kill in war would have great difficulty readjusting to peaceful living. A great many articles appeared in newspapers and professional journals saying, "When those men who had been trained to kill return, they might become violent at the slightest provocation." That never happened because the men who had seen so much killing and devastation only wanted to get home to a peaceful life and return to normalcy. Their goal was to get a job, education, to return to their previous job and/or get married. Hence, the postwar baby boom. They became busy with life and just wanted to forget the suffering and heartache they had known. It was for that reason many refused to talk about their experience for over fifty years.

After many of those WW II veterans had reared their children and retired, they began to reflect on their lives. They realized again just how fortunate they were to have survived. Many felt an obligation to tell their story in order to keep alive the memory of those who did not return. Most men interviewed for this book agreed they were telling their story after fifty years hoping that America would remember the men who did not return as well as the horror, pain, and suffering caused by war. Sadly some died after being interviewed and before this book was published.

Those citizen soldiers of WW II had seen so much death and destruction caused by war. They wanted Americans never to forget the horror of war. Prior to September 11, 2001, mainland USA had never been touched by the devastion of war. But that all changed on September 11, 2001, when this nation watched horrified, live and in living color, the death, and destruction caused by mad men. Sadly, it took that terrible tragedy of September 11, 2001, to cause Americans to really understand what the servicemen witnessed during WW II. They had seen cities leveled by bombs. They had personally witnessed starvation, suffering, devastation, death, and disease firsthand.

This writer returned home from WW II in Europe after seeing cities leveled by bombs and children starving. I also went through the infamous Dachau concentration camp where 237,000 innocent people were killed by the Nazis. When I returned home, I tried to tell my friends and neighbors what I had seen, but they never could really understand. But after September 11, 2001, America understands more clearly that there is evil in this world that must be opposed at all times. When this nation's freedom is threatened, it must be preserved at all costs.

Many historians have divided recent US history by the attack on Pearl Harbor. December 7, 1941, was considered a hinge of US history. Those living at that time, who were at least of elementary school age, never forgot where they were on that sad Sunday. We knew something tragic had happened that would forever change our lives. It had and it did! Similarly, those living on September 11, 2001, at least of elementary school age, will never forget where they were as they watched, stunned and horrified as airplanes crashed into buildings and thousands perished as those buildings came crashing down. Never again will Americans have to be told about the suffering, death, and devastation of war because they have now witnessed it first hand.

This book is written as a reminder of the horror of war. It is a testimony of man's inhumanity to man under wartime conditions. It is also a reflection of the resiliency of the human spirit while living in subhuman conditions. It is a record of the indomitable human nature that never gives up hope even under the most hopeless conditions. That has been the record of the American soldier, sailor, and marine in WW II and throughout history. That whenever and wherever this nation's freedom was threatened, its citizens answered that call to protect and preserve that freedom.

The servicemen of WW II believed that no sacrifice was too great and no suffering too severe to preserve this nation's fragile freedom. Those citizen soldiers of WW II were the freedom fighters of their generation. It may be that following September 11, 2001, every American of every background and culture may again be called upon to sacrifice some of their personal freedom in the fight against evil madmen.

Jack D. Ellis

Walking the First Mile as a POW

With their guards on each side and the Tiger tank trailing behind, the thirty-two prisoners were marched back down the road they thought was controlled by the Americans. As they marched two abreast out of the aid station, they looked over in the edge of the woods at the dead bodies of their beloved buddies. It was a traumatic sight of mangled, bloody bodies. The face of one of the band members had been blown away, and it was obvious the five dead men went quickly and never knew what hit them.

PART I

MEDIC TO POW: SOME WALKED EAST

Sergeant Phil Hardin's Story

Welcome to Hell

We climbed the rugged hills in Tennessee
And marched through Indiana's mud and rain,
A winter in Kentucky's snow, yet we
Were warmed by fire of youth and hearts aflame.
Farewell, mighty woman with torch in hand
For Lafayette and you we do or die:
Once more we sail to that invaded land
In answer to the call of freedom's cry.
But there, no welcome lady on the beach...
Wrecks and twisted steel scattered on the shore;
And out at sea as far as eye could reach
Were barges, cruisers, battleships and more.
And yet there was a stillness on that day
As if each one was given time to pray.

We quit the beach and entered hedgerow land
Cattle tokens gave thoughts of farm and fun;
No mercy given here to beast or man
And all the cows lie swollen in the sun.
"Welcome to Hell!" this sign near Carentan
The Screaming Eagles gone for needed rest;
A lad too young to shave became a man
For we were facing Jerry at his best.
July fourth, independence on the brink
The roar of all the guns became a flood;
Oh, Jefferson--what you declared in ink
Each hedgerow claimed a thousand times in blood!
Sweet passing youth, yours not to reason why,
Too young to vote, yet old enough to die!

Phil Hardin

CHAPTER 1
Beginning Steps as a Medic

And he went to him and bound up his wounds…
and took care of him. Luke 10:34

During WW II there were millions of men who could be called heroes given today's definition of "hero" in the military service. But chief among those countless unsung heroes of WW II were the men of the Medical Corps. Those men were found in the thick of battle bravely facing enemy shells, bombs, and bullets with only first aid equipment, blood plasma, pain medicine, and crude litters for transporting wounded soldiers. Their only defense was the bright red cross on a white background displayed prominently on each shoulder. They hoped and prayed enemy soldiers would respect that international humanitarian symbol as they peered through their gun sights. Sometimes they would and sometimes they wouldn't. Even when the medics themselves became targets, that did not stop them from their dedicated task of helping the wounded and dying. Around the world during WW II wherever deadly bullets, bombs, and artillery fragments brutally tore through an American uniform into American flesh and bone, spilling American blood, the first cry heard was "Medic." Wherever that plaintive cry for help went out there was usually a medical aid man that responded without regard for personal safety. Those military medical men moved quickly to find the wounded, provide whatever aid they could to ease the pain and suffering, and get the wounded back to safety and more professional medical care.

This is the story of Phil Hardin, one of those medical aid men who bravely faced the enemy's weapons without regard for his own personal safety and provided aid and comfort to America's wounded soldiers on the battlefields of France. He was later captured by the Germans and survived eight months of what he described as "hell" in a German prisoner-of-war camp outside Berlin.

Philemon A. Hardin was born February 25, 1922, on a small family farm located on Ramey's Creek in rural Rowan County, Kentucky. It was in an isolated area deep in the hills of Eastern Kentucky. He was the oldest of five boys born to Dorsey, Sr., and Zona (McKenzie) Hardin. Phil, as he was known by his friends, attended the McKenzie School, a one-room school located near the banks of the Licking River about one mile from his home. During the elementary grades, he was in school with a lovely little girl by the name of Margena Ellington, who would later become his lifelong companion.

As a child of the depression, young Phil was no stranger to sacrifice and hard work. As the oldest boy in the family, he began work at an early age in order to help support the family. Each boy had daily chores to do before and after school. There was milking, feeding the animals, and working in the fields of corn and tobacco. Also, as the boys got older, they went to work at their grandfather's sawmill and in the log woods to supplement the family income. Jobs were scarce and the outlook bleak in rural eastern Kentucky in the 1920s and 1930s, and Phil would sometimes work on neighboring farms chopping tobacco and thinning corn for 5 cents an hour.

As the nation's economy began to improve, sixteen-year-old Phil Hardin, like thousands of other young people from the Eastern Kentucky hills, moved north across the Ohio River for greater job opportunities. He lived with his aunt, Pearl Holler, near Middletown, Ohio, and did farm work. In 1940 Phil moved farther north to Shelby, Ohio, and went into construction work. He was there on December 7, 1941, when Japan bombed Pearl Harbor drawing the U.S. into WW II. Following the outbreak of the war, he returned to Middletown, Ohio, and went to work in the steel mills. It was hot, hard, back-breaking work but the pay was good and Phil worked cheerfully because he was building a future. During that time he kept in close touch with his childhood sweetheart, Margena Ellington. On April 11, 1942, Phil and Margena were married following her high-school graduation. After a brief honeymoon, they began their life together in a small apartment in Middletown, Ohio.

Beginning in 1940, every young American male between the ages of 18 and 30 was required to register to be drafted into military service. Young Phil Hardin was one of the first to register, and the specter of being drafted into the Army cast a pall over his marriage. It was exactly five months following his marriage that he, like millions of American men during WW II, received a letter from the president of the United States. The letter began with: "GREETINGS: You are hereby directed to report for military service."

Volunteered for the Medical Corps

Phil was ordered to report to Ft. Thomas, Kentucky, for his Army physical exam. He passed with flying colors and was sworn into the Army on October 14, 1942. Following his exam, he returned to Middletown, Ohio, to await his orders to report for basic training. In Middletown R.C. Caudill, the Middletown Church of God minister from Morehead, Kentucky, gave Phil a small pocket-sized New Testament and Psalms. Phil carried that small book with him throughout his entire military life, and it was a constant source of spiritual strength for him. Phil Hardin was ordered to report to Camp Atterbury, Indiana, for basic training on November 1, 1942. Following aptitude tests and psychological screening, he volunteered as a medical technician and was assigned in the 2nd Battalion Medical Training Unit of the

330th Infantry Regiment in the 83rd Infantry Division. There he became friends with four men and together they later became known as the fabulous five of the 2nd Battalion Medical Corps. Those five would serve together for the next two years.

Those five men were:

(1) Phil Hardin was from the hills of Eastern Kentucky and was tough and wiry as the proverbial pine knot and as stable as the giant oak trees that cast their roots deep into the soil of his beloved Kentucky hills. He was deep of faith and strong of heart. Phil Hardin grew up walking everywhere he went because the family had no car. That walking would serve him well later in his military career.

(2) Bud Friend was from northern Ohio near the Indiana border. He grew up in a small rural village where everyone knew his neighbor and was always willing to help others. Bud Friend was a shy, quiet, and reserved young man. His last name was Friend and he was indeed a friend throughout two years of trials and tribulations. He was a man you could trust with your life.

(3) Dale Hill was from Marshall, a small town in northern Michigan. Although he was extremely near-sighted, he memorized the eye chart and managed to pass the exam to get into service. In spite of wearing glasses, he had been drafted by the St. Louis Cardinals baseball team and had played a couple of years in their minor leagues. But his dream of becoming a major league baseball player ended when his Uncle Sam drafted him into military service.

(4) Alex Scepanski was a burly, first-generation Polish-American fisherman from the state of Connecticut. His father and mother had migrated to America from Poland after WW I. Al had a deep love for his native Poland and an intense hatred for the Germans. Little did he realize how much of his native Poland he would see before the war ended.

(5) Ben Johnson was a soft-spoken southerner who grew up south of Nashville, Tennessee. He was a country music fan, and, like most

servicemen, was proud of his heritage. But when things got tough, as they did many times, Ben Johnson was like a rock and never allowed the circumstances to get him down.

These five men began their military service together, trained together, served together, and suffered many harrowing experiences together.

Those five homesick young soldiers received their basic training at Camp Atterbury, Indiana. There were five months of grueling physical exercise, forced cold winter marches in the snow, training films, first aid classes, and firearms training. But the worst part of basic training was being away from home and family. Although Phil was in the Medical Corps, he was still required to qualify with a rifle on the firing range. When the time came for him to fire for record, he did not even have a rifle, but had to borrow one to fire for score. Phil had grown up with firearms, and he scored as an expert marksman even without practicing. Also during basic training all soldiers come into contact for the first time with their first sergeant. Phil's first sergeant was six-foot-four, two-hundred-ten pounds, lean and mean. He was a hard-driving, tough-talking typical first sergeant responsible for turning one-hundred-fifty raw recruits into tough fighting men. He bragged about how tough he was and how he couldn't wait to get into combat. He was the best drill sergeant in the company. He intimidated the men at first, but as soon as they toughened up, they didn't let him scare them one bit. Unfortunately, he did make life miserable for the Mexican-Americans in the outfit and abused many of them.

In April, 1943, all of the medics of the 83rd Division were ordered to report to Missouri for advanced first-aid training. That part of Phil's training included how to splint a broken limb, apply pressure bandages to bloody battlefield wounds, treat for shock, give blood plasma, and give injections for pain and wounds. The remainder of the 2nd Battalion was ordered to the hills of east Tennessee for battlefield maneuvers. After completing his advanced training as a medic, young Hardin was ordered to report back to the 2nd Battalion in Tennessee.

He was especially glad to get back with his friends; however, they were there only two weeks before the whole division was transported to Camp Breckinridge, Kentucky.

Phil remembered the winter of 1943-44 as a winter with lots of snow even in the relatively southern area of the Kentucky-Tennessee border. That winter, the men of the 83rd Division lived outside in tents most of the time even in the rain, snow and sleet that sometimes came out of the angry sky with a vengeance. (The men of the 83rd Division did not realize it then, but they were being trained for brutal winter warfare the following year). However, the men's morale remained high despite the harsh weather and primitive living conditions. Phil recalled, "They were all young tough and strong, and filled with the fire of youth and wonder about what their future held."

Rumors were always rampant in the Army. One of the rumors flying from the latrines of the 83rd Division was they were going to Alaska because of their cold-weather training. Another rumor was they were going to the Bavarian Alps in southern Germany to capture Hitler's alpine fortress. In any event, by February 1, 1944, they had received their orders to ship out, and they knew not where they were going. Before leaving the states, every man was given a two-week furlough home. One half of the men were furloughed the first two weeks and the other half were given their leave the second two weeks. Phil Hardin recalled he received his furlough in the second group during the last half of February, 1944. The men of the 83rd Division had not been home for one year.

Phil wrote in his memoirs, "Waiting at home for me was Margena, my beautiful twenty-year-old wife and Larry, my precious one-year-old son." He recalled that those two weeks were the most fleeting time of his life and that each 24 hours seemed only a passing moment.

Margena and Phil spent those two weeks visiting family and friends in Morehead. They also were trying to find out where every one of their Morehead friends now in the military service was sta-

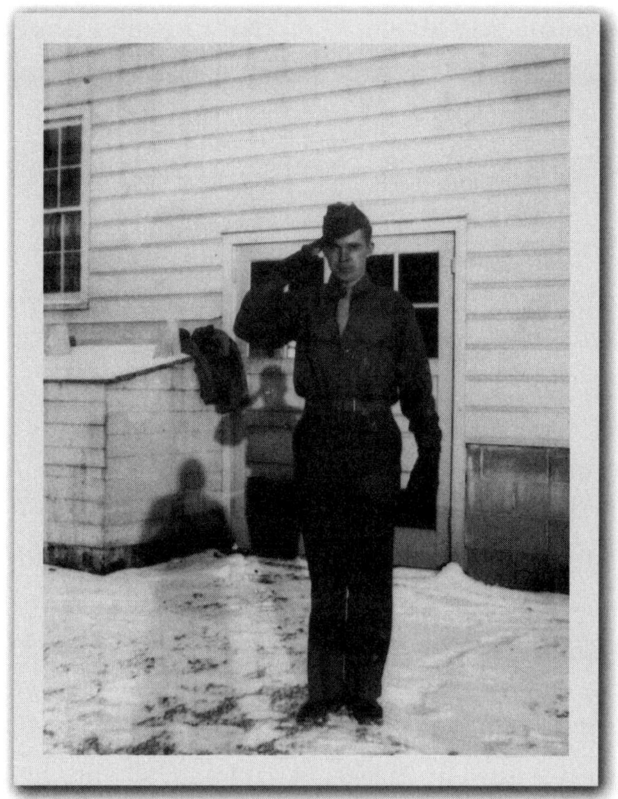

Phil Hardin during winter training in the states.

tioned. They soon learned they were stationed all over the world, even in places unknown to them. It was then Phil pondered where he would be going upon his return to duty.

When at last the time came for the young couple to say goodbye, it was a tearful farewell at the Morehead train station. Phil did not know where he was going or how long he would be gone. Neither of them knew when they would see each other again, or *if* they would ever see each other again. Phil only knew, as did millions of GI's in WW II, that he was in for the duration of the war plus six months, if he survived that long. It was a heart-rending time for the two young people, and Phil wrote in his memoirs a portion of an Emily Dickinson poem which said, "Parting is all we know of heaven and all we need of hell." The young soldier said, "At that time and unknown to me, I had a rendezvous with destiny which involved far more hell than our parting." The couple said their tearful goodbyes, and Phil returned to duty at Camp Breckinridge, Kentucky, on March 1, 1944.

The 83rd Division Ships Out

The last week in March the men of the 2nd Battalion were transported on a crowded troop train from Camp Breckinridge to Camp Shanks, New York. There they were reunited with the rest of the 83rd Division. The men then received their shots and were processed in preparation for sailing out to parts yet unknown. On April 5, 1944, 5,000 of the 20,000 men of the 83rd Division lined up on the dock with all their equipment and were packed like sardines into the British troopship *Orion*. As the *Orion* sailed that afternoon out of the busy New York harbor it passed near that majestic symbol of freedom, the Statue of Liberty. Phil Hardin, like millions of men whose last image of home was the "Mighty Lady" with her torch of freedom held high, wondered deep within his heart, "Will I ever see her again?"

As the *Orion* sailed northeast out of the harbor, it joined a mighty convoy of troopships forming in the Atlantic Ocean. Those ships held the remainder of the 83rd Division plus other units. He recalled, "Our troopship was one of the troopships with each carrying 5,000 soldiers. The convoy soon joined a mighty armada of naval military might. Mingled among the transports were four cruisers and one battleship." As they peered toward the horizon the men could see several destroyers had formed a circle around them, and they assumed there were American submarines under the sea. Even with all that naval firepower for protection, those "ground pounders" were somewhat apprehensive and wondered if a German U-Boat might slip through that protective net on a dark night and fire a lucky torpedo.

The eleven-day voyage across the cold North Atlantic in April was uneventful except for the rough seas and forty-foot waves. There were also white, ghost-like icebergs that appeared on the horizon, and occasionally a whale would be spotted as it cleared its blow hole and blew a spout of water high into the air. The rough seas caused many of the men to become seasick. They would be bent over in the heads (Navy word for bathroom) as well as hanging over the rail on deck heaving when there was nothing left to heave.

The troopship carrying Phil Hardin and the 83rd Division went north of Ireland then south through the Irish Sea and landed at Liverpool, England, on April 16, 1944. The men disembarked from the *Orion* and were transported by rail to Wales where they spent more time training under combat conditions. They were there on June 6, 1944, when they received the news that the Allies had embarked on what General Eisenhower called the "Great Crusade." It was the invasion of fortress Europe by the Americans, British, French, and Canadians. The medics of the 83rd were thankful when they received the report that the Allies had successfully gained a foothold in France. But all of them knew that soon they would be involved in that bitter struggle. That was why they were there and why they had been trained.

The Great Crusade Begins

Following the June 6, 1944, D-Day invasion, the 83rd Division moved to southern England and ports on the English Channel. On June 24, 1944, they were transported across the Channel on board the British ship *Rapier*. They landed on Omaha Beach about noon on June 24th. As they disembarked, they could see hulls of partially sunken ships and twisted steel fortifications up and down the beach. Also there were ships everywhere amid those wrecks still unloading the tools of war.

The men disembarked from their ship and quickly moved across the hallowed sand where so much American blood had been spilled 18 days before. Although they were not yet under fire, the men of the

83rd moved rapidly inland into the green fields of France. Everywhere they looked the earth was scarred by war. There were deep bomb and artillery craters partially filled with putrid water. Trees were blown out of the ground blocking the roadways, and everywhere there were bloated carcasses of dead cattle rotting in the hot June sun. As Phil Hardin and the 83rd division moved farther inland, he recalled seeing a crude sign nailed on a tree along the roadside saying, "Welcome to Hell," courtesy of the 101st Airborne. At that time Phil thought to himself what kind of hell must it have been to the men who landed here on June 6, but little did he realize his own personal hell lay ahead of him.

By the end of the day on June 26, 1944, the men of the 83rd Division had moved one mile inland and set up camp for the night. On the morning of June 27, the men broke camp with orders to move south and relieve the men of 101st Airborne Division who were the first Americans to land on D-Day when they parachuted out of their C-47 transport planes behind enemy lines to disrupt German transportation and communications during the invasion. The Screaming Eagles of the 101st Airborne Division had been in combat for 18 days without rest. They had taken heavy losses during that time, and those beleaguered men urgently needed rest from the battle.

As the 83rd Division moved south through France, Phil said the terrain began to change. They went through beautiful farmland, orchards, woodlands, and some swamplands. The green pasturelands were surrounded by hedgerows. Those hedgerows were mounds of dirt about six feet high and six feet across with closely planted hedges and tangled vines intertwined on top of the mounds. They served as fences for farmers and were almost impossible to cross. They could sometimes even stop a tank. Phil recalled, "As we marched southward we could hear the roar of artillery fire and see our planes flying overhead, and we knew we were approaching the enemy lines."

The 83rd Division made contact with the 101st Airborne Division on June 27, about eleven miles inland and one mile south of Carentan, France. To say that those Screaming Eagles were glad to see their relief arrive was a vast understatement. The paratroopers hugged their relief troops and there was a great deal of back slapping, hand shaking, and well wishing as the men exchanged positions. Each group wished the other well, and the 101st moved to the rear for some well-deserved rest and recuperation after 18 days and nights on the battle line. As the 101st moved out, the 83rd Division moved forward into battle.

One division of infantry consisted of about 20,000 men, and a battalion consisted of about 1,000 men. Each battalion of 1,000 men was supported by a mobile medical aid unit. Phil Hardin was a sergeant with 2nd Battalion's Mobile Medical Aid Unit. Captain Delucci and Captain Stacks were the doctors in charge of the unit and they were assisted by four medical technicians, one sergeant, one corporal, and two jeep drivers. There were also twelve litter bearers and twelve aid men. All of their equipment, tents, and medical supplies were transported in a large trailer pulled by jeep. Each company had a chaplain attached to their unit. Those thirty-two medical assistants and two doctors and a chaplain were responsible for the battlefield care and treatment of 1,000 U.S. soldiers. Phil said, "Those thirty-two men were very close to each other and 90 percent of them had served together for almost two years, yet Captain Delucci expressed some concern about a few late replacements among the aid men and litter bearers." Among those replacements were Mexican-American litter bearers, who all performed well under fire.

Heavy Casualties—Few Medics

Throughout the night of July 5, the medics continued bringing in more wounded. There were men with limbs missing screaming in pain. Others had bloody stomach wounds and were holding their intestines in place with their hands. Many others were mercifully unconscious and could not feel their pain or hear the low moaning of those around them.

CHAPTER 2
Calling All Medics

Is there no balm in Gilead; is there no physician there? Jeremiah 8:22

When the medical aid unit was within one mile of the front lines, Captain Delucci ordered the men to set up the tent, dig their foxholes, break out the medical supplies, and prepare to go forward to search for wounded soldiers. Unlike the classic TV series M*A*S*H (Mobile Advanced Surgical Hospital) which provided medical care for wounded soldiers in the Korean War where the wounded were picked up by helicopter and flown many miles behind the enemy lines, the Mobile Medical Care for wounded soldiers in WW II was usually about one mile behind the front lines. Also, the Medical Aid Men and litter bearers themselves were the ones that went into the thick of battle and brought the wounded back for treatment. Also unlike the M*A*S*H TV program, the medical care givers lived in extremely primitive conditions. They slept in fox holes, ate packaged C-rations, shaved in their helmets with cold water, and used the bathroom in temporary open slit trenches. There were no beautiful nurses there for the men to chase and no hot food for the men to complain about. There was just no comparison between the Mobile Advanced Medical Care Units of WW II and the M*A*S*H Units portrayed in the TV series. The WW II medics crawled over battlefields and through muddy fox holes in the face of enemy fire wherever there was a wounded soldier crying "Medic." They were the great unsung heroes of WW II, and their casualty rate was higher than the infantry soldier because they were constantly exposed to enemy fire.

As soon as the aid station was prepared to receive the wounded, Captain Delucci asked for volunteer aid men and litter bearers to move forward to search for wounded men and those that needed help. Phil Hardin and close friend, Dale Hill, along with four Mexican-American litter bearers, volunteered for the humanitarian mission to search for the wounded and rescue the dying. The six men moved cautiously into the front lines of battle with no one between them and the German army. Occasionally the men could hear rifle fire and for the first time heard the unmistakable sound of a German machine gun. It was easily distinguished because it fired much more rapidly than an American machine gun.

As night approached, Phil, Dale, and the litter bearers received orders from Captain Delucci to dig in on the front line and remain there until daylight. The six medics went to sleep in their foxholes that night with the sounds of war all around them. Phil Hardin was always a light sleeper and about midnight he heard an urgent call for "Medic" coming out of the blackness of a moonless night. He slipped quietly out of his foxhole, and, as his eyes adjusted to the darkness, moved cautiously toward the cry for help.

The call came from an infantry sergeant who said one of his men was wounded and asked Phil to go down the road he had just traveled and someone would be there waiting for a medic. Phil awakened Dale and the four Mexican-American litter bearers. The six men walked quietly down the middle of the road in the pale moonlight. Since Dale could not see well, and the four Mexican-Americans spoke little English, Phil led the group down the dark shadowy path. As he walked that unknown path, Phil remembered the 23rd Psalm he had learned in sunday school back in the Kentucky hills. "Yea, though I walk though the valley of the shadow of death, I will fear no evil, for thou art with me." Just remembering those words gave him courage.

About every thirty or forty yards there would be the command, "Halt! Who goes there?" Then there would be the call for the password. After giving the password "Bees wax" they would then be allowed to continue. After they moved about 300 yards farther down the road, a sergeant met the medics and escorted them to the body of a dead GI. He had been ordered forward to replace a fellow soldier on the battle line and did not give the password "Bees wax." He had been shot twice through the heart. Phil placed a KIA (killed in action) on his clothes, and they carried the body back to the aid station. After that the medics never returned with a dead body because Captain Delucci ordered his men not to bring any more bodies back. There were other men with burial and grave duties that took care of the dead. The task of the medical aid men was to help those still living.

During the next week the 330th Battalion was pinned down by crack German SS troops in control of the hedgerows. Although there was no forward movement, the litter bearers and aid men had brought in about fifty casualties that ranged in severity from superficial (they were bandaged up and sent back into battle) to critical (they were triaged back to England for surgery).

About 6 p.m on the evening of July 3, 1944, a young lieutenant fresh out of officer candidate school and assigned to F Company called all of the men from the Medical Unit together for a briefing. He said that at 0530 the next morning there would really be some fireworks. Although it was July 4th, it was not to celebrate the fourth but to dislodge the Krauts from their deeply entrenched positions hidden in the hedgerows. He said that Army Intelligence reported there was not much out there ahead of them that would slow them down.

Sgt. Hardin slept very little that night, July 3, 1944. His thoughts were on the following day and the uncertainty of what lay ahead. Phil prayed that the medics would not fail the wounded in the days to come. All the medics must have had trouble sleeping that night because all were up long before daylight preparing for their mission of mercy amid the hell and killing of war.

By dawn's early light on July 4, 1944, the heavy artillery of the 83rd Division began belching their fury of fire, smoke, and deafening noise all up and down the battle line as far as one could see in either direction. At one point Phil could see the Stars and Stripes blowing briskly in the breeze silhouetted against the backdrop of the cannon fire. He began to hum to himself the words of the "Star Spangled Banner" and remembered the story of how it was written by Francis Scott Key during the British naval bombardment of Fort McHenry in 1814. The flag, then, was still flying by dawn's early light just as it was this morning. As far as anyone could see to the right and to the left there was one solid sheet of flame and fire accompanied by the noise of the big guns. Phil remembered saying to his friend Dale that, "Any Germans out there are surely dead by now."

After 15 minutes the barrage lifted and Company E was ordered to move forward and shove the "Krauts out of the hedgerows." As they moved out, F Company and the medics took their position. Captain Delucci said most of their casualties would probably be from short rounds of artillery but that they were prepared for any casualties. Captain Delucci wished all of the medics "God speed" and said, "Men we'll be home for Christmas." He was trying to be as upbeat and positive as he could to keep up the morale of the men of the Medical Corps. It was hard to keep up one's morale amid such pain and death.

Pleas for "Medic" Heard Everywhere

Shortly after F Company moved up into the position vacated by E Company, there was the sound of German machine gun fire. The men were surprised that any Germans had survived that blistering artillery attack but the sound was unmistakably German machine guns.

Five minutes later a second German machine gun opened fire and was soon followed by enemy mortar fire as the Germans zeroed in on the advancing GIs in the hedgerows ahead. Soon the pitiful cry of "Medic" could be heard up and down the line from different directions at the same time. It was evident that the men from the F Company had taken heavy casualties as they advanced.

Phil and four aid men moved quickly into the battle zone to answer a cry for a medic. When he reached the wounded soldier, he found the young lieutenant that had briefed them the night before. He was hit in the elbow and was bleeding badly. Phil quickly bandaged his arm and put it in a sling. The young lieutenant assured him he could walk back to the aid station and Phil answered another plea for a medic. Crawling on his stomach across the battlefield to the next foxhole dragging his medical supplies with him, Sgt. Hardin found another GI wounded in the arm. The young soldier insisted he was all right but said, "Go see about my buddy in the next foxhole." Phil crawled to the next foxhole where he found the man already dead. Returning to the first soldier, he bandaged his arm and wanted to send him back to the aid station, but the young soldier would not leave the body of his friend. Phil referred the dead soldier to the graves registration team and they came out and recovered the body.

Hearing no more cries for a medic and seeing no more wounded, Phil returned to the aid station. He was needed there to help the many wounded soldiers rapidly coming in from all up and down the battle line. At the end of the day his station had handled over 250 casualties. Their battalion strength had been reduced 25 percent in one day. Also, they were short of blood plasma because they had used over 250 units on that one day's casualties. Phil recalled, "That he had never suffered from fear like he did on that July 4th, and he kept telling himself that his best chance for survival was to remain calm and do his job of helping the wounded." Phil said, "It was then he pacified his psyche and kissed her out of her gloom."

Heavy Casualties—Few Medics

Throughout the night of July 5, the medics continued bringing in more wounded. There were men with limbs missing screaming in pain. Others had bloody stomach wounds and were holding their intestines in place with their hands. Many others were mercifully unconscious and could not feel their pain or hear the low moaning of those around them. Captains Delucci and Stacks worked frantically throughout the night doing the best they could to stabilize the wounded long enough to get them back to be flown out to a hospital in England. But the wounded began to back up at the aid station waiting for transportation. Captain Delucci requested more manpower to help transport the wounded, and his commanding officer sent the battalion band members to help transport the wounded.

The next morning, with 25 percent of the men out of action, the battalion managed to fight its way forward about one half mile. As Phil moved up with the men, caring for the wounded as best he could, four of the Mexican-American litter bearers came running up, yelling frantically and motioning for Phil to follow them. They ran quickly to their right, zigzagging their way across the battlefield until they reached a hedgerow. As they peered through the dense underbrush, they could see an open field, and about 300 yards out in the middle of the field was a wounded GI. Several of his squad where crouched down behind the hedgerow. They told the medics the wounded man was the point man in their squad that day. They said, "As he reached the middle of the open field, he was met with a hail of machine gun fire." They believed he was still alive because he had crawled several feet after he was hit. Two hundred yards beyond him was another dense hedgerow that hid the German machine gun nest. Of course, the Germans would see whoever entered the field.

Daring Rescue

Sgt. Hardin was in charge, and any action taken would be his decision. Phil knew they would be risking their lives; therefore he asked each man what should be done. Every man said they should attempt a rescue, and when Phil called for one volunteer to go with him to attempt the rescue, every man volunteered. The four men drew lots and the winner got to risk his life with Phil to save the soldier.

Making sure the large red cross on a white background was clearly visible on their helmets and shoulders, the two men prepared to enter the open field in the face of possible death. They had no idea whether the Germans would respect their humanitarian emblem or open fire on them. The two moved through the hedgerow out into the open field pulling a litter fitted with bicycle wheels so that the two men could easily carry the wounded soldier.

The two medics walked side by side at an average pace straight toward the wounded soldier. To Phil it seemed more like three miles than three hundred yards. Knowing they might be struck with machine gun fire at any moment, the young sergeant remembered a verse of scripture from the New Testament and Psalms he carried close to his heart in his pocket. It was the words of Jesus: "Greater love hath no man than this, that he lay down his life for his friend." But he hoped and prayed he would not have to lay down his life just at that moment.

After what seemed like an eternity, the two medics reached the wounded soldier. It was obvious his leg was shattered. The medics had been taught to splint and give morphine shots wherever soldiers fell, but this was an extraordinary situation. They were under the eye of the German machine gun nest and "Jerry" could change his mind and open up on them at any time. So the two men carefully lifted the wounded soldier onto the litter fitted with two bicycle wheels. As they lifted him he screamed in pain causing them to move much more quickly. They ran back toward the cover of the hedgerow, pulling the wounded soldier on the bicycle-wheeled litter as fast as they could, expecting bullets to fly at any time. But the German soldiers had respected their red cross.

After they reached the safety of the hedgerow, the wounded GI was given a shot of morphine, pressure bandages were applied to stop the bleeding, and his leg was splinted. Then the two medics wheeled him back one mile behind the battle line to their aid station. There Drs. Delucci and Stacks performed emergency surgery before sending the young GI by ambulance to the rear to be flown back to England. Phil Hardin never did know if he survived, but he had done his best to save him. One of the difficult things about being a medic was that you never knew if the wounded GIs you picked up on the battlefield survived. The job of the medic was to help ease the pain and suffering of the fallen GIs on the battlefield and offer them some hope. They were men of mercy not only for the Americans but also for the enemy soldiers that were wounded, for they treated captured enemy soldiers in the same way they treated their own wounded.

On July 6, the medics moved into no man's land separating the two armies. There they found five wounded German soldiers, one with a Luger automatic pistol. Taking the pistol they administered morphine, gave blood plasma, bandaged their wounds, and sent them back to the aid station. The Luger was turned over to the first sergeant at the aid station. It would later almost get him killed.

The afternoon of July 6, 1944, a messenger informed Captain Delucci that the 330th Regiment had moved forward about three miles. The captain then ordered the men to strike their tents, pack their equipment and supplies, and prepare to move forward. So with all of their gear packed in a trailer pulled by a jeep and Captain Delucci leading the way, they moved forward over bomb craters and around destroyed tanks and trucks. Soon they heard the sounds of battle ahead of them.

This time the medics set up their aid station in a battle-scarred two-story farm house with several broken windows, located at the edge of a green field that had been used for grazing cattle. But the only cattle remaining were lying dead, stinking and swollen in the sweltering summer sun. As they moved in, the young Kentucky Medic wondered where the people were who had lived on the farm and prayed that his farm in Kentucky would never have to endure the ravages of war.

Before the men finished setting up the aid station, the wounded began arriving. As each wounded man arrived, he was treated as promptly as possible by one of the doctors and aid men while the rest of the men continued to set up their temporary quarters. The wounded GIs continued to be brought to the aid station all afternoon with all types and severity of wounds. One teenage GI was brought in with both legs blown off and four men in an artillery crew near the aid station took a direct hit on their gun emplacement and all were killed.

As night descended, the roar of the guns diminished, and the men were thankful they had survived another day of bitter fighting. But even though the big guns had become silent, there were wounded soldiers on the battlefield that needed help. Shortly after darkness fell on the night of July 6, 1944, Sgt. Hardin and his medics began answering the pleading cries of wounded soldiers throughout their sector. About midnight as the medics crouched behind a darkened hedgerow, Phil heard that intense pleading call for a medic. Sgt. Hardin ordered his men to stay back as he crawled forward into the darkness trying to locate the wounded man. Five minutes later he found him down on his knees holding his lower abdomen. As Phil touched the young soldier, he seized his arm in a vise-like grip so tightly Phil could not free himself.

The young medic then placed his light on the ground and with his right arm gave him a shot of morphine. After a few minutes the soldier relaxed his grip, and, as Phil shined light on his face, he realized it was one of his buddies that he had served with for two years. He was from the hills of east Tennessee. The two had gotten together many times during their training and after coming overseas, too. Phil recalled that whenever they got homesick they would often get together and talk about home. This GI was not just another wounded soldier on the battlefield; he was also a close friend. The young Tennessean had enlisted at age 17 and now had fallen on the battlefield before he was nineteen.

As Sgt. Hardin gently pulled the young soldier's hand away, he identified himself and he called him by name and said, "I need to see where you're hit." He said, "Phil, am I going to make it?" and Phil replied, "You're going to be back in those beautiful green Tennessee hills before you know it and I wish I could go with you as far as Kentucky." But as the light shown on the wounded area it revealed that the shell had torn his trousers into shreds. As he cut away his trousers, Phil's heart sank as the light revealed a bloody mess of skin, muscle, and intestines. Also, the young soldier's genitals were blown away. Although the wounds were deep, surprisingly he did not seem to be in immediate danger of bleeding to death. Nevertheless, Phil put pressure bandages on the wounds. He called for other medics and after the morphine took effect, they bandaged the young soldier's awful wounds as best they could. Then four litter bearers took him back to the aid station. As he was carried away, the critically wounded soldier had a slight smile and a peaceful expression on his face, almost as if he could see the Tennessee hills. Phil Hardin never saw him again but doubted that he ever reached home.

Sgt. Phil Hardin, POW photo in Stalag XII A

——————— ☆☆☆☆☆ ———————

Oh Jefferson—what you declared in ink

Each hedgerow claimed a thousand times in blood!

Phil Hardin

——————— ☆☆☆☆☆ ———————

CHAPTER 3
From Battlefield to POW

They shall lay their hands on you and persecute you, delivering you up...into prisons. Luke 21:12

July 8, 1944, is a date that will live forever in the mind of Phil Hardin. On the night of July 7, the medics got very little sleep because wounded men were being carried in from the battlefield all night long. About daybreak Phil was finally able to get in a little "sack time." However he was rudely awakened about 9 a.m. by the roar of artillery fire coming from behind their aid station away from the front lines.

Phil quickly jumped up, washed his face in cold water, and dry shaved with a razor he carried in his pocket. Shortly after he went back on duty, a badly burned GI walked into the aid station and reported the Germans had mounted a counterattack and broken through their lines. He said that a German Tiger tank had scored a direct hit on his tank and it burst into flames. He was the only survivor. After being treated for his burns, he was quickly loaded into an ambulance that sped back down the road to what they thought was safety. The ambulance returned in five minutes saying a Tiger tank was blocking the road that supposedly led back to safety. Captain Delucci then realized the aid station was surrounded by German troops and he ordered that two of the most severely wounded be loaded onto litters with four men to each litter. They were then ordered to move out on foot through the woods in an attempt to bypass the German tank.

As the first four litter bearers moved out carrying one of the wounded soldiers, they went through an open-ended shed and moved out through the woods. Just as the second litter moved into the shed the Tiger tank fired one shell that struck the first litter crew killing the four bearers and their patient. A second shell struck the edge of the shed wounding the second group of bearers and their patient.

The men still inside the aid station heard the shelling and the cry for help and rushed outside. The shocking scene before them was indeed traumatic. Five men were dead at the edge of the woods and five were wounded inside the demolished shed. The four litter bearers that were killed were battalion band members pressed into temporary duty as bearers. In combat there are no absolutely safe places. Quickly the medics carried the wounded back inside the aid station leaving the dead where they fell. By that time, there were twenty wounded men inside the aid station and five lay dead outside. Knowing they were surrounded by enemy troops gave them a helpless feeling of uncertainty. But that uncertainty did not last long.

Five minutes later a German soldier stepped out from behind a tree about 100 feet away at the edge of the clearing. He was wearing a camouflaged uniform, and slung over his shoulder was a small caliber machine gun (burp gun). He motioned behind him and nine more soldiers appeared, each in camouflaged uniforms carrying burp guns. They waved "potato mashers" (German grenades) at the station and shouted "Alles raus mit der, mach schnell," which meant "everyone come out right now." Leaving the wounded behind, the men cautiously moved outside with their hands up, not knowing what to expect from their German captors.

As the medics, along with the walking wounded moved outside, the German soldiers spread out around them in a semicircle menacing them with their automatic weapons. But they stayed back a few feet from them shouting orders and lining them up. They were then ordered to put their hands on top of their heads as their captors began searching them for weapons.

As the men stood there with their hands laced over their heads, they were carefully searched for weapons. Sergeant Cooms, their tough-talking first sergeant, had the German Luger in his belt that had been taken off of a wounded German soldier. When the guard saw the Luger, he became so angry he rammed his burp gun barrel hard into the sergeant's belly and rapped him viciously in the head with the gun butt. Sarge fell to his knees clutching his belly and his head touching the ground in mortal fear and pain. Another soldier rushed up and grabbed Sarge's head and bent it backwards and put a knife across his throat. Phil closed his eyes and whispered a prayer, sure that they were going to cut Sarge's throat. But the officer barked an order and the sergeant was released in a crumpled heap on the ground. The old sergeant had forgotten what every GI knew, that if you're captured by the enemy and have enemy weapons or souvenirs on you, you had better get rid of them. After that Sgt. Cooms became a marked man.

Even as the men were being searched they could hear the ominous sound of a tank, its cleats clanking, as it came up the road behind their aid station. As the German tank came creaking up, the arrogant tank commander was standing up in the turret with the upper half of his body outside the tank. He was dressed in the black uniform of the dreaded German SS Troops, with the SS insignia on his helmet and collar. Also the SS insignia was on the collars of all of the camouflaged uniforms of the soldiers. That insignia identified them as Hitler's best trained, most experienced, and certainly among the most cruel soldiers in the world.

One major example of the cruelty and barbarism of Hitler's elite SS troops was their massacre of 642 French civilians in the small village of Oradour-sur-Glâne. On June 10, 1944, four days after the allied invasion of Normandy, Hitler was moving his SS troops toward the Allied advance when the French resistance, in an attempt to slow down their troop movement, bombed the railroad station in that small French village and captured an SS officer. There was an unconfirmed report that he was executed in Oradour-sur-Glâne.

In retaliation, witnesses claimed, the SS troops circled the village, divided the men into five or six groups and herded them into barns. The women and children were then locked in a church. The men were taken out in groups and shot. Then a fire was started on the altar of the church and when the women and children tried to escape the fire, the Germans stuck their guns through the windows and killed every one of them.

Smoke was later seen rising from the village and farmhouses as the Nazis ransacked the town and countryside. That, however, was not the end of that bloody day of killing, for the Germans stopped the incoming 6 p.m. train outside the village and arrested everyone bound for Oradour. They were mercilessly murdered and their bodies thrown into the giant fire burning in the village. Six hundred and forty two men, women, and children were brutally massacred by those SS troops. Following the Oradour massacre, they moved up to engage the 83rd Division capturing Phil Hardin and the medics of the 2nd Battalion. Certainly, the Americans captured by those SS troops had every right to be fearful of their treatment as POWs.

The fact that Captain Delucci spoke fluent German helped their situation tremendously. Although he told the German commander they had badly wounded soldiers inside and tried to bargain with him, there was no bargaining at all with the arrogant German commander. He ordered that only two doctors and four medics could remain with the wounded, and the others were now prisoners of war. The Americans were then ordered to remove their belts and shoe laces and to place their hands on top of their heads and lace their fingers together. Anyone failing to obey immediately would be shot.

Walking the First Mile as a POW

With their guards on each side and the Tiger tank trailing behind, the thirty-two prisoners were marched back down the road they thought was controlled by the Americans. As they marched two abreast out of the aid station, they looked over in the edge of the woods at the dead bodies of their beloved buddies. It was a traumatic sight of mangled, bloody bodies. The face of one of the band members had been blown away, and it was obvious the five dead men went quickly and never knew what hit them. Phil said to the man marching beside him, "At least they did not suffer." Then a guard shoved a machine gun into Phil's back and said, "Nicht sprechen" (no talking). So the men walked in silence as they marched toward an unknown fate.

After marching about a mile down the road, the SS captain and the Tiger tank turned the prisoners over to another group of soldiers and quickly disappeared back down the road toward the sounds of battle. Their new guards ordered the men to start walking down a narrow trail through a wooded area. They were forced to march until sunset and then were crowded into a small stone building where they spent their first night in captivity.

Starvation Hill

The next morning the men were given a slice of bread and a cup of water. Then they were commanded again to start walking, they knew not where, helpless to control their fate. They were prisoners and their captors never let them forget that fact. After walking continuously until late afternoon of the second day, they were herded inside a building crowded with prisoners of war from the 101st Airborne, 82nd Airborne, and several infantry units. Many had been captured on D-Day or D-Day plus one. They had been prisoners for over a month. Those POWs were anxious to hear how the war was going, but Phil Hardin and the medics of the 2nd Battalion had no good news to tell them.

That stark, stifling hot prison had been appropriately named "Starvation Hill." The gaunt emaciated soldiers wearing uniforms that appeared three sizes too large indicated the place was properly named. After remaining on Starvation Hill for three days with one slice of bread and a cup of water each day, Phil was glad to hear they were being moved to another place. Surely it could not be any worse.

At twilight on the third day, about one hundred American POWs were ordered outside, and, flanked by about a dozen guards, were told to start walking across the French countryside. For the next six nights they walked from twilight until dawn. Because of American planes flying overhead, the men were concealed in barns or woods during the day. Although they tried to get some sleep during the day, hunger pangs and the noise of low-flying planes made it difficult to rest. The men had nothing to eat and only an occasional drink of water for four days.

On the evening of the fifth day, those starving one hundred POWs were ordered outside the barn and told to line up and count off. As the men stood in line in the twilight, two priests and four nuns slowly emerged from a nearby Catholic church. They began talking quietly to the German officer in charge and pointed toward the prisoners. Following their conversation, the nuns went back inside the church. Soon they emerged with four large baskets filled with boiled eggs. They gave each famished POW a boiled egg and a cup of water. Phil said, "That was the best egg I ever ate. I can still taste it." That one boiled egg kept some of the men alive, because they had been prisoners for a month longer than Phil Hardin and the men of the 83rd Division. After devouring the boiled eggs, the men again began walking into the blackness of another night. During that night two of the POWs made an unsuccessful attempt to escape. They were soon caught and severely beaten as the other POWs watched.

Misery Motel

At dawn of the sixth night the weary starving men walked into the small French town of Alençon. There they were herded into a transient prison camp. During their imprisonment at Alençon, their food rations were increased to one pint of watery soup flavored with either potatoes, greens, or sauerkraut each day. Also there was one loaf of bread for every seven men, and they were able to get water from a small, hand-operated pump in the middle of the courtyard. After living on those rations for two weeks in what the men called "Misery Motel" Phil recalled that he was really beginning to feel the pangs of hunger. Little did he realize it, but it would get even worse before it got better.

After two weeks in Misery Motel a German SS officer, flanked by a dozen guards armed with rifles and bayonets, ordered the men to line up outside the building. There were also men in menacing machine gun emplacements on each side. Then they were ordered to empty the contents of their pockets into their helmets and turn their pockets wrong-side-out. The eagle-eyed guards moved through the rows of men making sure that the orders were obeyed. Phil recalled that in his billfold he was carrying a one-page letter with no envelope or address from a cousin stationed somewhere in England.

Phil hesitated to drop his billfold into his helmet until one of the guards prodded him in the back with his bayonet. He then knew there was nothing to do but to obey. The guards then moved among the men collecting the helmets and carried them inside to their commanding officer while the men were kept standing in the hot July sun. After four hours their helmets and contents were returned, but Phil noticed the letter from his cousin was missing. Then the officer ordered all the men whose names were called to board the trucks that were waiting to transport them to another camp. After the last name was called, Phil and five other GIs were left anxiously standing in the parade ground as the last trucks carrying their friends disappeared from sight.

The remaining six men were then informed that they were being held for interrogation and were returned to their barracks. When he heard the word "interrogation" Phil immediately remembered a lecture given by an American officer in England. The officer had instructed the men on how an American prisoner of war was supposed to conduct himself during an interrogation. Phil recalled that, according to the international Geneva convention, you were required only to give your name, rank, and serial number. Also, you were never supposed to look the interrogator directly in the eye because he could tell if you were lying. You were supposed to look him between the eyes and think how you would like to put a bullet there. Sgt. Hardin was determined to follow that advice if and when he was interrogated.

One by one the five other men were escorted by armed guards out of the barracks. None had returned when two guards came for Phil and he was marched outside at gunpoint. He was taken into another building and down a long, dimly lit hallway. As he walked down that long hallway he wondered what had been the fate of the other five men ahead of him. When they reached the end of the hall, one of the guards opened the door and motioned with his rifle for him to enter.

As the nervous young sergeant walked into the dimly lit room, he was confronted by a huge German officer seated behind a desk. Phil recalled, "He was not only huge, but he had a scowl on his face and a scar running from his right ear to his chin. He wore the black uniform and insignia of one of the elite SS officers." When Phil entered the room, the officer nonchalantly raised his head, and the young sergeant came to attention and saluted him. The salute was never returned. The interrogation had begun.

Pointing to Phil's insignia, he said, "I see you're in the 83rd Division and we know you were stationed near an airbase in England." Phil had never heard of the airbase he mentioned, and when the young sergeant told his interrogator repeatedly he knew nothing about such an airbase, the officer became extremely angry and agitated. He repeatedly made threatening gestures with his pistol and then got up in Phil's face and screamed more questions and threats at him in broken English.

The officer claimed that the Americans had tortured German prisoners of war in North Africa, and repeatedly said, "Sergeant, the war is over for you. If you cooperate with me, you will have care and protection and will be placed in German industry. If you do not cooperate, we in the SS have ways of torturing you until you will cooperate. Many of our men take pleasure in forcing Americans to cooperate."

Phil Hardin wrote in his memoirs, "Fifty-four years have passed since my encounter with that German interrogator, yet I believe the following is very close to the answer I gave him in the summer of 1944." "Sir, you have my identification which is proof that I am a Medical Technician. Before we were taken prisoner, the German soldiers in our sector retreated a short distance. As our soldiers advanced we found five wounded German soldiers. We administered morphine, dressed their wounds and carried them to our aid station on a litter where two physicians treated them and gave them blood plasma. Our ambulances then transported them back to a field hospital. They were given the same medical treatment as our own wounded soldiers. That was all done without interrogation or threat of torture. Sir, I carry no weapons but am trained and dedicated to saving lives. That's the honest truth. If I told you a lie, you or the SS would recognize it as a lie. My fate is in your hands.'"

After two hours of grueling questions, the interrogation abruptly ended. The officer issued a command and the same guards that brought Phil there escorted him at gunpoint out a different doorway that opened directly into a narrow alley. Once outside, Sgt. Hardin was marched across the alley into an open field. When they reached the middle of the field the order was given to halt! As Phil halted he looked apprehensively over his shoulder at the two guards who had moved about 30 feet away from him. Then looking to his right about fifty yards away, he saw a German soldier sitting behind a machine gun pointed directly at him. Thinking they meant to kill him, Phil fell to the ground in a cross-legged sitting position.

Sitting on the ground in front of that machine gun for just a few minutes waiting for the worst to happen seemed like hours. But then a loud command came from the building, and the two guards pulled the young soldier to his feet and, motioning toward the gun, marched him directly toward it. Thinking they were getting him closer to the machine gun in order to make sure he would be killed on the first burst, Phil marched slowly forward praying every step. But the guards marched him right past the machine gun for about 100 yards and ordered him into a windowless building and locked the door. He was held there in solitary confinement without food or water in total darkness until the next morning. It was impossible to sleep on that hot sweltering July night in a room without a window. Phil's greatest fear was that he would be taken back to the SS officer for more brutal interrogation.

After midnight the room cooled considerably and Phil dozed off into a sweet sleep of forgetfulness. He was awakened before dawn by the guards pounding on the door yelling, "Raus mit der, schnell!" (come outside right now.) The hungry POW was then given a slice of bread, a metal bowl of watery soup, and a tin cup full of water. It was not very much to eat but it was his first food and water in 48 hours, and he "wolfed" it down.

No Shelter At Chartres

Following his slice of bread and glass of water breakfast, he was loaded into the back of a truck with a dozen other American POWs and transported on a six-hour journey over rough back roads to Chartres, France. At Chartres he was placed in a prison yard surrounded by a 12-foot-high wire fence with a guard at each corner. There were no buildings in the compound, and there was no place for shelter from the weather or from a bomb attack. However, there were shallow foxholes for the guards in case they were bombed or strafed from the air.

At Chartres he was reunited with some of his friends from the 83rd for the first time since he and five other men stood on the parade ground and sadly watched their comrades being driven away leaving them to be interrogated. Phil was overjoyed to see his buddies from the 83rd Division again. Just to see his buddies again raised Phil Hardin's spirits .

Phil remained at Chartres for a week and the city was bombed every day. The first day the men thought surely it was the end for them because they had no place to hide as the bombs came whistling out of the air toward the compound. All the POWs could do was lie flat on the ground and pray. But the bombs landed a few hundred yards to the east. Each day, following the bombing attacks, the POWs would wait for the dust to clear to see if the ancient cathedral of Chartres, built in 1288, had survived. When Phil left the prison camp in August, 1944, he could see that the west wall of the stately old church was still undamaged.

The Hellish Journey Begins

On August 1, 1944, the American POWs at Chartres were packed into boxcars about half the size of American boxcars. Each car was loaded with fifty-four men, twenty-seven seated shoulder to shoulder on the floor on each side of the car. The men on one side of the boxcar could not lie down at the same time without infringing on the space of the men across from them. Therefore the men would take turns lying down and sitting up. They slept in shifts.

The boxcar walls and roof were solid wood, but high up on each side of the boxcar were two horizontal openings about four inches wide by four feet long. In the middle of the boxcar was a five-gallon zinc bucket used as a toilet for fifty-four men. As the train moved slowly out of the station and crawled across the French countryside, the men could not see outside and had no idea of their destination. Since there was no fresh air, the boxcar soon began to feel like an oven in the August heat. After the first day, the men had all stripped down to their shorts. By the end of the second day, all the water was gone from their canteens, and many men were beginning to dehydrate. Also, with no fresh air, the stench inside the cars was almost unbearable.

Every day about noon the puffing steam locomotive would creak to a stop and take on water and coal. Every day at that time one of the guards riding in the caboose would open the boxcar door, hold his nose because of the putrid stench, and take a count of the men. The men would plead with him for water, but to no avail. On the evening of the third day two men became so dehydrated they passed out. But after they were given a little more room and fanned with a hat, they revived. Phil recalled that was the first time, and probably the last time, that he did not think of food because the thirst for water was so much worse than the pangs of hunger.

Thirst Becomes Unbearable

As the sun came up on the fourth day in their boxcar oven, it was evident that some of the men would not survive another day unless conditions improved. Phil did not believe he would survive another day without water, and he wrote his family a note on a blank page torn from the small New Testament he carried in his pocket. He gave the note to one of his buddies with instructions that if he didn't survive to try to get the message back to his wife.

Just before noon as the August sun beat mercilessly down on them causing the conditions to worsen in the boxcar, Phil Hardin stood up and said, "Men, I believe in the power of prayer and I believe we ought to pray." Everyone became quiet and the only sound that could be heard was the rhythmic clickity-clack of the train wheels as Phil began to lead the men in prayer. With a soft earnest voice, with no "thees" or "thous," the young sergeant pleaded for God's mercy and help for the weak and suffering men in their pitiful condition. He then lead the men in the Lord's Prayer.

Not a word was spoken for several minutes after the men recited the Lord's Prayer together. Each man was pondering his own physical and spiritual condition and the only sound heard was the continuing clickity-clack of the train wheels as they sped across the German countryside. Then one of the men begin to sing an old Irish tune about his mother. Phil recalled some of the words from that song: "My mother, God bless her, I love her." The song leader had a beautiful tenor voice and the singing seemed to help the men's morale. But Phil Hardin, the young medic from Kentucky, was the stabilizing force under those unbearable POW conditions in Germany. Thirty-six years later, on August 12, 1980, James Noel Bryan wrote Phil Hardin thanking him for being there and helping him survive that terrible time. Mr. Bryant wrote: "It has been 36 years since we walked across France followed by that nightmarish train ride across Germany. That is an experience I shall never forget as long as I live. Phil, I want to thank you again for being the man of the hour on that terrible train ride. I have said many times, I wasn't scared of the devil himself as long as I could see you." What a tribute to the young Kentucky medic who continued to offer hope to others under horrendous conditions.

Two hours later the train pulled into a small German village and stopped to take on water and coal. As usual the guard came up and, holding his nose, opened the boxcar door and counted the men. Some of the men near the door looked outside and saw the "Jerries" pumping water from a hand pump across the street from the station. Pointing to the pump, the men once again pleaded with the guard for water. The guard called the officer in charge and he told them they could have water if they had a container. It was at that moment that one of the men grabbed the putrid five gallon zinc bucket that had been

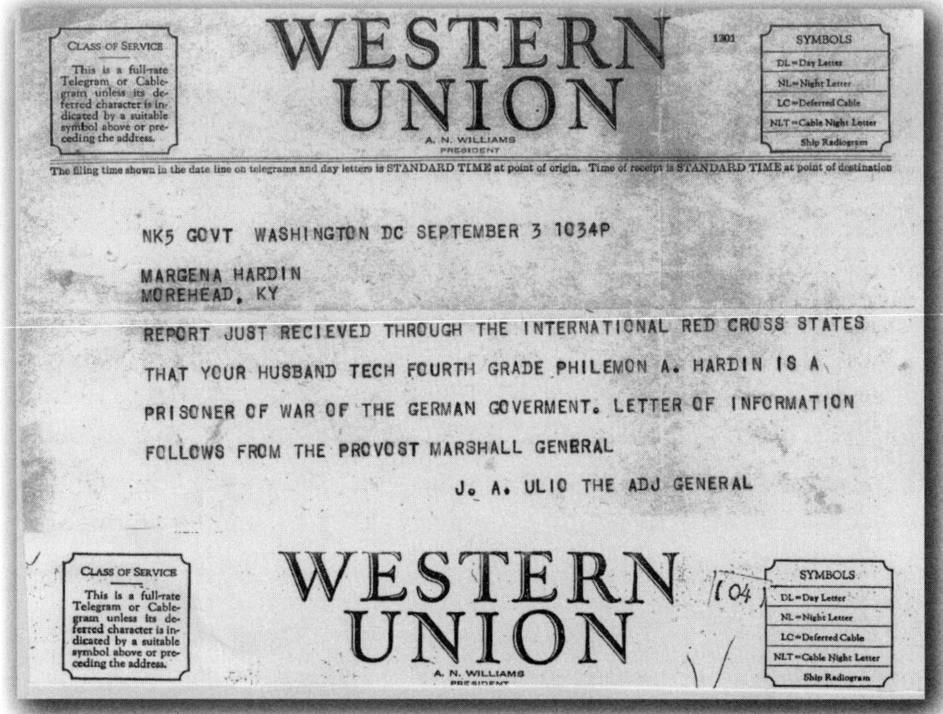
WESTERN UNION

CLASS OF SERVICE
This is a full-rate Telegram or Cablegram unless its deferred character is indicated by a suitable symbol above or preceding the address.

A. N. WILLIAMS
PRESIDENT

1201

SYMBOLS
DL=Day Letter
NL=Night Letter
LC=Deferred Cable
NLT=Cable Night Letter
Ship Radiogram

The filing time shown in the date line on telegrams and day letters is STANDARD TIME at point of origin. Time of receipt is STANDARD TIME at point of destination

NK5 GOVT WASHINGTON DC SEPTEMBER 3 1034P

MARGENA HARDIN
MOREHEAD, KY

REPORT JUST RECIEVED THROUGH THE INTERNATIONAL RED CROSS STATES THAT YOUR HUSBAND TECH FOURTH GRADE PHILEMON A. HARDIN IS A PRISONER OF WAR OF THE GERMAN GOVERMENT. LETTER OF INFORMATION FOLLOWS FROM THE PROVOST MARSHALL GENERAL

J. A. ULIO THE ADJ GENERAL

WESTERN UNION

CLASS OF SERVICE
This is a full-rate Telegram or Cablegram unless its deferred character is indicated by a suitable symbol above or preceding the address.

A. N. WILLIAMS
PRESIDENT

104

SYMBOLS
DL=Day Letter
NL=Night Letter
LC=Deferred Cable
NLT=Cable Night Letter
Ship Radiogram

After being listed as missing in action for almost two months, this telegram to Sgt. Hardin's wife was welcome news.

used as their toilet from the middle of the boxcar floor and jumped out the door emptying its contents as he ran frantically toward the pump. He rinsed the bucket as well as he could with the guard yelling, "Schnell, schnell!" (Hurry, hurry). He quickly pumped the bucket full and ran back to the boxcar.

As the bucket of water was handed through the door the men farthest from the door began frantically to press toward the water, afraid that they might not get their share. There was grave danger that some of the weaker men might be trampled and that some of the water might be spilled. At that moment Phil Hardin stood up and in a strong voice called on the men not to panic, assuring them that each man would get his fair share of the water. The men then stopped crowding toward the water and waited their turn. Phil recalled the water was rationed with one canteen lid full for each man. That was about one sip. Phil waited until last and there was no more water for him. But several of the men shared a few drops from their canteen lids allowing Phil to have one sip of the precious fluid. That water tasted almost as good as the pure cool spring water that flowed from the limestone cliffs in eastern Kentucky. It was the most satisfying sip of water that Phil ever had in his life. No one commented on what had been in the bucket before it was filled with drinking water.

Showers of Blessings

Late that afternoon a hard rain fell on the little train loaded with POWs. Some of the rain seeped through the cracks in the wooden ceiling and walls, and the men were able to catch it in their hands.

Phil said, "I shall never forget that shower of blessing. That handful of cool rainwater, which I caught in my hands, was even more refreshing than the drink of water I had at noon from the five-gallon zinc bucket. Maybe it was because I knew it was much purer." Also the rain cooled the temperature and made the remainder of their journey a little more bearable. As the train carried the prisoners deeper into Germany, the guards became more liberal with their water. Many of the men recalled how conditions had changed following that humble prayer that morning. During WW II there was a saying that there were no atheists in foxholes, and Phil was convinced there were no atheists in the POW camps either.

British POWs Share Food

Those starving American POWs on that train in the heart of Nazi Germany had not eaten for five days. As they received more water their terrible hunger pangs became more acute. The men did not know it then, but the hunger would only become more intense. After seven days on the prison train subsisting on nothing but water, the POWs were unloaded at Stalag IV B. It was filled with British POWs. Some of them had been captured during the British defeat at Dunkirk four years ago in 1940. But most of them were airmen that had recently been shot out of the skies over Europe. The British POWs had just received a Red Cross shipment of food, soap, toothpaste, and personal items which they generously shared with the American POWs. Phil Hardin and the American POWs were at Stalag IV B for almost three weeks. Each day they received one slice of bread and one cup of watery soup with either a cabbage leaf, sauerkraut, or a potato. It was hardly a subsistence diet, and the young sergeant was losing weight every day. But it would get even worse.

The last week in August Phil Hardin and about 1,000 other American POWs were loaded into twenty small German boxcars, headed toward another unknown destination. On September 1, 1944, they arrived at Stalag III C. That was an infamous POW camp located 35 miles east of Berlin just east of the Oder River. After being unloaded at Stalag III C, the first sight that met their eyes was about 1,000 Russian POWs slowly starving to death. Since the weather was still warm they were outside, stripped to the waist soaking up the sunshine. Their emaciated bodies, gaunt expressions, and distended stomachs were evidence they were starving to death.

An inner fence separated the Russians from the Americans, and the American POWs were warned to keep their distance from the Russians because many of them were infected with tuberculosis, leprosy, and other diseases. They were a heart-rending sight, treated with little mercy or care by their German guards and were slowly being reduced to skin and bones, hopelessness, then death. At Stalag III C there had been no packages from the Red Cross to the Russian prisoners because the Soviet Union did not contribute or belong to the International Red Cross.

For the next two months Phil Hardin and the other American POWs subsisted on the same rations as the Russians. That included one slice of bread a day, one cup of thin soup flavored with a cabbage leaf, turnip, or potato. It was a starvation diet. Also, their morale and resistance began to weaken even as the cold German winter approached.

As the weather grew colder, the hunger pangs and craving for food grew even more acute. The men tried to get their minds on other things, but the gnawing emptiness inside their stomachs kept their minds returning to their intense hunger. In early November a truck load of food parcels from the American Red Cross finally found its way to Stalag III C. There was a package for each man, and each parcel contained canned food, chocolate, and four to nine packs of cigarettes. American cigarettes could buy anything you wanted in Germany. One pack could be traded to a guard for one loaf of bread; therefore the choice for many was to smoke or eat. Most chose to eat and traded with the guards for food.

By the middle of December, winter descended on Stalag III C with cold and snow. As Christmas approached, the American POWs' morale began to sink. But on December 15, 1944, their morale improved as more packages from the American Red Cross found their way to Stalag III C. Those parcels were life savers. In addition to food, candy and cigarettes, there were coats and shoes. Phil received a much-needed pair of shoes. The soles of his shoes were flapping, and his feet stayed wet. He also received a GI overcoat. Both the shoes and overcoat would be life savers for him in the future. Phil also remembered he received a picture postcard with a scene in New York city which he traded to a lad from Brooklyn for a scene depicting a log cabin in Kentucky. Sights and scenes of home were most welcome in the POW camp.

Prisoner of War Camp

St. XIIA

(Nb. of Camp only; as may be directed by the Commandant of the Camp.)

Date August 12, 1944

I have been taken prisoner of war in Germany. I am in good health — ~~slightly wounded~~ (cancel accordingly).

We will be transported from here to another Camp within the next few days. Please don't write until I give new address.

Kindest regards

Christian Name and Surname: Philemon A. Hardin

Rank: Tec. 4th Grade

Detachment: Army Medical Department

(No further details. — Clear legible writing.)

This postcard from Sgt. Hardin to his wife was received after she was notified he was a POW.

CHAPTER 4
Suffering in Winter Warfare

I reckon that the sufferings of this present time are not worthy to be compared to the glory that shall be revealed in us. Romans 8:18

As Christmas, 1944, approached, the guards became more belligerent and arrogant. They constantly bragged that their armies were pushing the Allied armies back into the English Channel. However, that beleaguered bunch of Americans POWs considered their story little more than propaganda until they brought in another group of American POWs that had been captured in the Ardennes. One of the men was from Phil Hardin's 83rd Division, and he told an incredible story of bitter fighting during the cold December weather. He said, "The Germans had mounted a major counter offensive. I was with my company on the night of December 17. It was a snowy cold night, and we had taken shelter in a bombed-out abandoned farm house in the Ardennes." He said he decided it would be warmer in the barn so he crawled under the hay in the barn loft. When he awoke the next morning, his company had disappeared and the farmhouse had been taken over by the Germans. He said, "I tried to sneak out through the woods but a perimeter guard caught me." That bit of news of the war was a blow to the morale of the POWs in Stalag III C.

Fighting Equipment Failure, Weather and the Germans

It was discovered during the battle for Europe that some of the American equipment was inferior to the German equipment, e.g. the magazine loader for the American machine pistol and tommy gun was inferior to the German loaders. Therefore, under certain conditions American soldiers had to load those weapons by hand. The importance of a good loader was especially important during street fighting when fire power was needed in a hurry and an empty magazine was a desperate thing. Therefore, failure of those American magazine loaders sometimes caused loss of life.

The men of the 83rd also found a deficiency in the magazine release of their M3 automatic "grease gun." It was too loose, and when slight pressure was exerted on it in just the right spot, it would release and fall out. The first time that happened was when one of the gunners raised his M3 to fire at the enemy and the magazine dropped out. But the men quickly remedied that problem by taking a ball pin hammer from a jeep and pounding the release slightly tighter making it more secure. That might not have been acceptable to the ordnance company but it worked well under battle conditions.

Battle of the Ardennes

Between December 10-15, 1944, the German army managed to successfully concentrate 250,000 men along an 80 mile front without allowing Allied intelligence to define their objective. On December 16, 1944, they launched a surprise counterattack that consisted of 20 divisions, led by Field Marshal Von Runstedt against Allied troops who had plans to be home for Christmas. In sub-zero weather the German drive northward toward the English Channel became known as the "Battle of the Bulge."

Among those troops standing directly in the path of that major German counterattack were the men of the 83rd Infantry Division. They were thrown into the conflict on December 16, 1944, in what became known as the Ardennes campaign. The German attack at first was a tactical success. But when American troops were re-deployed, the attack was stopped in the Ardennes. Even though the Battle of the Bulge eventually failed, it proved to be the largest battle in American history. Even when it became apparent that the Battle of the Bulge had failed, the Germans did not withdraw from the Ardennes until January 21, 1945. The results were catastrophic as the Allies' casualty list totaled 76,890 men and the Germans lost 120,000 men including those taken prisoners.

What made the Ardennes Battle so terrible was the extreme cold and heavy snowfall. It was the worst winter in fifty years and caused many major disruptions in the movement of men and equipment. It increased the casualty rate because, even if a soldier received a minor wound, unless medics could get to him quickly, he would die of shock or freeze to death. Also frostbite was a common enemy for both Germans and Americans, in the extremely cold weather.

83rd Division Fights Dual Enemy: Weather and Germans

While Phil Hardin was suffering from starvation and the winter hardships of a POW, the men from his 83rd Division were fighting the winter weather and the German advance known as "The Battle of the Bulge." It was the strongest German attack they had faced since the early days of the invasion where Sgt. Hardin was captured in France. The men of the 83rd were fighting almost daily snow storms, freezing temperatures and icy winds which doubled the difficulty of defending their positions against the German advance. Although the 83rd Division had trained during the previous winter by living outside in tents in the hills of Kentucky's Camp Breckinridge, they never faced the severely cold weather they encountered during the Battle of the Bulge. Even though they were trained in winter warfare, they had to learn a lot by trial and error. Some learned it through frostbitten hands and feet, pneumonia, and various other debilitating and bronchial ailments. Besides physical problems, there was the added trouble with frozen weapons, equipment and even frozen water and food. But throughout the battle the men of the 83rd Division improvised by using good old "American ingenuity" to overcome the twin enemies of weather and Germans.

Line company men of the 83rd fought a bitterly contested eight-day battle that successfully repelled the German attack in their area. It was the 83rd Division's success in holding their line that enabled the American armored spearhead to break the back of the German advance. In that battle they learned a lot about winter warfare that would become "Standard Operating Procedure" (SOP) in the future (especially in Korea).

GI Ingenuity Prevails

The U.S. methods of winter warfare were often makeshift and crude because there was little time to waste on details. They certainly had never been written in any Army manual of procedure. But the fact is that the men's hastily improvised methods of keeping themselves moderately warm and dry and their weapons and equipment workable played an important part in their ultimate success of stopping the German advance in the Battle of the Bulge.

T/Sgt. Wilburn McQuinn of Helechawa, Kentucky, a platoon sergeant in the 330th Regiment, tried the usual methods for frostbite prevention by insisting that the men do frequent finger and toe clinching exercises to keep the blood circulating to their extremities. But he and his men learned some other tricks, too. Some of the men took off their overshoes in their foxholes and dried them by holding them near burning GI heat rations (fuel tablets). Others used waxed K-Ration boxes which burn with very little smoke but give off a good flame for a few minutes. Both GI heat tablets and K-Ration boxes were also used for drying their socks and gloves. Some of the men used straw inside their overshoes to keep their feet warm while marching. Others used old newspapers, strips of blankets, or old rags to help keep their feet warm and dry. That was reminiscent of the problems faced by George Washington's troops during the Revolutionary War.

Captain Robert F. Windsor, Company A commander, 330th Regiment, had another method of trying to keep the men's feet from being frostbitten. They found that their feet stayed warmer if they didn't wear their leggings. During the day when their leggings got wet with melted snow, they would then freeze at night and tighten up on their legs cutting off circulation which caused frostbite. That was also true of the snug fitting GI Arctic cloth overshoes. They were too tight fitting which also froze and cut down on blood circulation. From that experience the Army began issuing shoes and cloth Arctic overshoes two sizes larger than the men ordinarily wore.

Another method of fighting frostbite was for the men to remove their Arctic overshoes at night whenever possible. Also it was apparent that wearing those cloth Arctic overshoes caused the men's feet to sweat profusely making them even colder. Of course the best way to stay warm and dry was to have a heated "Drying Tent" so that the men could be pulled out of the front line occasionally and let them get thoroughly dried out and warm.

The drying tent was a pyramid shaped tent set up in a sheltered location several hundred yards behind the front line with a GI stove inside to provide heat. But only about seven men could get inside a drying tent at one time. That procedure required about 45 minutes to two hours to dry the men and their clothes. All the frontline companies in the 83rd Division used that method, but there were never enough drying tents to accommodate the number of wet and freezing soldiers.

On a particularly bitter cold night before Christmas 1944, Sgt. Estelle Jacoby of Canton, Ohio, set up a stove in his foxhole to help protect himself from the frigid temperatures. He first stretched a shelter half over the foxhole for a roof, leaving a few inches uncovered at one end. Then he rigged up an empty metal ammunition box as a stove and gathered tree branches for fuel. The opening at the top of the shelter half allowed the smoke to escape and a better draft for the makeshift stove.

Other men in the 83rd Division used a similar method to fight frostbite and cold weather. Some of those even stretched a blanket over their foxhole leaving an opening at one end and used GI heating rations for fuel and a metal cup for a stove. Fuel tablets, which were used primarily for cooking purposes, were issued to the men in packaged units of three, similar to D-rations. Each tablet was burned one at a time for about 15 minutes giving off a fair amount of heat. They would be placed in a metal cup at one end of the foxhole to control the draft and smoke. When used for cooking, the fuel tablet was sufficient to heat one can of C-ration and one cup of coffee.

Other men of the 83rd who were farther behind the battle line could do much more detailed and creative improvising. They found that a pretty fair stove could be made by cutting off the tops of the used "jerry" cans and using an 8mm mortar tube as a stove pipe. The same procedure could be used with empty gasoline drums (after they were thoroughly emptied) to make a homemade stove which would give out enough heat for a large tent or an empty cellar .

Because of almost continuous fluctuation of positions, it was almost impossible to get sleeping bags and straw up to the frontline troops. Instead of straw the men used branches and trees on the floor of their foxholes. Logs and more branches overhead were used to protect them from bursts of snow blown from trees above them. GI pioneer tools, which included axes and saws, were issued to each unit for foxhole construction. GI raincoats, overcoats and blankets were used for foxhole covers. Two or three men would sleep in each foxhole, close enough so they could pool their blankets and body heat. They usually wore their helmets for added warmth.

Keeping Warm and Dry Difficult

In the brutally cold weather the men had difficulty carrying their own blankets. They would get wet in the snow and then freeze at night making them hard to unroll and heavy to carry. The same was true with GI overcoats which became water-logged and frozen after several days in the snow, slush, and freezing temperatures.

Keeping their feet dry was a continuous struggle for frontline troops. The men of the 83rd Division were issued a dry pair of socks every day. However, wading through icy streams and plodding through knee deep snow drifts often resulted in a soldier soaking two or three pairs of socks within a few hours. When that happened the men would wring out their socks thoroughly and place them inside their shirts or under their belts where their body heat would gradually dry them out. Also, at night the men would put their soaked socks under their blankets and sleep on them in order to dry them out.

S/Sgt. Leslie C. Hoessley from St. Paul, Minnesota, was accustomed to winter weather but remarked that he had never had to suffer through a winter such as the winter of 1944/45. Sgt. Hoessley said, "When we had to wade through snowdrifts and icy streams, our pants would be wet to our knees and our legs would soon become numb. Then our pants would freeze solid and would form a windbreaker around our legs and keep us a little warmer. But when it got a little warmer, our pants would thaw out again and our legs would get numb again. Also, another thing that bothered us was that we couldn't always take off our wet shoes at night. If we did, and didn't have time to dry them out before going to sleep, then our shoes would be frozen solid in the morning and we couldn't get them on."

Some of the men of the 83rd Division preferred to let their pant legs drop outside their overshoes to keep the snow out (certainly in combat there was no such thing as a dress code). All of the men agreed that the so called GI Arctic cloth overshoes were not very good for winter warfare because they soaked through easily and then froze stiff which made them difficult to take off. The men fighting the winter war in Germany agreed that combat boots and rubber overshoes were the best type of foot wear for winter warfare. Unfortunately there always seemed to be a shortage of combat boots and rubber overshoes.

There were only 40 pairs of combat boots available for Company A of the 83rd Division. The men much preferred combat boots to leggings which always snagged in fences or brush. But it seemed the so called "Blue Star Commandos" (rear-area troops) had all the combat boots and combat jackets. There was some resentment among the infantry soldiers because they had been told that combat boots and combat jackets could only be issued to the Tank Corps and the Army Air Corps. While on leave in Paris, some of the infantrymen saw the fur-lined jackets with hoods issued to the Army Air Corps and they became the envy of the infantry soldiers.

The infantry soldier was issued a field jacket for winter wear. The first ones issued were not very warm or practical, but the new ones with a draw string were warmer and had more pockets for grenades and ammunitions. Also, the jungle pack carried on their back didn't seem very practical. It was too big and bulky and had too many straps. The infantry soldiers preferred the musette bag carried on their back in a horseshoe blanket roll.

Terrain and Camouflage Difficult

The type of terrain also was a factor in winter warfare. The marshlands in some areas posed special problems for the men of the 83rd Division as they battled the Germans and winter weather. Adding to the infantry men's troubles, were the marshlands where sometimes they were forced to dig their foxholes at night. In that terrain they would hit water about two feet down. That meant three or four inches of water would accumulate in their foxholes during the night. That forced them to line the bottom of their foxholes with branches. During the night they would have to move around very gingerly in order to keep from sinking into the water. One night a platoon of the 83rd Division had to dive into their muddy foxholes without proper preliminary preparation as a German tank suddenly came along a forest path spraying them with machine gun fire. By the time the tank retreated every man in the platoon had his field jacket, pants, shoes and socks soaked thoroughly. Enemy pressure was so strong that night that none of the dripping soldiers could be spared to go back to the drying tent. They all had to spend the entire night shivering in wet clothes in temperatures near zero.

Some of the men of the 83rd Division were issued white snow capes for winter camouflage. But after using them a few days, the men were extremely critical of the capes. They claimed they were too loose for fighting and were constantly getting snagged on bushes and tree branches. That caused the already over burdened soldiers to have to take time out to untangle themselves. Also the thin white fabric soaked up rain and snow quickly. After freezing they rattled like a tin suit of armor. One soldier returning from a scouting patrol said they were unfit for use when strict silence was necessary. In some units the men managed to "liberate" bedsheets and other white cloth from deserted villages, but most men operated without any camouflage at all after their GI issued snow capes proved impractical.

The men of the 83rd Division complained that the standard GI gloves were un-satisfactory for winter fighting. When wet, they froze up and prevented the free movement of their trigger fingers. Also, they were not very durable and wore out after a few days under the tough conditions of forest fighting. When their gloves wore out many of the men used spare socks as substitutes.

Most of the infantrymen wore cloth hoods impregnated with rubbery material to keep the snow from dropping down the back of their necks. Others found that a GI towel could be used as a muffler or even earmuffs when wrapped around their heads under their helmet. Still others improvised by using their sleeping bags as combat suits. To be sure of having their sleeping bags with them at all times, some of the men cut leg holes in one end of them and pulled them up tight around their necks like combat jumpers. During the day they made a warm uniform and at night they served their original purpose as sleeping bags. The combat infantrymen claimed that sleeping bags were useless in winter warfare except for rear area troops. The men could not get out of them fast enough. Blankets proved much more practical under winter combat conditions. The webbing used to carry equipment also proved to be a problem in winter warfare. The webbing froze solidly on cold nights and had to be beaten against a tree in order to make it pliable enough for use the next morning. Another headache was water freezing in canteens. S/Sgt. Otho B. Upchurch, a Platoon Sgt. from Dohlgren, Illinois, said, "The canteens swelled up when the ice froze inside them and that made it difficult to get them out of the canvas canteen covers." Most of the men took their canteens to bed with them and kept them under their blankets to keep their water from freezing.

Freezing Weapons Fatal

Frozen weapons were among the most dangerous effects of the winter weather during the Battle of the Bulge. The extremely cold weather made many of the weapons and equipment difficult and dangerous to use. Automatic weapons such as BARs and machine guns were the most susceptible to freezing. But there was also some trouble with M1 rifles and carbines. Small arms weapons had to be cleaned twice daily because of the snow, and none of the larger guns could be left unused for any length of time without freezing. S/Sgt. Albert Runge, a platoon sergeant from Boston, Massachusetts, said, "The M1s worked well enough if you kept them clean and dry. But you had to be careful not to leave any oil in the chamber or the gun would freeze up and become stiff and difficult to operate. However, you could usually work the stiffness out quickly enough by pulling the bolt back and forth several times. Sometimes the carbines would stiffen up because of the freezing snow and wouldn't feed a shell into the chamber. If that happened it had to be worked out by ejecting a few rounds from the magazine. All that was well and good if quietness was unimportant and the enemy was nowhere near you. But it did cost some soldiers their lives under combat conditions."

During some of the most bitter fighting at Petit Langlier, Pvt. Joseph Hampton found himself in a tough spot with no time to fool around with a frozen weapon. Just as his platoon was about to be overrun by German infantry, he found that ice had formed in the chamber of his M1 rife. With no time to waste Pvt. Hampton urinated into the chamber providing sufficient heat to thaw it out. Less than five minutes later he killed a German soldier with his well functioning rifle. Pvt. Hampton's company commander later verified the incident, and GI ingenuity had prevailed again.

The heavier BARs (Browning Automatic Rifles) were also susceptible to freezing during the frigid weather. They froze quickly when not in use. Ice would freeze in the chamber stopping the round from going all the way into the chamber as well as retarding the use of the bolt. When that happened the men would sometimes cup their hand over the chamber or burn a heat ration pill near it until it let loose. The automatic weapons would work well after you got them warmed up and worked them manually a few times. Surprisingly enough the famous "Grease" gun never seemed to freeze up like the other automatic weapons. Some ordnance specialists reported that when the lubricants in the light machine guns and anti-tank guns froze that heat tables could be ignited to thaw them out so that they could be cocked manually and fired. But when the anti-tank guns froze, a blow torch had to be used to put them back into firing condition.

The men of the communications company of the 83rd Division had major problems with their equipment in the bitter cold weather during the heavy fighting in the Ardennes. As they spoke into their microphones their breath would condense into vapor and freeze in the microphones, breaking up their transmission or completely cutting it off. Most of the time their microphones were thawed out by using cupped hands or by placing them inside their sweaters. Pfc. Frank Gaus of Pittsburgh, Pennsylvania, said he solved the problem by inserting a piece of cellophane inside the mouthpiece preventing the moisture from accumulating there.

The intense cold weather continually caused their batteries to freeze up and suddenly go dead. Also Signal Corps maintenance crews were kept on 24 hour duty repairing numerous telephone lines torn loose when tanks and other vehicles slid off the icy roads ripping out the wires. There was also the problem of sending even written messages from the front to rear echelons because the intense cold made writing extremely difficult. Pfc. Arthur Hall, a company runner from Richmond, Virginia, reported that on many occasions platoon leaders had to use the radio instead of writing code messages because their fingers were too numb to use code slide deciphers. Pfc. Hall emphasized that there were times when even if he had a written code message, his jeep would freeze up or get stuck in the snow and he would have to walk. Communications were a major problem during the extreme cold weather and unfortunately lives were lost because of many messages that could not get through because of the weather.

While Phil Hardin was fighting the cold weather as a POW, his former comrades of the 83rd Division medics were also struggling to provide medical aid to the wounded under extreme war time winter conditions. The deep snow drifts made carrying the wounded on litters doubly difficult, requiring four men to a litter. Also the severe cold caused the morphine syrettes to freeze. Those morphine syrettes were in small collapsible tubes filled with hypodermic needles used for single doses of morphine. If a syrette froze, the medic would place it under his arm and thaw it out with body heat. But keeping the blood plasma from freezing was an even more difficult task. When GI stoves were not available to the medics, they would commandeer a jeep and place the frozen plasma under the hood of the jeep. They would then keep the motor running until the plasma thawed out; however, slippery roads and snow drifts in fields often stymied jeeps. It was then half tracks and tanks that were pressed into service to haul medical supplies and evacuate wounded.

Some medics often improvised crude toboggans made of strips of tin taken off the roofs of shell damaged buildings. They would use two by four planks as runners for their sleds. Those crude toboggans carrying the wounded were hand pulled by medics or towed by jeeps. They were also used to transport supplies as well as evacuate the wounded soldiers over the frozen landscape.

"Weasel" Best Snow Vehicle

According to Company A Commander Captain Marion B. Cooper of Hillsboro, Indiana, the Army's M-29 "Weasel," or "Doddle Bug," was the most effective snow vehicle and every rifle company needed their own "Doddle Bug." They were the only vehicles that could buck those roads and snow drifts without getting bogged down causing loss of valuable time and, more importantly, loss of life in the case of more seriously wounded men. Many of the jeeps were taken away from the motor pools and replaced with "Weasels." Although they were excellent in snow and ice the "Weasel" did not do well on hard surfaces. When used on hard surfaces, "Weasels" wore out in less than 1,000 miles and the worn out metal tracks fell off. But one would last 3,000-4,000 miles on snow and off road soft surfaces.

The Mess Sergeants of the 83rd Division had their problems with cold weather cooking. On one cold morning Mess Sgt. Joseph L. Ornge of St. Louis, Missouri, left his tub full of pancake batter early one morning for an hour to load a "chow" jeep heading out to feed the front line troops. When he returned the pancake batter had frozen stiff and he had to thaw it out with hot water poured into powdered milk. The men ate watery thin pancakes that morning but they were always glad to get any hot food and coffee. Sgt. Ornge also used straw, shelter halves, and blankets to wrap around a marmot can that carried hot food to the front line. That was the only way to keep food and coffee warm during the drive from the battalion mess tent to the front lines.

The men of the 83rd found only one compensating factor in all of the winter weather in the Ardennes. That was because when they accidently plodded across a snow covered mine field the mines sometimes failed to explode. The melted snow seeped down around the firing pins of the buried German land mines and froze preventing them from detonating. Some chemicals in other land mines turned to mush when frozen and failed to explode. That was about the only positive thing that the men of the 83rd could say about winter warfare.

Necessity Mother of Invention

Under certain battle conditions, such as house-to-house fighting, the soldiers found that a weapon was needed that was somewhere between a hand grenade and a bazooka. The projectile fired by a bazooka would sometimes fail to explode if it hit too light an object or sometimes it just scooted across the ground before hitting a solid target. A weapon was needed to blow out doors and shoot through windows spraying a room with shrapnel. The ordnance company did not have such a weapon. Some of the GIs in the 83rd Division improvised by developing their own weapon that worked like a charm for their needs. The men took a 60mm mortar shell and removed the increments. Then they took an adapted hand grenade and fit the fins of the mortar shell into the prongs of the adapted hand grenade and secured the two together. That hybrid weapon could then be fired as a hand grenade from a regular rifle grenade launcher. It gave a flat trajectory of about 135 yards, and a trajectory range of 300-400 yards.

The range was increased by elevating the rifle, and was also increased more by putting the butt of the rifle firmly on the ground thereby lessening the kick and increasing the range.

With that hybrid weapon every rifleman was a potential mortar man and each company went into action with three mortar shells to each squad. That brought mortar fire to the very front line. When the infantry ran out of mortar shells they borrowed from the mortar squad. That system saved bazooka projectiles. The GIs of the 83rd started using those new gadgets on November 22, 1944 in Germany, at Mariadorf, and improved them during the battle at Stavelot. The Germans never knew what hit them in those two encounters. But it was another example of GI ingenuity adapted to meet unforeseen circumstances.

Phil Hardin back home in Kentucky with his wife, Margena, and son, Larry, after his harrowing experience as a Medic-POW in WW II

CHAPTER 5
Five Walked East

Let my people go. Exodus 5:1

The winter of 1944-45 was one of the coldest on record in northern Europe. In the early part of January there was a lot of snow, but as the end of January arrived the weather cleared and it became bitterly cold. While the men of Phil Hardin's 83rd Division were fighting the severe cold and the Germans in the Ardennes, the men of Stalag III C were also suffering. They had little food, clothing, or heat. But as the weather cleared the prisoners gained hope, for they could hear Allied bombers bombing Berlin day and night. Also the prison "grapevine" began to say that the Russians were advancing westward, and the Americans, British, and Canadians had reached the Rhine River.

The Germans at Stalag III C published a newspaper once a month called the "Overseas Kid" that was distributed to the prisoners. The latter part of January, 1945, the POWs at Stalag III C received a copy of the "Overseas Kid." Though it was always filled with German propaganda, by reading between the lines the POWs could sense that the Germans were losing the war. In that same issue the Germans admitted that the Russians had entered Warsaw and the Germans had made a "strategic withdrawal."

The news that the Russians were driving the Germans back into Germany on the Eastern front and the Allies were driving the German army back into Germany on the Western front made the POWs anxious about their fate. Would the German guards kill their prisoners before they were overrun by the Russian army? Stalag III C stood east of the Oder River directly in the path of the advancing Russian army. Certainly the guards wanted the Oder River between them and the advancing Russians. That meant the guards would either move their GI prisoners toward Berlin, kill them, or abandon them.

The GI POWs realized their precarious position, and they prayed not to be caught between the two armies when they fought the battle for Berlin. Their worst nightmare was that their German captors would force them back across the Oder toward Berlin, ensuring that they would be caught between the armies. Nor did the possibility that their guards would just abandon them offer a much better solution to their dilemma.

There was one 30-watt light bulb in the ceiling of each of the flimsy barracks in Stalag III C. The light was turned off at dusk and turned on again at dawn. On the morning of January 31, 1945, the lights in all the barracks were turned on well before dawn. The men knew something was happening, and they anxiously milled around and waited for the worst. Soon the guards came in and ordered them to prepare immediately to vacate the prison.

After the guards left, the men held an informal meeting and discussed whether they thought they were about to be shot, turned loose, or ordered to move back toward Berlin in advance of the Russian Army. They decided if they were to be shot that they would all scatter in different directions at the same time and maybe some would live to tell the story.

Shortly after daybreak a light German reconnaissance plane flying from east to west back toward Berlin swooped low over the prison signaling to guards and prisoners to head west across the Oder back to Berlin. It was apparent that the Russian army was not far away and the POWs did everything they could to slow down the evacuation. Some that were crippled walked a little slower; some that were carrying personal belongings dropped them and were slow picking them up; and some purposely slipped and fell on the frozen ground getting up very slowly. The GI POWs still thought they might be marched out of the prison to some isolated field or forest and be shot. Phil Hardin and twenty-four other men refused to leave their barracks until a dozen guards returned with fixed bayonets and changed their minds. But even then those twenty-five came out very slowly and joined the rest of the crowd of prisoners and guards.

Two hours after the time the plane flew over the camp motioning the men to evacuate, they departed from the prison camp. Even then they marched slowly out of Stalag III C. The long column of 1,000 GI prisoners headed north and west at a snail's pace toward the Oder River. After the column had moved about a quarter of a mile outside the prison gates, they suddenly heard gun fire at the front of the column. Also, artillery shells were exploding to the right and left of the marching prisoners. As the incoming shells exploded all around, many of the guards ran into the fields heading toward Berlin leaving the POWs and a few guards behind. The men quickly passed the word throughout the column to return to the prison. Those guards that had not run away remained with the prisoners.

After returning to Stalag III C, the men learned that the Russians thought they were a German column and fired into the front of the column killing 45-50 Americans. Back in the prison camp the GIs held a meeting and decided they were going to remain in camp and wait for the Russians to liberate them. It was then that the prison commander ordered the POWs to march west again out of the prison camp. He threatened that if they refused, he would order German artillery to destroy the prison camp and all those remaining inside.

As soon as the German commander had issued his orders to vacate the prison, he and many of the guards jumped into the remaining vehicles and sped quickly out the gate and headed back toward

Berlin. They were no sooner outside the gate when they were met with a hail of incoming Russian artillery. Most of them survived and continued on in their vehicles, while others escaped by fleeing toward the open fields, intending to cross the Oder River and get back to Berlin. However, several of the guards returned to the prison and attempted to disguise themselves as POWs and hide among the American GIs. That lasted only a few hours because Russian POWs soon found abandoned guns and quickly ferreted out every German guard trying to hide in the camp. One by one as the disguised guards were discovered, they were taken out into the parade grounds and killed in cold blood. Those Russian POWs showed no mercy on their former guards and brutally executed them as they pleaded for mercy.

Another meeting was soon called by the GI POWs in an attempt to decide what course of action was best for them. They decided that they should leave the prison camp immediately because the German prison commander might make good his threat to call in the German artillery to destroy Stalag III C. The men were also worried that the advancing Russian tanks and artillery would shell the prison. The GIs decided that for the present their best chance for survival was to remain in the prison camp even as some of the healthier Russian POWs headed east to meet their advancing army. For the next two days the men of Stalag III C witnessed some of the fiercest fighting of WW II. It was the beginning of the Battle for Berlin as German fighter planes dueled with the advancing Russian tanks.

On February 2, 1944, the American POWs decided to evacuate the prison for the third time. Before leaving, they scrounged all the food they could find and took it with them, not knowing when they would eat again. Phil recalled he had a can of beans and three potatoes in his pockets. But this time there was no delay as the 1,000 men lined up and marched out of the camp north toward Landsberg, Germany, a small bombed-out deserted village two miles north of the camp. The town had already been evacuated in the face of the advancing Rus-

Kriegsgefangenenlager

Datum: Nov. 26, 1944

Dearest, This is a time when we must
live by faith. We prisoners must live from
day to day, thinking nothing of to-morrow
because to-morrow looks dark sometimes.
But God always sees us thru. See Red
Cross, they will tell you what you can
send me. Send all you can. Love, Phil

This postcard reflected Phil Hardin's faith in the future even though each day as a POW looked bleak.

sian army. The remaining Russian POWs accompanied the Americans to Landsburg and invited the Americans to go with them because they were on their way to Berlin with their own army. They thanked the Russian POWs but after gathering all the information possible, some of the GIs decided they would have a better chance for survival by heading east toward Warsaw, Poland. They hoped eventually to get through the advancing Russian army to freedom in Poland. Others believed their best chance was to head west toward Berlin even though they knew that by heading west they might always be in "no man's" land between the two armies locked in mortal combat for many months.

Although neither option offered too much hope, Phil Hardin and his four friends decided to walk east into the teeth of the advancing Russian. By doing that, they might at least move beyond the "no man's" land between the armies. These five GIs were: (1) Ben Johnson, a soft-talking southerner from near Nashville, Tennessee; (2) Al Sapanski, a first generation Polish-American from Connecticut who spoke broken German; (3) Bud Friend from Antwerp, Ohio, near the Indiana border; (4) Dale Hills, from northern Michigan, who had been a near-sighted professional baseball player in the St. Louis Cardinal minor leagues; and (5) Phil Hardin from the hills of Eastern Kentucky, who understood hard work and sacrifice and was both physically and emotionally strong. These men had sacrificed, suffered and survived a lot together during the past two years, and they were determined that nothing but death would ever separate them. Certainly sub-zero temperatures, snow, and the advancing Russians were not going to stop them now that they had survived the suffering at Stalag III C.

The five weak and cold GIs began walking west at daybreak on February 3, 1944, in a temperature of 10 degrees above zero. Phil Hardin said in his memoirs, "We didn't know how far it was or how long it would take but our final destination was Warsaw, Poland." That had been their destination ever since they heard before leaving Stalag III C that Warsaw had been liberated by the Russians. The desperate, displaced GIs walked only during the daylight hours because they were afraid the Russians would mistake them for Germans and the Germans would mistake them for Russians. Therefore, they wanted to get out of Germany and reach the Polish border as soon as possible. They would stop at twilight each night and scrounge for food. As they crossed the east German rural countryside, every house they passed was abandoned and most of them had been shelled and were uninhabitable.

On the second night they approached an abandoned farmhouse and yelled out to see if anyone was home. Hearing no response, they cautiously entered the house and searched the rooms. In an upstairs attic bedroom they found the bodies of a middle-aged German man and woman hanging in a closet, victims of cruelty by the Russian soldiers. The men moved on to another empty house, because if they were found by the still retreating German soldiers, they might be held responsible for the death of the German couple. Every house in eastern Germany was abandoned and the men had no trouble finding shelter at night.

As they walked through eastern Germany, the roads were filled with German civilian evacuees moving west trying to escape the Russians. These displaced civilians were carrying their personal belongings, pushing carts, or riding in one-horse wagons loaded with what precious furnishings and personal belongings they could transport. It was a sad sight to see in the freezing winter weather. As the five men walked eastward, they saw many more cruel and brutal signs of war. East Germany was a surreal, barren moonscape—a land of abandoned houses, dead animals, and dead German soldiers.

As the men continued toward the Polish border, they began to meet the advancing Russian army. They met Sherman tanks, Studebaker trucks, Willys jeeps, and Plymouth staff cars, all evidence of American products shipped to Russia to aid them in fighting a common enemy. They were making good use of all of those arms and equipment. Soon they began to meet what they most feared—the advancing Russian infantry. Some of those armed men were riding in horse-drawn wagons or in jeeps, or were on foot. Every group the men encountered held them at gun point and threatened to kill them. Also many were drunk, undisciplined, and itching to kill Germans. The American GIs were afraid they would shoot first before asking questions.

Phil Hardin said, "Because of the language barrier, it was difficult to explain to the Russians that we were American POWs who had been liberated by the advancing Russian army. But when the Russians finally did understand that we were Americans, they insisted on hugging us, kissing us on each cheek twice, and slapping us on the back as a gesture of comradeship."

There were times when they could tell that the soldiers were not really convinced that they were Americans. Phil said, "We made it a point never to look back after we walked away after being questioned, because when we did, those suspicious soldiers were eyeing us belligerently with rifles at the ready position." Also Phil said, "I had on a new pair of shoes and I kept them muddy all the time because I was afraid some drunken Russian soldier might kill me for my shoes."

After eight days the hungry, weary, and cold GIs reached the Polish border. They later learned that it was 80 miles from Landsberg, Germany, where they had started their wintry walk. Their fear that the retreating German soldiers would force them back toward Berlin proved unfounded. But the landscape of east Germany was literally a battleground with signs of death everywhere, and, as they crossed into Poland, there were even more signs of death.

In Poland they found every village and town full of bodies of young German soldiers where they had fallen. Their barefoot frozen bodies were not only stripped of their shoes but also their coats. Many were in the streets where trucks and tanks had run over them and flattened their bodies like pancakes. Obviously the German retreat had been so disorganized, they had no time to bury their dead, and the Russians were not about to stop and bury the bodies of their hated enemies. Many of the streets were almost paved with the bodies of German soldiers. Although Phil Hardin and his friends estimated they counted over 10,000 dead German soldiers, they never knew how many had been killed and their bodies moved. They had no idea of how many Polish and Russians had been killed and buried. But they did not see a single dead Russian soldier. The Russian army and the Polish people had taken time to remove their dead from the battlefield. But the carnage of dead German soldiers was a sight that still haunts Phil Hardin.

As the five former POWs moved deeper into Poland, they were received by the Polish people as if they were their own. In each town they were escorted to the Russian commander of that sector and were given passes and identification that allowed them to move freely toward Warsaw. Phil Hardin said, "Those passes saved our lives many times because every time we were stopped by the Russian soldiers, we showed them our identification and were allowed to pass with the usual hugs and kisses twice on each check." In some instances, the Russians would even call ahead to the next village, and they would be met and welcomed by the local villagers. Also, they were provided with food, lodging, and friendly conversation. Although those people were starving, they graciously shared what little they had with the cold American GIs.

Without the help of the Polish people and the security of their Russian identification papers, these American GIs could never have survived their walk through the middle of no man's land between the two armies. They continued to be halted by the Russian soldiers many times during the day. However, when they produced their passes they were permitted to continue without incident. Each night they were taken into the home of a different family who gave them lodging and shared their meager food supply with them.

On the night of February 24, the men arrived in a small village west of Warsaw. Sure enough they were met in the street by a family who took them into their home and provided them food and lodging. The next day as the GIs prepared to leave, an elderly man brought two young women in, and through the means of broken English and sign language, asked Phil if the two women could accompany the men on their journey to Warsaw. Sgt. Hardin recalled in his memoirs, "We were more than willing to take them along with us and wished we could have done more for those benevolent people who had done so much for us." The family was grateful to them and gave the small band of travelers food for their journey.

The next day, February 25, 1945, was Phil Hardin's 23rd birthday. It was a birthday he would never forget because, about 3 p.m. that afternoon, the five weary GIs and two women walked into the city of Warsaw. It was a city in turmoil, with evidence of war everywhere. The city was crowded with Russian soldiers headed west over the same route toward Berlin that had brought the GIs to Warsaw. Phil

Hardin said, "There were hundreds of French, British and American ex-prisoners of war still streaming into the city from the west." The women who accompanied them on their last day left them in the town square and went on their way.

Standing there in the center of battle -carred Warsaw, Phil recalled that every building as far as he could see had been damaged. The five men moved under the partially damaged roof of a building and tried to decide what they should do next. They had a two-day supply of food remaining, but because of the large crowds, were very anxious for their own safety. However, they had agreed they would not go any farther east than Warsaw, and even though they were unsure of their future, decided to remain in the city. Sgt. Hardin in his memoirs wrote, "As I stood there with troubling thoughts crossing my mind, a small slender woman approached me. She spoke in Polish which we did not understand, but she motioned for us to follow her." The five weary walkers looked at each other and agreed to follow the woman, not knowing where she was leading them or why she had selected them from among the thousands of men milling around in the town square.

They followed her on faith as she led them though the narrow streets of Warsaw. The streets were filled with bomb craters and rubble from fallen buildings. After following her for 30 minutes, the men began to worry that they were being lured into a trap. Phil said, "As we were walking she finally made us understand why we were chosen. She had seen us walk into the town square with the two women who accompanied them." Those were women she happened to know and she was trying to help the GIs because they had helped her friends. That relieved some of their fears about why they were selected but they still didn't know where they were going.

As darkness began to fall, their unknown slender female friend led the men to a building that had suffered only minor damage. She took them around to the rear of the building and up two flights of stairs and ushered them into a single room. In one end was a mattress on the floor covered with two or three tattered but clean blankets. At the other end was a small gas stove, a table, and three chairs. Their mysterious benefactor pointed to the chairs and motioned to the men to sit down. After they sat down she said something to them they did not understand and left them alone in the room.

Their guardian angel returned in about ten minutes with two lovely children, a little blond-haired girl about eight years old and a boy about six. She then warmed the food the men had carried with them and served it to them. The generous GIs tried to share their food with her and her children but she refused. She then prepared food for herself and the children. The food she prepared for her children appeared less nourishing than what the men were eating. Following their meal, the mysterious hostess decided the men's extra pair of socks and underwear they carried in their pockets needed washing. She then took their extra clothes and departed with the children. They returned in about an hour and handed the GIs their neatly folded socks and underwear.

That night they all stayed in that one tiny room. Although their hostess tried to give the men her mattress for the night, they refused, insisting that she and her children keep their mattress. The five men slept at the other end of the room on the cold hard floor as they had been doing for the past 23 nights on their walk from Landsberg to Warsaw.

They had survived their dangerous journey through sheer determination. By the grace of God they had completed their 22-day walk through no man's land between the Russian and German armies. That night before entering Warsaw, Phil prayed and thanked God for a safe journey though hellish conditions and for being part of a miracle.

The next morning the woman heated a piece of bread and a potato (all she had) and insisted that the men eat it. But the five GIs refused and insisted that she and her children needed the food more than they did. As the men rolled up their blankets and prepared to leave, it was a poignant farewell. The language difficulty denied the men the words to express their deep appreciation to the slender, unknown woman for her help. They shook hands with her, hugged the little girl and boy, and parted from them forever.

After saying their goodbyes, the five GIs walked back down into the center of Warsaw where about one thousand other American POWs were congregated. There, they found a joyous celebration and heard the greatest news they had heard since their liberation. The Russians had prepared a large warehouse where they could sleep and would furnish them food and medical care. Also as soon as possible, they would be transported by railroad boxcar south to Odessa, Russia, located on the Black Sea.

The first day under the care of the Russians the American ex-POWs had their clothes fumigated. They were all given a bag and told to strip naked and wrap up in their blankets and put all of their clothes into the bag. When those one thousand GIs stripped, put their clothes in bags with their name tag tied outside, and piled those bags into one huge pile in the middle of the warehouse floor, they never thought they would ever get their own clothes back. About an hour later however, each man got his own fumigated clothing back, and their blankets were taken and fumigated.

The third day in Warsaw the American GIs were told they were to be examined by Russian doctors. But before being examined, they were told they had to strip naked again. The men thought nothing of that until they found out all of the Russian doctors were women. That made it a little tense since the Americans had never been used to standing naked before women doctors. But the physical exams went quickly and some of the men were placed in a Russian medical center for further care. Phil and his four companions were declared fit to continue their homeward odyssey.

On March 4, 1945, the American, French, English, and Canadian ex-POWs were loaded into Russian boxcars in preparation for their

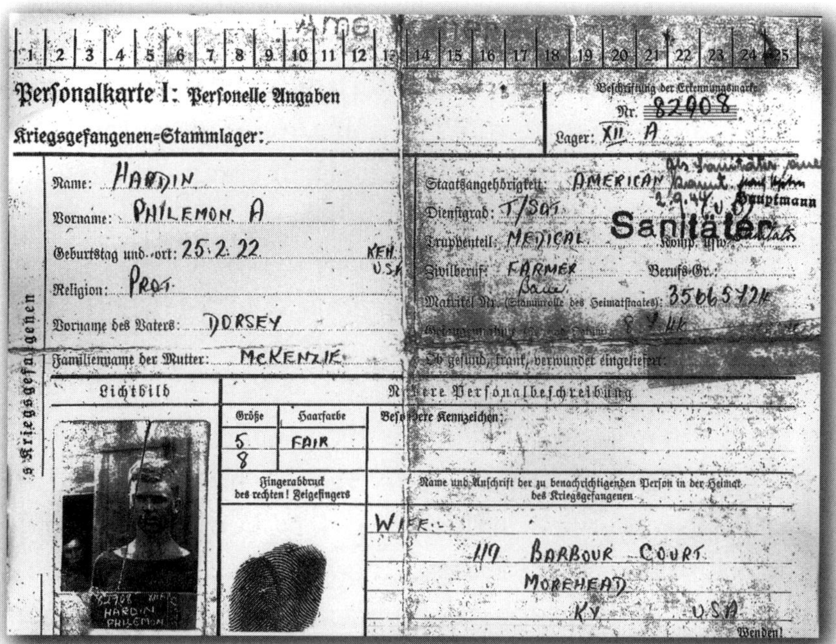

1 2 3 4 5 6 7 8 9 10 11 12 13 14 15 16 17 18 19 20 21 22 23 24 25

Personalkarte I: Personelle Angaben

Kriegsgefangenen-Stammlager:

Beschriftung der Erkennungsmarke
Nr. 82908
Lager: XII A

Name: HARDIN
Vorname: PHILEMON A
Geburtstag und -ort: 25.2.22 KEN. U.S.A
Religion: PROT.
Vorname des Vaters: DORSEY
Familienname der Mutter: McKENZIE

Staatsangehörigkeit: AMERICAN
Dienstgrad: T/SGT
Truppenteil: MEDICAL Komp. usw.:
Sanitäter
Hauptmann
2.9.44
Zivilberuf: FARMER Bauer Berufs-Gr.:
Matrikel Nr. (Stammrolle des Heimatstaates): 35665724
Gefangennahme (Ort und Datum):
Ob gesund, krank, verwundet eingeliefert:

Lichtbild

Nähere Personalbeschreibung

Größe	Haarfarbe	Besondere Kennzeichen:
5 8	FAIR	

Fingerabdruck des rechten! Zeigefingers

Name und Anschrift der zu benachrichtigenden Person in der Heimat des Kriegsgefangenen:
WIFE:
119 BARBOUR COURT
MOREHEAD
KY. U.S.A.

Wenden!

Sgt. Hardin's photo, fingerprint and POW record at Stalag XII A

journey back to home and health. That cold winter afternoon the boxcars carrying their precious cargo crawled slowly out of war-torn Warsaw and headed south toward the port city of Odessa. The men were told the journey southward would take several days but the weather would moderate slightly each day as they moved southward.

The journey through southern Russia took the men through very sparsely populated country. Four years earlier the Germans had conquered that region, and before being driven out, the Russians had burned their crops and villages leaving little for the Germans. It was the scorched-earth policy of the Russian people to keep the Germans from making use of the land or buildings during their occupation. Phil Hardin recalled they would travel for miles and never see a single dwelling in the bleak, uninhabited countryside. During the seven-day journey southward, the Russians managed to supply the ex-POWs with one meal each day.

The train pulled into Odessa at sunrise on the seventh day and unloaded the ex-POWs near the waterfront. The port was crowded with ships unloading the tools of war provided by the U.S. that would allow the Russians to continue their conquest of Germany. Also, the city was filled with thousands of ex-POWs that had been held in east Germany and had been liberated by the Russian army. Phil Hardin recalled they were all housed in a large warehouse near the waterfront. There they awaited their turn at boarding a ship to take them home.

After three days, it finally became the American ex-POWs turn to board a ship to take them home. There were about fifteen hundred Americans, one thousand British, and 200 French ex-POWs loaded on board the large British liner HMS *Bedford*. Their ship sailed south across the Black Sea, through the Bosphorus Straits into the Sea of Marmara, and on through the Dardanelle Straits. While passing through the Dardanelles, the ship passed very close to land, giving the men a magnificent view of the ancient city of Constantinople. They could clearly see the beautifully domed Moslem mosques and slender minarets reflected in the sunshine. That was in an area of the world where St. Paul, the Apostle of Jesus Christ, preached Christianity. As the ship sailed on through the Mediterranean Sea, the weather was warm and spring was in the air. It was far different from Germany, Poland, and Russia with their ice, snow, bitter cold, and biting winds.

The HMS *Bedford* docked at the Island of Malta on March 22, 1945, and all of the British were unloaded. They were to be transported by air for the remainder of their journey back to Merry Old England. The *Bedford* resumed the mission of mercy and landed next at the southern French port city of Marseilles on March 24. All two hundred former French POWs cheered wildly as they sailed into their homeland, tears of joy came down their cheeks.

As soon as the French disembarked, the *Bedford* turned eastward through the balmy Mediterranean and docked at Naples, Italy, on

March 25, 1945. There the fifteen hundred emaciated American former POWs disembarked from their mercy ship. Phil Hardin recalled that upon landing, the first thing they did was to be fumigated and bathed. Then they were given a complete physical exam by about twenty American army male doctors. Although they were prodded, poked, and punched in typical army fashion, they never complained. Many of the men were sick and were placed in the local army field hospital. But Phil Hardin and his four friends were considered well enough to continue and were issued new GI uniforms. Phil said he never thought he would ever be so glad to see new government-issue clothes. The next step for the men was the usual army orientation classes and debriefing interviews by the psychologists. The men were asked where they were captured, when they were imprisoned, what kind of treatment they received, and how they were liberated. It was all entered into their personnel records for future evaluation.

Phil recalled they were in the beautiful ancient city of Naples for four days. Following their orientation, they were given 24-hour passes to travel throughout the city. Although there was much to see, the only thing on the mind of those former POWs was getting home. They didn't have to wait long. On March 31, 1945, they sailed out of Naples on an American Liberty ship headed back to their homeland. Phil remembered the poignant homecoming of the French POWs when they saw their homeland and wondered if he would react in the same way when he reached the USA. Seven days later, their Liberty ship sailed into Boston harbor. Phil remembered there were tears, cheers, and prayers of thanksgiving as they approached the harbor. That made it perfectly clear to him that soldiers around the world reacted the same way when they returned home. Every soldier on foreign soil lives for the day he can return to his homeland.

Phil Hardin wrote in his memoirs, "We arrived in Boston Harbor April 8, 1945. I had not heard from home for 10 months and others had waited even longer." The day after they disembarked, the men were permitted to call home. They were on the base in a large room with few phones and long lines of soldiers waiting their turn to call home, when one of the long distance operators exclaimed, "The President is dead!" Phil said, "The low drone of voices became still and a great hush descended upon the room. It was as if Gabriel had proclaimed a moment of silent prayer for our beloved leader."

Phil continued in his memoirs, "Soon it was my time to call home, but my fingers trembled so that the operator graciously dialed for me. Then my wife, Margena, said, 'Hello,' and we were talking for the first time in over a year. We didn't have long to talk but she gave me the important news: Wilbur, my brother, was a soldier in Germany; Uncle Fant was a prisoner of war in Bad Orb Stalag XII in Germany; Adrian McKinney, a good friend, had been shot down over Truk Island in the South Pacific and was missing in action; Robert McKinney, a neighbor who lived down river from us, was killed in Europe. Before we ended our conversation, Margena emphasized that she and our little son, Larry, were in good health as were my four brothers, her brother and sister, and both of our parents."

Phil Hardin left Boston by train on April 11 and arrived the next day at Camp Atterbury, Indiana, where his GI journey had begun two years earlier and where it was now ending. Phil said, "Some General gave a speech which was long forgotten, but not the sixty-day furlough that began the next day." On April 15, 1945, as the train slowed to a stop in Morehead, Kentucky, Phil Hardin saw his wife and son waiting for him near the station. Then he trembled with the brief question: Is this only a dream? But thank God it was not! The war was really over for one American GI who had answered his country's call during WW II and who was forever changed as a result. But one question plagued him for fifty years . . . what would have happened if he had walked west back toward Berlin instead of walking east toward Warsaw, Poland?

PART II

FIRE AND ICE: SOME WALKED WEST

Sergeant William Hall's Story

★★★★★

Center of the Bull's-Eye

On the fourth night of the train ride, they pulled into a railroad siding and were told they would spend the night there because of higher priority rail traffic that needed to pass them. The boxcar doors were locked and the guards left the boxcar on the siding. The POWs train was left on a siding surrounded by German munitions trains. The possibility of their being blown to bits was very real.

CHAPTER 1
From Combat to Capture

Whence come wars and fightings among you.
James 4:1

This is the story of a POW at Stalag III C who walked west toward Berlin as he fled for his life during the closing weeks of WW II. It is the dramatic story of Sgt. William P. (Bill) Hall.

William P. Hall was born on a bitter cold winter day in St. Paul, Minnesota, on February 10, 1924. He was the son of George W. and Helen (Carroll) Hall. Following his discharge from military service, he married Catherine Mancuso, the daughter of an Italian emigrant and veteran of World War I. They have three children, Mary Catherine, William J., and Thomas, as well as eight grandchildren.

Bill Hall grew up in St. Paul and attended the local public schools and graduated from high school in 1942. Following high school graduation, he enrolled in a business school and planned to enter private business or banking. But in March, 1943, the young student, like millions of American men at that time, was called into military service. He was assigned to the infantry and, following basic and advanced training, was shipped to England as a staff sergeant in Company K, 115th Infantry of the 29th Division that was preparing to invade fortress Europe in what General Dwight Eisenhower called "The Great Crusade."

Sgt. Hall landed in the second wave to hit Omaha Beach on June 6, 1944. He was a replacement light machine gun squad leader in a group that had suffered 80 percent casualties in the first wave. After heavy fighting on the beach, Sgt. Hall and the 29th Division slowly fought their way inland across the French countryside and through the hedgerows. The 29th Division fought valiantly through the bloody battles of Normandy, St. Lo, Brittany, and the French port of Brest. By mid-September, the 29th Division had fought their way well into Germany despite heavy resistance.

On September 25th Sgt. Hall and Company K slowly approached the small German village of Kreuzrath. It had been evacuated and the men entered the village with very little opposition from the few retreating German troops stationed in the village. The 115th Infantry quickly set up a line of defense in and around the town and awaited further orders. By that time Sgt. Hall's weapons platoon was at full strength and his light machine gun squad included one 30-caliber machine gun, complete with ammunition, one gunner, one assistant gunner, two ammunition bearers and, Squad Leader Hall. They quickly set up their machine gun nest on a small hill at the edge of the village. In that vantage spot, they were concealed from frontal observation by trees and bushes and had a clear field of fire overlooking a flat open field. In the distance they could just barely make out what appeared to be farm outbuildings, haystacks, and fences.

In more peaceful times, perhaps that small village numbered five or six hundred, but now it had been evacuated by the local population. Since there were no civilians in the village, Sgt. Hall and his men moved into a nearby vacant house. For the first time since Bill Hall had landed on Normandy almost four months earlier, the young sergeant sat in an easy chair inside a house with a roof overhead and saw himself in a mirror. He was shocked at the man who stared back at him from the oval mirror on the wall. That man had a heavy growth of beard, dirty helmet, rumpled uniform, and combat gear that reminded him of a character in a cheap Hollywood war movie. But for a few nights, the young sergeant and his men were able to sleep in a soft bed. That was a luxury he had almost forgotten, but the men did remove their combat boots and equipment in order not to soil the bed. However, that luxurious living was soon to come to an end.

A Deadly Patrol

On the morning of October 1, 1944, Company K Commander, Captain Waldo Schmidt, called for a volunteer to lead a patrol to investigate the farm buildings in the distance at the far edge of the field. Also, the purpose of the patrol was to probe the German defensive positions that might be ahead. Captain Schmidt believed that was necessary in case the company was suddenly ordered to advance across the open field. Sgt. Joe "Red" Smith volunteered to lead the five-man patrol. Red was a seasoned combat veteran who appeared fearless in battle. He was well respected by the men, and the patrol followed him as he moved cautiously over the open terrain. Red carried a cumbersome "walkie talkie" (portable radio), keeping in constant contact with Sgt. Hall as he approached the distant haystacks. His response was, "All is quiet and there are no signs of the 'Jerries.'" But suddenly all hell broke loose!

Red shouted into the "walkie talkie" that the Jerries had been camouflaged in the haystacks and hidden in the barn, and the patrol was under heavy automatic weapons fire from the front and both flanks. Sgt. Hall could hear small weapons fire, yelling, and screaming above the radio static. Red's hoarse voice came through the radio, "I've lost two men already and I'm hit in the thigh." Sgt. Hall continued to hear the fierce sounds of battle over the radio, but there was no more report, from Red or the patrol. Suddenly the sounds of battle stopped, and in spite of repeated attempts, nothing more was heard on the radio but static. Captain Schmidt called for reinforcements, but none were available until the following day.

The next day the men moved forward toward the haystacks in company strength and met no resistance. But sadly they came upon the common grave of four of the patrol members. The Jerries had buried them in a shallow grave and marked it well with each patrol members' rifle stuck in the ground, with helmet and dog tags identifying each victim. The only name Sgt. Hall could recall among the victims was Dominic (Lucky) Luchiano. Squad Leader Red Smith was not among the victims. (It was later learned that he survived the war in a German hospital and returned home to live a relatively long life.) Following that incursion, the company returned to Kreuzrath to await further orders.

The Attack at Schierwaldenrath

On the evening of October 3, 1944, Company K received orders to move out and take the next German village of Schierwaldenrath about 10 miles ahead. The weather was cloudy and misting rain at 3 a.m. the next morning as Company K moved out past the haystacks where the four men in the advanced patrol were buried. The men were somber and silent as they moved past the graves. The attack force that morning consisted of Company K's riflemen, one mortar platoon, and two light machine squads. One of those squads was under the command of Sgt. Hall. The captain had left one radio man and one mortar platoon at Kreugrath.

Company K's attack force was also supported by three light tanks. Those tanks were lightly armored and each carried one 30-caliber machine gun and a small 47-millimeter cannon. Their firepower was weak at best, but it was all that was available. Sgt. Hall recalled his rifle had been misplaced the day before the squad moved out, and one of the radiomen left behind in the village gave Hall a .45 Colt army automatic pistol. When daylight came, they moved across an open field and the outskirts of Schierwaldenrath in a picture-perfect skirmish line. As they neared the village, they were met with some small arms fire but, thankfully, had not taken any casualties. Suddenly, three Jerries stepped out from behind a small clump of brush with their hands over their head. They were minus their helmets and weapons and indicated they wanted to surrender.

The three Germans seemed to think Sgt. Hall was an officer because he was the only one with a pistol and indicated they wanted to surrender to him. Sgt. Hall later confided they didn't know he couldn't hit the side of a barn with that weapon. The young sergeant motioned the Germans forward with his menacing pistol, and hoping to play on his sympathy, the Jerries took out their wallets and wanted to show him photos of their family. But Bill Hall indicated he was not going to shoot them, and the men broke out in big smiles. After searching the men for weapons, Sgt. Hall marched them to the edge of the village and ordered a rifleman to stand guard over them until they could be turned over to the MPs.

As Company K began to move farther toward the center of the village, they began to receive heavy automatic weapons fire from the farthest edge of the village. Soon they were taking mortar and heavy artillery shelling from beyond the village. It was then apparent that the men of Company K had met heavy resistance from the Jerries. Quickly, the men took positions in and around the houses, and Sgt. Hall set up his five-man machine gun squads upstairs in an abandoned residence. From that spot they had a commanding view of an apple orchard about 300 yards away, they could see enemy soldiers moving in and out at the apple trees and they opened fire on them with a withering burst that dropped eight or ten before they could withdraw from the orchard.

The Counterattack

Throughout the day, the Germans infiltrated in and out of the orchard in spite of the withering fire from Sgt. Hall's dropped several more of the unfortunate infiltrators. By sundown there were over a dozen dead and wounded Germans lying among the apple trees.

About 7 p.m. that evening, the Jerries began a bloody counterattack determined to retake their small village. They unleashed heavy cannon fire on the deeply entrenched American positions. The firing was coming from the dreaded German self-propelled (SP) guns running up and down the roads on the American flanks. (An SP gun is a cannon, usually a 75 mm or an 88 mm, mounted in a tank-like vehicle.) The SP guns quickly destroyed two of the American light tanks, and as the third one tried to race to safety across the open field it was blown to pieces by an SP gun.

The battle was raging and Sgt. Hall was firing his machine gun at German troops now working their way back through the apple orchard. The Germans lost several more men but continued to advance toward the village in great numbers. As Sgt. Hall looked down the street, he could see an SP gun coming straight toward his position in the second floor of the house. Sgt. Hall's squad concentrated their machine gun fire at the SP gun, but their fire power was not enough to even slow it down. Then the SP gun stopped right in front of the house where they were located and swung its long-barreled cannon directly at the second floor window. The five Americans scrambled to get the hell out of the house, but were too late because just as they reached the stairs, the explosion came. The entire upstairs wall collapsed, and they rode the stairway, in a cloud of dust and a pile of bricks, all the way into the basement. Although dazed by the fall, they miraculously survived with only minor cuts and bruises. Still dazed, the five men huddled in the darkened basement discussing their next move.

Captain Schmidt saw the hopelessness of the situation and called regimental headquarters for help. He was told to hold their position until further notice because there were no reinforcements available. By that time, the scene was a nightmare, and the entire company was forced to abandon their positions and seek cover in the houses that remained standing. It was then that Captain Schmidt received permission to retreat, but by that time all avenues of retreat were cut off by the deadly SP guns.

Captain Schmidt, in a desperate attempt to hold off the German advance, called for American artillery to fire on the village. The American troops were then caught between the deadly SP guns and a murderous barrage from their own artillery. During this barrage Captain Schmidt was killed by his own artillery fire. He had sacrificed his own life in an attempt to save his men.

The Capture

When the American artillery fire finally lifted, Sgt. Hall, platoon leader Jim Jordon, and the rest of their men lay huddled in the basement after being hit by SP cannon fire. They were just thankful to be alive when they heard heavy boots walking on the floor above near the basement entrance. Suddenly the door was forcefully flung open and a voice in broken English said, "If there is anyone down there they had better come up in two minutes or a hand grenade would be tossed down to clear the area." The embattled troops agreed that it was over for them. Sgt. Jordon yelled, "Don't shoot, we're coming up." However, for a brief moment as the men climbed out of the basement, they thought they would be shot, especially since it was their machine gun that had killed so many German troops in the apple orchard.

They were not shot, but marched through the village as they were being fired upon by their own artillery. At the edge of the village they were turned over to a German officer who spoke good English. He asked if anyone had an American cigarette and Sgt. Hall gave him his pack. He offered each American a cigarette and lit it for them and put the remaining cigarettes in his pocket as he ordered them to be marched out of town.

The filing time shown in the date line on telegrams and day letters is STANDARD TIME at point of origin. Time of receipt is STANDARD TIME at point of destination

MA193 45 GOVT=WUX WASHINGTON DC 4 855P 1945 MAR 4 PM 8 05

MISS LOTTIE C HALL=

741 EAST MONTANA AVE STPL=

BASED ON INFORMATION RECEIVED THROUGH THE PROVOST MARSHAL GENERAL RECORDS OF THE WAR DEPARTMENT HAVE BEEN AMENDED TO SHOW YOUR BORTHER SERGEANT WILLIAM P HALL A PRISONER OF WAR OF THE GERMAN GOVERNMENT ANY FURTHER INFORMATION RECEIVED WILL BE FURNISHED BY THE PROVOST MARSHAL GENERAL=

J A ULIO THE ADJUTANT GENERAL.

This telegram announced that Sgt. William Hall was no longer listed as missing in action.

CHAPTER 2
Stalag XII A: Beginning of Misery

They made their lives bitter with hard bandage.
Exodus 1:14

Following his capture on October 4, 1944, Sgt. Bill Hall and about 20 other POWs were herded together and marched out of the battle-scarred village of Schierwaldenrath. They were forced across an open field and up a small hill and confined in the darkened basement of a small shell-damaged house. A guard was posted at the top of the stairs to insure that no one tried to escaped. But at that point the men were so battle weary and thankful to be alive that even though they were apprehensive about their future, they made no attempt to escape.

Their German guard spoke almost perfect English and told them the war was now over for them. He also said that very soon a new German secret weapon would bring the war to American soil and then the war would be over for everyone. But though fearful of the future he faced, Sgt. Bill Hall fiercely determined in his heart to survive his captivity.

On October 5, the little band of American POWs was moved out of the basement and assembled outside in the yard. Bill Hall recalled the guards took away their helmets, packets of precious sulpha pills, and all of their personal belongings, such as watches, rings, and other personal items. While standing at attention in front of the house, an imposing German colonel by the name of Hauptman Eggert approached the POWs and in perfect English, informed the men that he was the commander of Task Force Peters that had recaptured the town and they were now prisoners of the Third Reich.

Colonel Eggert was polite and addressed the Americans as "Combat soldiers who had fought valiantly" and complimented them on their strong resistance. He did not interrogate them, but ordered them transported by truck behind German lines to a holding area. He said, "From there you will be transported to a prison of war camp deep inside 'The Fatherland.'" By that time, Bill Hall's thoughts were of his family back in Minnesota. He was worried about how they would react when they received the "Missing in Action" telegram from the War Department. To many families that term meant they were probably blown to bits, lying in an unmarked grave, or were lost somewhere in an ocean. Sgt. Hall was sorry for what his family would go through, and he was wondering if he would ever see them again.

Beginning of Sorrows

About noon that day, the POWs were loaded in the backs of trucks and headed off toward an unknown destination. As they traveled across the German countryside, there was little conversation among the men because each man was quietly withdrawn into his own thoughts, wondering what the future held for him. About sunset the trucks came to a grinding, squeaking halt in front of a group of houses. The men were then ordered out of the trucks and assembled on the outskirts of a small rural village. By that time, the GIs were all getting hungry, and were told they would soon be fed. An hour later they were given two slices of sour black bread and a cup of "ersatz" coffee (substitute coffee usually made from soybeans). But it was the first food they had eaten since their capture and the men devoured the sour bread and washed it down with the hot, oily liquid. But Bill Hall's stomach was sending signals that he was not ready for the food.

Sgt. Hall recalled that most of his meals during his days in combat consisted of Army C and K rations, with just an occasional hot meal. He said, "My empty stomach would not tolerate the sour black bread and oily coffee and I threw it up fifteen minutes later." By that time, he was feeling miserable, lonely, and depressed. None of the men seemed to want to talk very much, nor did Bill Hall feel much like talking. Each man seemed content to withdraw in his own private thoughts of home and future fate.

Sgt. Hall recalled that after being fed about sundown, they were locked up in darkened houses. During the night, there was a torchlight parade of a Hitler Youth group marching up and down the street singing patriotic songs and shouting, "Sieg Heil." They carried huge red and white banners with a black swastika in the center. They held the flag high as it waved in the evening breeze. Sgt. Hall recalled he had read about those raving fanatics in the "Stars and Stripes," and they made him feel uneasy as they marched up and down the street in front of the defenseless POWs. Finally, they proceeded on their way without incident as if they were unaware that there were even American POWs in their village.

At daybreak the following morning, the band of POWs was given more of the black sour bread and ersatz coffee. After forcing himself to eat, Sgt. Hall was sure it would not stay down, but it did. After that unsavory meal, the men were ordered outside where they were faced by a squad of German soldiers armed with rifles and bayonets. The squad leader was the typical movie image of the German soldier. He was about six feet tall with an athletic build and, on one side of his face, from his hairline to his chin, was an ugly scar. He had a trench knife stuck in his jack boot and wore a fur-trimmed cap. He was menacing looking and all business as he carried a German Schmeisser submachine gun slung over his left shoulder. That deadly weapon could fire 650 rounds per minute. The German sergeant was wearing the standard German Army grey-green uniform and spoke broken

English. He ordered the POWs to form up in columns of two and march along behind him across the German countryside.

From time to time as they marched through the countryside, the German sergeant would fire the submachine gun at game birds. But Bill Hall recalled that he never seemed to hit anything; however, the deadly sound of that rapid fire weapon sent cold shivers up and down his spine. As the weary band of American POWs marched through Germany, they passed through several small villages. Each time they passed through a village, many of the residents would open their windows and throw garbage on them and then spit on them. They also shook their fists at them and shouted words and phrases the men could not understand, but they knew they were by no means welcoming them to their village.

Stalag XII A's Sadistic Sergeant "Turncoat"

After a grueling march of several days, they arrived at Stalag XII A near the town of Limberg, Germany. It was a rectangular, barbed-wire enclosed camp with massive gates and a tower at each corner manned by guards armed with machine guns. The German guards were somber and mean compared to the combat troops who had captured them. Sgt. Hall would very soon discover just how brutal and barbaric they actually were.

Bill Hall recalled as they marched through the gates of Stalag XII A, he beheld a sight that he could hardly believe. It was an American who was collaborating with his German captors. He was dressed in a pressed and immaculate GI uniform and wore the patch of the 82nd Airborne Division. You could slice bread on the creases of his shirt and trousers. His black combat boots glistened in the sunshine. The POWs later learned that the turncoat's name was Sgt. Keeting, who had been captured on D-Day and had probably landed with his hands up.

He was a sadistic fellow who seemed to enjoy his new-found power. The first thing he did was curse them all out and call his own countrymen the "scum of the earth." A German officer stood behind him smiling his approval as he slapped the top of his boot with a riding crop. It was obvious he enjoyed seeing Americans being "chewed out" by another American. Sgt. Keeting ordered the men to form up in a column of twos and double timed them down the camp's main street to the mess hall. He threatened to punch the eyes out of any man who did not keep up the pace. Of course, the men were bone tired after their long march, and several of the men were really struggling to keep up the pace.

The turncoat sergeant had his own private room near the main prison gate where he maintained a large supply of Red Cross food, supplies, and cigarettes while the rest of the American POWs were living in lice-infested filth on a starvation diet. After the war Sgt. Keeting was court-martialed for consorting with the enemy when several men reported his actions. He was sentenced to ten years in the military prison at Fort Leavenworth, Kansas. But according to the men who knew him, he should have been hung.

While Keeting marched the men to the mess hall, some of his henchmen sat up two large kettles in front of the mess hall and issued the men tin cups and plates. They were then told that if they lost them, they would be beaten and their plates and cups would not be replaced. Sgt. Hall recalled that first meal consisted of a ladle full of long green roots that turned out to be garbage and a cup of that oily "ersatz" coffee

Interrogation and Daily Routine

After eating that rancid meal, the men were marched across the prison yard into a large building where several long tables were set up. German soldiers were seated behind each table. As Sgt. Hall faced the burly Nazi across the table from him, he gave him his name, rank, and serial number. That was all that was required under the Geneva Convention. Hall's interrogator wanted to know more personal information, e.g., where he was born, names of relatives and what state he was from. Sgt. Hall refused to divulge any personal information except that he was a student before entering the Army. No matter how much yelling, screaming, and threatening occurred, Sgt. Hall refused to give him any more information. The Nazi interrogator groaned, screamed, and slammed his fist on the table, but to no avail. Fortunately for Bill Hall, no further action was taken against him for his refusal to answer more questions.

Following their interrogation, the men were marched up the street to their new barracks. It was located in a long, narrow one-story building built to house 150 men. There were rows of bunks two high up and down each side of the bare-walled barracks. Their so-called beds consisted of wooden slats with straw stuffed in a rough tarpaulin canvas cover and called a mattress. There were no pillows and only one thin moth-eaten blanket. The floor was filthy, and the stench of vomit and dried excrement was almost unbearable.

There were many men already bunked there, and as they lay on top of their straw mattresses, their gaunt, emaciated faces looked like waxen dolls. It was a dismal, depressing sight for anyone to see. Sgt. Hall recalled he was assigned to a bottom bunk which was only a few inches off the floor. As he lay on his bunk, his stomach churned within him. That first night was a sleepless, restless, nightmarish experience. He shivered under the thin blanket and the sounds of the night kept him awake most of the night. Fits of coughing, snoring, moaning, and groaning filled that frightful place.

The next day, Sgt. Hall was introduced to the daily routine of Stalag XII A. They lined up outside at 8 a.m. to await their morning ration of "ersatz" coffee and one slice of sour bread that had to do them until evening. Then each evening they lined up outside their barracks to await their thin soup without any meat or vegetables of any kind. However, it did contain small white worms that swam around in the gruel. Their meals were delivered to the barracks each day by two men from their barracks. Each day two different men were designated to bring the slop from the mess hall to the front of the barracks about three blocks away. Once there, it was slopped into their tin plates and splashed out over their hands. Once, when it was Sgt. Hall's turn to fetch the filthy food, he and his delivery partner had scarcely left the mess hall when they were tripped by one of the sadistic guards. Fortunately they saved most of the soup or the men would not have had anything to eat that evening.

Dysentery Result of "Garbage" Soup

Bill Hall's stomach seemed to become less tolerant every day of those daily meals of garbage and worms. Little did he realize it then, but the camp conditions would only get worse, especially at the latrine. The latrine was a long, low wooden building constructed over an open cesspool. There were holes cut in the floor which the men straddled to answer nature's call. One day as Sgt. Hall was leaving the latrine, he met three British POWs entering. In just a few minutes the Germans entered the latrine with a fire hose and proceeded to hose down the floor with the powerful water hose. In the process, they washed the three British POWs down the holes into the cess pool. Bill Hall said, "It's a sight I shall never forget watching those three men struggling and floundering in that six-foot-deep sea of sewage." It was one of the low points in his memory of his life in a German POW camp.

The weeks of garbage soup and unsanitary conditions began to take its toll on the health of many of the men. One night Sgt. Hall became delirious with a high fever. Two of what he called "the greatest friends I ever had," Jim Jordon and Bill Shortall, carried him over in the middle of the night to the makeshift camp hospital. He was suffering with dysentery.

Sgt. Hall recalled that was as near dying as he had ever been. He was later told by his two friends that he was screaming, frothing at the mouth, and literally burning up. He lay in the hospital for several days not knowing where or who he was. His insides were on fire and he lost most of his body weight.

The crude hospital was staffed by one British doctor, and the only treatment he had for dysentery was powdered milk. It was in short supply but was a staple shipped in Red Cross parcels. However, the doctor still had to scrounge and beg the Germans and the turncoat Sgt. Keeting for even Red Cross supplies. The hospital looked like it belonged on an 18th century army base. The bunks had straw-filled canvas bags for mattresses, no pillows, and even thinner blankets than were in the barracks. There was one toilet and washroom at the far end of the ward with a long row of leaking faucets with no soap or hot water, and the floor was wet and filthy.

In the middle of the night when Bill Hall had to go to the bathroom, and with dysentery you go often, he had to grope his way through the darkness to the toilet. His insides felt on fire. Since he had little control of his bowels, his clothes became quickly soiled, and he had no means of personal hygiene or cleaning himself. Men were dying, and two or three would be carried out every day and buried in the prison graveyard that was fast filling up.

British Doctor's Heroic Efforts

The British doctor had no real medical supplies but worked heroically with what he had. Bill Hall said, "I can only thank God for delivering me from that den of iniquity and not allowing me to shrivel up and die." He began to gain strength. The powdered milk, his youth, and strong determination seemed to contribute to his recovery. Bill Hall wrote in his memoirs, "Of course, I shall always be eternally grateful to my two buddies and the British doctor for what they did for me."

The young sergeant could not recall how many days he spent in that hospital. But he did remember waking up one morning with a mass of red welts from his neck to his groin. The doctor told him it was from the lice that had infested his clothing, and about all that could be done was to take all of his clothes off, turn everything wrong side out in order to reach the lice that had buried into the seams of his pants and shirt. After turning his clothes inside out Bill could clearly see the lice buried in the seams of his clothing. He soon learned from the other men how to pluck them out of the seams and crush them with his fingernails, a routine he followed every night. There was no salve or remedy to ease the terrible itching that was almost driving him out of his mind. Constantly scratching the inflamed blisters caused them to become infected, break open, and bleed until the young sergeant looked like a piece of raw meat. Although his condition improved slightly as time passed, he was bothered by that rash throughout all of his days as a POW.

One afternoon as he continued to improve slowly, the Sgt. Hall gazed out the window and saw several men being addressed by Sgt. Keeting's henchmen. He overheard them telling the men that they would receive ten cigarettes for the trip. As Bill Hall looked more closely he could see his good friends Bill Shortall and Jim Jordon were in the group. He immediately became alarmed that his two best friends were going to be leaving without him. He walked over and yelled out the window at his two comrades and they came over and told him the barracks they were in had been ordered to move to another Stalag.

Bill became frantic because he knew if his friends left him, he would be stuck in that terrible hospital for weeks. Also he would have to contend with Keeting and his henchmen, as well as the sadistic guards at the mess hall. Sgt. Hall had not been discharged from the hospital and was still carrying a fever, but he felt the British doctor would be glad to get rid of one more headache so he told his two friends he was coming with them. He jumped out of the hospital window to join them as his two friends braced themselves to help break his fall in his weakened condition. He landed pretty hard, but nothing was broken, so he lined up with Shortall and Jordon in the middle of the group and held out his hand for his ten cigarettes for the trip.

As the German guards ordered the men to march out of the camp, the men had no idea what the future held for them, but whatever it was it couldn't be any worse than Stalag XII A.

Sgt. William Hall weighed 94 lbs. when he was released as a POW. Months later, back home he still had not regained his weight.

CHAPTER 3
Terror on the Train

Fearfulness and trembling are come upon me and horror hath overwhelmed me. Psalm 55:5

As sick as Bill Hall was, it was a wonderful feeling to be out of that prison compound and headed anywhere else. At that point he didn't care just where as long as it was as far away from Stalag XII A as possible. Between six or seven hundred men marched out of camp that day down to the railroad yard where a train was waiting for them. The train was made of European boxcars about one half of the size of U.S. boxcars. The cars were old, rickety, and weather beaten with no logos on the sides to identify them. It appeared each boxcar would hold about fifty men.

As the men loaded into the tiny boxcars, they found that each car had a heavy wire partition down the center and fifty men were packed like sardines in one half of the car. There were two guards that had the entire other half to themselves. There was barely enough room in each car for the men to sit and no room to lie down. Before the train pulled out, each boxcar was given two five-gallon zinc buckets—one for a toilet and one for a water bucket. But there were no cups. Each boxcar was given a putrid looking piece of yellow cheese with a brown liquid spilled over it. Just the sight of it made Sgt. Hall sicker than he already was. But to his surprise some of the men were willing to trade cigarettes for his share of that sickening mess, and he gained five precious cigarettes in the trade.

Heading for the Heart of Germany

On October 25, 1944, the train packed with American POWs jerked, creaked, and groaned as it pulled out of the railroad station headed somewhere deep in the heart of Germany. But it was to be a nightmare experience for all of the men and an even more hellish experience for the weakened and sickly sergeant cramped in one half of a small boxcar, that made normally uncomfortable conditions almost unbearable. The men became edgy, surly, grouchy, and morose. Beyond the dividing wire, the guards played cards and paid no attention to the POWs' requests for more water.

The first full day on the train was even more difficult for Bill Hall. He was so sick at his stomach that the mere thought of eating that nauseating cheese made him gag. He tried to keep his mind occupied by peering through the slots in the side of the boxcar and watching the German countryside roll by. It reminded him of the American midwest and made him feel a little homesick. The train continued to puff along into the oncoming darkness. Sleep was almost impossible since no one could lie down. The men could only nod in short naps as they shivered in the cool, damp darkness of the crowded car.

Starvation, Dysentery, and Red Rash

Sgt. Hall was fighting more than the cool night because he was still suffering with the pain of his dysentery and a high fever. His stomach felt on fire with a rope bound tightly around his midsection which was constantly being pulled tighter and tighter. His cramping became more intense, and he was doubling over with pain until he could stand it no longer. He had to walk over several men trying to sleep as he finally reached the bucket used for a toilet. The resulting stench caused many of the men to yell at Bill. The fever was running rampant inside his body causing him to become drenched with sweat even in the cool night air.

Just when Bill Hall thought the end was near, his two loyal buddies, Jim Jordon and Bill Shortall, came to his rescue. Jim had managed to scrounge a half a can of Nestle's powdered milk, and they fed him the dry milk powder in an attempt to dry up his dysentery. It was all they could do but it seemed to help. From time to time the train would stop and the guards would open the door, and one of the men would empty the bucket they had to use for a toilet. But the breath of fresh air was like a tonic to the men. Although the POWs were not allowed to get off the train, occasionally when the train stopped, the guards would open the screened partition in the boxcar, and they could stretch their legs in the other half of the car. But those rest periods were too few and far between.

During the occasional stops the men were given a slice of black bread and a bit of sausage. It was that little bit of nourishment and the dry powdered milk that enabled Sgt. Hall's condition to improve slightly. But he was still suffering the symptoms of dysentery. Also he continued to be plagued by the red rash on his skin, but he gradually was learning to live with it.

Center of the Bull's-Eye

On the fourth night of the train ride, they pulled into a railroad siding and were told they would spend the night there because of higher priority rail traffic that needed to pass them. The boxcar doors were locked and the guards left the boxcar on the siding. However, before leaving the guards did open up their half of the boxcar which allowed the men to move about more. Late in the evening, Sgt. Hall suddenly heard the mournful wail of air raid sirens and the ominous sounds of airplanes in the distance. It was apparent that an air raid was about to take place, and the men waited for the guards to return and let them out to enter an air raid shelter. But that never happened!

The POWs train was on a siding, surrounded perhaps by German munitions trains. The possibility of their being blown to bits by their own aircraft became very real. The men knew the night attacks were carried out by British heavy Lancaster bombers, and they could deliver a devastating load of destruction. As the drone of the aircraft engine grew louder, the anti-aircraft fire became more intense, and at any moment the bombs would begin falling on the rail yards. The little band of POWs was trapped and could do nothing but pray.

As the first wave of bombers flew over the rail yards, their bombs fell with a deadly whistling sound. The concussion caused the tiny boxcar to shudder and bounce as they struck dangerously close. At that moment the roar of the aircraft engines seemed directly overhead, and the boxcar shuddered with each new blast. The men could look through the cracks in the boxcar wall and see fires burning and flashes of anti-aircraft guns all around them. They felt like rats in a giant trap with no way of escape, with pieces of debris hitting the top and sides of the boxcar. After what seemed an eternity, the bombing stopped as suddenly as it began, and the aircraft engine sounds faded away into the night.

Following the bombing raid, the guards returned from their shelters and opened the boxcar doors. They were joking and laughing and wanted to know how many of the men had soiled their pants during the air raid. The shaken POWs were then allowed to get out of their prison and walk around on the ground under the watchful eyes of their German guards. The scene around them was unbelievable. The railroad yards were engulfed with flames, and the POW train engine had been hit. Although the engine seemed to be leaking steam, it was able to continue running.

It was a miracle that all of the POWs survived that night of terror. "To this day," Sgt. Hall said, "I can never forgive the Germans for leaving us trapped in those boxcars while hell fire itself descended on us. It was a cowardly act and reflected just another example of their inhumanity and disregard for their fellow man."

Before leaving the battered railway station, the guards told the men that they had shot down half of the planes. The POWs took that with a grain of salt since they could see no signs of airplane crashes. As a result of the bombing, the POWs' transport train was delayed another day before departing. During that time the men had no food, water, or clean toilet facilities. It was as if the guards were punishing the POWs for the bombing raid. Sgt. Hall could not recall just how many more days after the air raid they were on the train, but he clearly remembered when the train arrived at the little town of Kustrine on the Oder River. There they were marched off the train across the Oder River into Stalag III C near the Polish border.

1 2 3 4 5 6 7 8 9 10 11 12 13 14 15 16 17 18 19 20 21 22 23 24

Personalkarte I: Personelle Angaben

Kriegsgefangenen=Stammlager: ~~III C~~ XII A

Beschriftung der Erkennungsmarke Nr. ~~76569~~

Lager: XII A

Des Kriegsgefangenen

Name: HALL

Vorname: William

Geburtstag und -ort: Feb 10, 1923; MINN.

Religion: Cath.

Vorname des Vaters: GEORGE

Familienname der Mutter: HELEN

Staatsangehörigkeit: AMERIKANER

Dienstgrad: Sgt.

Truppenteil: U.S.A. Komp. usw.:

Zivilberuf: STUDENT Berufs-Gr.:

Matrikel Nr. (Stammrolle des Heimatstaates): 37555225

Gefangennahme (Ort und Datum): GERMANY

Ob gesund, krank, verwundet eingeliefert: Well

Lichtbild

Nähere Personalbeschreibung

Größe	Haarfarbe	Besondere Kennzeichen:
5'10½"	BRNN	

Fingerabdruck des rechten! Zeigefingers

Name und Anschrift der zu benachrichtigenden Person in der Heimat des Kriegsgefangenen

MISS. LOTTIE HALL
741 E. MONTANA AVE
St. PAUL MINN.

Wenden!

Sgt. William Hall's POW record at Stalag XII A

CHAPTER 4
Stalag III C: Winter of Discontent

There was no bread in all the land.
Genesis 47:13

To Sgt. Hall the outward appearance of Stalag III C seemed to be quite an improvement over Stalag XII A, he was looking forward to better treatment at the new camp. As the men marched up to the main gate, their German guards turned them over to an American master sergeant. He addressed the men and said he had been placed in charge of the camp by the Germans. He informed them they would receive adequate food while there and a part of that food would be from Red Cross parcels. Bill Hall was somewhat skeptical of that because so far he had only heard rumors of Red Cross parcels, and all he had ever received from them was just a few cigarettes. But, unlike the American turncoat Sgt. Keeting at Stalag XII A, this new sergeant delivered on his word and was able to provide one Red Cross parcel shared by two men every three weeks. The Red Cross parcels usually contained powdered milk, cigarettes, candy, biscuits, sugar, articles of clothing, and personal items such as soap, razors, blades, toothpaste, and toothbrushes.

The Red Cross parcels were made possible by terms of the International Geneva Convention which governed the treatment of prisoners of war among its member nations. (Russia and Japan chose not to be members of that group.) Member nations were permitted to send packages and mail through the International Red Cross to their prisoners of war being held by other member nations. But in many instances, like Stalag XII A, the Germans kept the packages themselves, which was a violation of the international agreement. (Following WW II some Stalag commanders were prosecuted for that violation.) But, needless to say, those parcels were welcome sights by the POWs, and in many cases saved their lives. At Stalag III C where they only received about half of the packages actually shipped to them, the guards would torment the POWs by delaying two or three days before delivering the parcels.

Subhuman Living Conditions

Stalag III C consisted of one-story, plain wooden barracks divided into blocks. Each barracks slept about 100 men in rows of upper and lower wooden bunks with canvas-covered straw mattresses. Each barracks had a wood burning stove and two long tables in the middle of the room. The walls were bare and there was one small light bulb in each building. Sgt. Hall and his two friends, James Jordon and Bill Shortall, were all housed together in the same barracks along with other members of the 29th Division.

The latrines (toilets) consisted of open holes in the floor over an open pit and were located at the far end of the camp about a block away. Inside the latrine there was a washroom with no hot water where the men could at least maintain some semblance of personal hygiene. The POWs were issued one razor and one razor blade for each ten men. Because of the shortage of razor blades (and soap) and no hot water, many of the men were bearded and not very clean.

At Stalag III C the men were still on a starvation diet of one slice of black bread and a cup of oily, ersatz coffee each morning, and at night, they ate a watery soup. But the Red Cross packages supplemented their diet and barely kept them alive. The men talked and dreamed of food. They even prepared mental menus of their favorite meals. Planning meals served to keep their minds occupied; however, it did little to curb their appetite.

There were playing cards packed in some of the Red Cross parcels. That resulted in several poker games with cigarettes as the pot. Gradually the men settled down into a daily routine of just trying to survive. Winter was approaching and the weather was getting colder. Each barrack received a small ration of wood each day for their stove. It was never enough, and the men in Sgt. Hall's barrack supplemented it by stripping up some of the subfloor, roof, rafters, and bed slats. It was a wonder the barracks did not collapse around them. But many of the men had lost so much weight they didn't have to worry about their bunks falling down with them.

Nightly Race with the Dogs

During the day the men could walk outside the barracks as long as they did not cross the trip wire near the barbed-wire fences that surrounded the camp. If that happened, the tower guards would immediately spray the area with machine gun fire. Needless to say the men shunned that area. Another real concern was having to go to the toilet at the far end of the compound about one block from the barracks. At night the guards released two vicious ninety-pound German Shepherd guard dogs. Anyone outside the barracks after dark was a prime target for dog food. Occassionally Sgt. Hall and other POWs who were bothered with recurring dysentery had to run the dog gauntlet several times each night. The men worked in pairs in order to make the run safely. The first man would divert the dogs' attention by rattling the doors at the far end of the barracks. Then the second man would run out the opposite door and, hopefully, make it safely to the toilet. Next they would repeat the process for the other men.

Although the guards at Stalag III C were abusive and firm, they did not seem to be as brutal as the guards at XII A. In fact, one of the main guards at Sgt. Hall's barracks was an old man who had served in WW I. He had experienced some of the horror of that war and seemed to have some compassion for the POWs. He actually was a kindly, old fellow who never gave them any trouble and often would sit and talk and smoke his pipe. Some of the men who could speak broken German would pump him for what little information he could give them. They did find out from him that the Russians were mounting a massive push westward from Poland.

Stalag III C was a camp for noncommissioned officers and, according to the Geneva Convention, "noncoms" were not required to work. The Germans were continually asking for volunteers to work outside of camp with the promise of better food. On one occasion, Sgt. Hall and several others volunteered out of boredom. Early the next morning, they were loaded into trucks and taken from the prison compound. Bill Hall said, "It felt good to get out of camp just for a few hours." As they passed by the edge of a small village, many of the local citizens jeered at them and threw rotten vegetables and rocks at the men. At one point the guards stopped the truck and threatened the townspeople and made them stop their harassment.

The trucks pulled up at a crossroads bordering some railroad tracks, and the POWs were ordered out of the truck. They were told to dig a trench across the road bordering the tracks and fill it with scrap steel stored beside the railroad tracks. It was to be used as a barrier for any Russian tanks and trucks should they decide to attack down that road. But as one man would shovel a load of dirt out, another would shovel it back into the trench. They were determined to do nothing to help the German war effort. Needless to say, they never did get the trench dug let alone filled with scrap steel. Also their barracks was never asked to volunteer again, and they never did get any special food. But they did get out of camp for one day.

Jewish Treatment

While on a detail pretending to dig a trench outside the prison Sgt. Hall first saw a group of Jewish prisoners walking up the railroad tracks followed by two armed guards. They were clad in dirty, ragged black and white striped uniforms with a yellow Star of David on their grubby shirts. Some were carrying sledge hammers and they appeared to be pounding loose spikes and checking for rail damage. They were closely guarded by brutal-looking guards. Every so often one of those sadistic guards would kick the rear end of one of those wretched Jews and laugh as the poor man fell head first to the ground. The Americans yelled at the guards in an attempt to stop the brutality, but to no avail as the guards continued to prod and drive the helpless Jews like cattle.

Sgt. Hall said, "As those Jews got closer to me, I could see more clearly their horrible condition. Their eyes were sunk deep into their heads resembling halloween masks. Their bodies appeared little more than a thin coating of skin stretched tightly over a bag of bones." At that time there had only been vague rumors of Nazi destruction of the Jews and their confinement in Nazi prison camps. But Sgt. Hall recalled that when he saw those pitiful human beings, he began to believe the rumors of brutal treatment of the Jews by the Nazis. Sgt. Hall said, "From time to time during my confinement, I did see other Jews being brutalized by those German barbarians. As long as I live and perhaps beyond, I shall never forget the pitiful plight of those pathetic people."

Early in December, 1944, the Germans had the POWs cleaning up their barracks, latrines, and grounds. The men were issued soap to wash their clothes and bodies. They were also issued razor blades, toothpaste, and new blankets. It became evident that something was up that the POWs did not know about, and they soon succeeded in coaxing it out of the old WW I guard. He told the men that representatives from the International Red Cross were coming to inspect the camp. The reason for the inspection was to make sure the camp was in compliance with the Geneva Convention rules that insured humane treatment of prisoners of war. Sgt. Hall never did see the representatives because none ever came to his barracks. But if the representatives ever came, all they would ever see was what the Germans wanted them to see.

If the representatives came they did not see how many ill fed men were starving to death in the camp. They did not count the number of men who were well below their weight minimum for their height. They did not see how many men had a bloody red rash all over their bodies or how they snapped the lice that crowded into the seams of their clothing. They never saw the nightly chore of men taking off their clothing and turning it wrong side out and spreading open the seams to expose the little white lice that were eating a meal off of their bodies. Also the representatives did not know that when they left the camp the men had to return their new blankets for the old tattered ones. No, they never saw any of those things and their report back to the American people was that the Germans were obeying the rules of the Geneva Convention regarding POWs. Knowing all of that made the Americans hate the Germans even more.

Christmas Party Courtesy of Red Cross

As Christmas approached, there were rumors in the camp that precious Red Cross Christmas parcels would arrive before Christmas Day. But the men would not let their hopes get too high because they had been disappointed so many times in the past, and they did not want to go through another big letdown. As Christmas Eve, 1944, arrived, the men were sure they would be disappointed again. But sure enough, about dusk on Christmas Eve several trucks marked with big red crosses on a white background pulled into the compound. The Red Cross supplies had arrived, and even better than that, each man received a parcel without having to share.

That meant one entire box went to each man. It meant Spam, cigarettes, chocolate, biscuits, instant coffee, powdered milk, and personal items. Some men even received GI overcoats and shoes. It was a wonderful Christmas for all the men and their best day since they were captured. (Though they did not know it them, it would be the last Red Cross food parcel they would receive for a long time.) That Christmas Eve in 1944 was one Sgt. Hall will never forget because he and several other men ate too much of the rich food. Their empty stomachs were unprepared to handle it and it all came back up outside the barracks door. But the celebration continued as the men sang Christmas carols and told stories of happy Christmases past.

About midnight Christmas Eve, the German Colonel Commandant of Stalag III C came through the door accompanied by his personal guards. It was only the second time Sgt. Hall had even seen the camp commander. But he was a typical German colonel out of a war movie. He was in his early fifties, with blond hair and blue eyes, and he stood very straight. He wore a full-length leather coat and carried a small swagger stick and he spoke fair English, as he wished the men a merry Christmas. He remained in the barracks for a few minutes, but during that brief time the men were impressed with his bearing and what he had to say. He seemed to be a decent man caught up in a war not of his own choosing, and he was simply trying to make the best of a bad situation. That night the POWs managed to have a merry old Christmas, thanks to the Red Cross parcels and the camp commander.

That night the old German WW I veteran was guarding the men during their celebration. Some of the men, filled with the spirit of goodwill, contributed some of their gifts and made up a Christmas package for the old man. Before he went off duty, they presented him with a generous Christmas box of goodies. He was surprised and when he opened the box, his eyes became as big as saucers. As he looked at the Spam, coffee, chocolate, etc., he began to cry. To those who could understand him, he said that was the first real food he had seen in months. He would share it with his wife and tell her about the men who had given them the wonderful gift. He had always been kind to the men, and Sgt. Hall said, "I never thought I ever would, but for the first time I felt compassion for a German."

CHAPTER 5
Hot Battle: Cold Walk

Pray that your flight be not in winter.
Matthew 24:20

The winter of 1944-1945 was one of the coldest in German history and by late January, 1945, the American POWs at Stalag III C was struggling to survive. Also, rumors were rampant that their prison compound on the Oder River was in danger of being overrun by the advancing Russian army. Then early one morning, the guards informed the POWs that within two days they would be moved for their own safety. (But the Americans knew it was more likely for the safety of the Germans.) It was then apparent that the rumors were true and Stalag III C was about to be overrun by the Russians. The American POWs were in a precarious position. The men held a meeting to discuss their options. Should they be abandoned by their guards, would it be better for them to (1) remain in the prison camp and risk being shelled by both armies; (2) walk west back toward the American lines and risk being caught up in the Battle of Berlin; or (3) walk east toward Poland into the advancing Russian army. But even as they met, their options were taken away as the guards ordered the men to assemble at the main gate.

During the last days of January, 1945, the Russians were fast approaching the Oder River, and the Germans were in disarray as they retreated before the approaching Russian onslaught. Sgt. Hall felt a sense of relief as the POWs were assembled at the main gate in preparation for fleeing the prison compound. Survival in III C had been difficult, depressing, and boring. Now with the temperature falling fast, it began snowing as they prepared to evacuate the camp. They had no idea where the main thrust of the Russian army would be, but each day had brought encouraging news of their imminent arrival. There was a rumor in Stalag III C that they were about to be liberated by the Russians. Obviously their German captors had other ideas and were not ready to abandon their prisoners as they ordered them to march out of the POW camp.

As Sgt. William Hall packed his meager belongings onto a makeshift sled, the jittery guards prodded him to move faster. That crude sled contained his journal documenting his life in Stalag III C, a few scraps of black bread, several cigarettes, a pair of gloves, poems, names and addresses of buddies, as well as his hopes and dreams for the future. Although much of the journal contained trivial comments, he felt that some day that book would be invaluable for remembering his life in a POW camp. It was his most cherished possession and was packed securely on the crude sled.

As they marched along the road, the temperature began dropping even faster and it began snowing harder. As the bone-chilling cold penetrated Bill Hall's standard issue field jacket, he realized he was not prepared for a sustained march under winter conditions. The young sergeant was a native of northern Minnesota and thought he was accustomed to cold weather, but those winters at home seemed mild in comparison to that winter in northern Germany. It began to snow harder as Sgt. Hall marched out of Stalag III C pulling his crude sled behind him. He recalled that day was the most depressing day of his life, not only because of the weather but because of the uncertainty about what lay ahead. As they marched down the road leading away from the prison, Bill Hall looked back and could see the anxious guards prodding the prisoners to move faster. It was obvious they were worried about the oncoming Russian army, and their actions expressed their anxiety. They were constantly yelling orders in a language Bill Hall never could quite comprehend. As the column marched along the roadside, several German staff cars passed them belching out blue smoke through the soft white snowfall.

Looking back toward the prison camp, the young sergeant surveyed the scene one last time. He could see clearly the dismal barracks and woven wire fences topped with three rows of razor-sharp barbed wire. He could clearly see the empty guard towers silently standing witness to the mass evacuation of the prison camp. Bill Hall recalled he had a deep sense of relief as he left that dreadful place, but he also remembered that he had a sense of fear. Where were they going? Why? Were the Russians near? Those questions were soon to be answered.

First March out of Camp

As the column of 1,000 American POWs marched slowly through the gate, Sgt. Hall recalled he was near the center of the slowly moving column. His precious journal was secured solidly on the sled under the personal possessions of some of his buddies. As the cold wind penetrated the paltry protection of his field jacket, it only added to his anguish. As each step took him toward an unknown fate, Sgt. Hall tried to concentrate on pleasant thoughts of home and family. His mind filled with flashing images of the past that seemed momentarily to crowd out some of his worry about the future.

The men had been marching for about 30 minutes when a command car carrying a German general pulled up beside the column and called one of the guards over to the vehicle. The men could plainly see the red tunic worn by generals. The guard came to immediate attention as the general issued some commands before roaring off in a cloud of blue smoke. That guard then moved up to the head of the marching column obviously carrying the general's orders to the rest of the Germans.

As their guards plodded alongside the column, they occasionally flapped their arms in an attempt to ward off the numbing cold. The muted clank of the marching men, the rattling of the equipment of the guards, an occasional order to move faster, and the whine of the wind were about the only sounds heard as that ghostly column of men moved slowly away from Stalag III C.

Suddenly the silence was broken by the sound of gunfire at the head of the column! However, the group continued to move forward even as the sound of small arms fire grew more intense. Then, the sudden, staccato sound of machine gun fire reverberated back through the column. Sgt. Bill Hall was a light machine gun squad leader before his capture, and he immediately recognized that deadly sound. Then the "whomp" of mortar fire added to their precarious position as those shells landed among the men at the front of the column. But it was the deadly whine of incoming artillery shells that drove the POWs and guards to break ranks and dive for whatever cover they could find.

As the POWs scrambled from the road to the ditch, they were subjected to a murderous barrage of shells. (It was later determined that fifty Americans were killed in that attack by the Russians who thought the POWs were German soldiers.) Sgt. Hall recalled that when the shelling began, he first froze in his tracks for an instant before instinct took over. In his desperate attempt to escape to safety, he abandoned his sled with his paltry possessions and his precious journal. The record of all of his fears, hopes, and dreams was lost forever. Sgt. Hall said he has bemoaned the loss of that book almost daily ever since.

Sgt. Hall recalled he never ran so fast in his life as he did going back toward Stalag III C. He ran past stumbling guards who gave no hint of a super race. Fear was etched on their faces as they flung equipment and weapons aside in an effort to lighten their load and hasten their retreat. As Sgt. Hall ran back toward the prison camp, it dawned on him that the Russians thought the column of POWs were German soldiers, and they were not going to take the time to make sure of their target.

The young sergeant recalled running past a house which several wounded POWs were attempting to enter. He hesitated for a second and considered the possibility of trying to get into that sanctuary with them. But he quickly decided it was already too crowded and continued to run back toward Stalag III C. The sound of mortar and machine gun fire seemed more distant as he approached the prison camp. When he neared the gate to the camp, he found many of the POWs had stopped at the gate and were considering going back inside the compound. Some of the men thought there were air-raid shelters inside the prison, but Bill Hall had never seen them and therefore he opted to stay outside the wire fence along with dozens of other POWs. By that time there were many regular German combat troops in evidence everywhere and it was obvious that the American POWs was about to be caught in the middle of a battle. As the POWs pondered what they should do, a German officer in combat uniform ordered them in perfect English to form up and move out again or they would be shot. Therefore, the POWs marched out of Stalag III C again, only this time they were under the control of German combat troops.

Second March Out of Camp

As the POWs marched down the same road the second time, they had not gone far until they came under Russian mortar and machine gun fire again. This time they all broke ranks and ran toward the town of Kustrine. The German crack combat troops made no attempt to stop the Americans because they were too busy preparing for the battle that was fast approaching.

On the way to Kustrine, they passed German combat troops digging in all along the roadside evidently preparing for a major fire fight. There was a five-man Panzerfaust team digging at a spot overlooking a bend in the road. The Panzerfaust was a German antitank weapon similar to the American bazooka. There were hundreds of German troops digging in along the roadside. Many of them were no older than teenagers and a few were even younger than that. They paid little attention to the Americans running past them as they assumed their assigned positions. Their grim faces made them all appear much older than their years. All acted completely oblivious to what seemed to lie in store for them at the hands of the Red Army. Leaving them to their own fate, the American POWs quickened their pace toward Kustrine. Upon arriving in the town, the first thing they noticed was the absence of people. There was no one on the streets and the inhabitants had all gone inside their homes, locked their doors, and closed their window shades. By taking those precautions, they must have thought they would be safe. However, if the Red Army came crashing through the town, their homes would offer very little protection.

Searching for a Safe Hiding Place

As the men walked along the empty streets, they examined each house in an attempt to locate a safe place to hide. As the day wore on, the POWs became more desperate to find shelter because they were convinced that it was just a matter of time before the two armies clashed. Certainly none of the men wanted to be caught unsheltered, unarmed, and helpless in the midst of a fire fight.

After searching the town thoroughly, Sgt. Hall and about eleven other men located a building they thought would offer them the best protection. It was a small wooden structure at the rear of a large residence. However, they found fifteen to twenty men already inside the small building, but they squeezed together to make room for twelve more men. By that time the men were packed in like sardines in a can. There was no room to sit down and barely enough room to allow the battered door to close. They did not take long to realize that the building was not adequate for so many men.

As Sgt. Hall and some of the late comers prepared to vacate the building to look for better shelter, the door was suddenly flung open. Silhouetted in the doorway was an old German civilian, pointing an ancient bolt action Mauser rifle at the POWs. He ordered the men outside. Once outside, the ancient German uttered a phrase they all understood—"Marsch!"

The old man evidently enjoyed his role as captor. As he marched the men down the street, the grizzled old Nazi mouthed a cadence, "eins, zwei, drei, vier," like the drill sergeant he probably was in WW I. Moving toward the sound of gunfire, the men became anxious about their fate and where their captor was taking them. Just as some of the men were planning to overpower the old man and get rid of him, an elderly lady came out of a house across the street. She shouted something at the wrinkled old German that made him throw up his hands in disgust and point to his captives. The lady moved forward and even in German the men realized the old man was being severely scolded. He appeared crestfallen and threw up his hands, spit on some of the men and began to walk back into town. But whatever the lady said to him probably saved the lives of some of those POWs and saved the old German from a fractured skull.

As the men began to consider their next course of action, the old lady motioned them to follow her to a wooden shed at the rear of her house. Although it was considerably weatherworn, it appeared substantial, and she motioned for the men to go inside. As they entered, they discovered about a dozen other POWs were already guests of that gracious lady. The building was dark inside but spacious enough to house all of the men. The plank walls were not butted against each other and allowed cracks of light to filter into the darkened room. Inside there were tools, an old car, sacks of grain, and lice-infested straw stored on a dirt floor. But the building provided a reasonably safe place for the men, and they hoped it would be a secure haven from the fire fight that was about to begin.

Bloody Battle Begins

The first night in their cramped quarters was a nightmare. The sounds of battle gradually moved closer. At one point the men, looking through the cracks in the wall, saw a Russian tank stop in the street directly in front of their hiding place and aim its cannon directly at the house in front of them while the crack of small arms fire and the shrill sound of artillery shells fell all around the helpless captives. It was evident that the brunt of the battle was taking place in and around the town. As the cold grey dawn broke, the fighting even grew more intense. Aircraft began bombing and strafing the town. The sound of aircraft machine guns sounded like ripping canvas above the whine of straining aircraft engines. The ground around them shuddered with the force of exploding bombs as the helpless men crouched down in their flimsy quarters with their hands over their ears. They could hear vehicles moving up and down the street and men shouting first in Russian and then in German. However, they had no way of knowing if the attacking aircraft were Russian or German, but the continuous bombing began to strain the nerves of the POWs. Sgt. Hall said, "All we could do was hope and pray that errant bombs or artillery shells would not seek us out, and that perhaps the Russians would win the battle and rescue us."

Sgt. Hall wrote in his memoirs, "Sometime during the next day a young boy came to the door of our shelter with several loaves of black bread and a large pitcher of cool milk. It was the first fresh milk I had tasted since landing on D-Day plus 1. I could only assume that the German lady who rescued us from the clutches of the old German man the day before was responsible for another act of kindness that provided us with the only food we had had in days. After his brief visit, I never saw the boy again, but I will always remember him and the German lady for their kindness." The young boy certainly risked his life to deliver those morsels to the starving men. Those acts of kindness by that unknown German lad and lady were proof that good does exist in the midst of evil. Sgt. Hall recalled that was a memorable meal of bread and milk to several starving men that day in 1945.

Unsure Which Side Was Winning

The battle for Kustrine continued for four days and three nights, and the men had no way of knowing who was winning the battle. On the second day one of the Americans peering through a crack in the wall saw Russian soldiers moving through an open field nearby. It was then suggested that a volunteer under a white flag of truce go outside and meet with the Russians. However, after discussing that option more in detail, the men decided it was not such a good idea as they remembered the Russians had shelled the column of POWs once, thinking they were German troops. In all probability it would have been foolhardy to attempt such a meeting in the heat of a ferocious battle.

Four days and three nights in those flimsy quarters during the battle for Kustrine seemed like a lifetime. That was especially true since they had no way of knowing who was winning. As the severity of battle subsided, most of the men huddling inside their flimsy shelter were stunned and shaken. They were afraid to venture outside and afraid to remain inside, and as they discussed what to do, the shed door was violently thrown open and their options were about to be taken from them.

Germans Won the First Round

A young German soldier, not much older than a teenager, stepped briskly through the door. Despite his apparent youth, his manner and actions were that of a seasoned combat veteran. His mud -pattered appearance and deadly Schmeisser machine pistol made it apparent that he had been in combat before. His eyes narrowed as he looked over the scene before him. Realizing he had captured a group of American POWs, he asked the men in broken English if they would rather be prisoners of the Russians or Germans. The POWs quickly replied, "Germans," because they were confident if they had said Russians they would have found out just how deadly his Schmeisser pistol could be.

Distraction and Devastation Everywhere

Having received the correct answer, the young German left without another word. He was gone perhaps an hour or so when he returned with an officer. This time they ordered everyone out of the shed into the street in front of the house. The sight that greeted them was unbelievable. The house in front of their safe haven was pockmarked by shell fragments and bullet holes. The windows were all blown out and part of the roof was gone, exposing the interior of the house. They had no idea as to the fate of the lady who was kind enough to hide them. She was nowhere in sight.

The scene in the street was catastrophic. Directly in front of the house was an overturned wagon with two dead horses lying in front of it. There were two or three bodies scattered upon what was once the front lawn. Further on up the street a burned-out tank still smoldered. A burned body lay half in and half out of the top turret. The treads were blown off and there was a gaping hole in the rear near the engine exhaust. One could see clearly the Russian red star on the side of the turret. Dead Russian and German soldiers littered the street and as the men moved forward they now saw parts of bodies in the street. One human leg, still with its boot intact, was lying next to what appeared to be a shoulder and an arm. The hand was torn off and was a few feet away. The trees were shattered by shell fire, and the houses all were badly damaged and in many cases simply blown apart. It now seemed obvious that the Germans had beaten off the Russian attack, but with heavy causalities on both sides. They now could see clearly the results of the battle they had heard raging around them while confined in the shed for three days and four nights.

Digging Out the Dead

As the POWs continued their forced march through the streets of Kustrine, the road curved slightly to the right. When they rounded the curve they came upon an even more grisly sight. The Germans had evidently dug a roadblock across the street. It was now a deep trench filled with putrid water and mud. Buried in that soft blackened ooze were dozens of German soldiers. The German officer leading the POWs informed them that they were to dig the dead out of that trench. Sgt. Hall recalled he and another man grabbed one dead German under the arms and pulled him from the mud. He was an officer and half of his head was missing. As they lifted him, some of his brains spilled out of the gaping cavity above his ear. Sgt. Hall immediately threw up. The POWs continued the grisly task of pulling the bodies of dead Germans out of that ditch for the remainder of the day. They would dig them out of the muck and throw the bodies into the back of an army truck parked nearby. All of this time they had nothing to eat or drink. It had now been about two days or more since they had any food. As it began to get dark a truck pulled up and two German soldiers unloaded some bread and a few bits of sausage. The starving men wolfed the stale bread down and savored the sausage. They had managed to dig all of the dead Germans out of the trench and that food was their reward. Also the German guards ate the same food as the POWs ate that day.

The Fatal Journey

Sgt. Hall recalled that bread and sausage tasted delicious and was badly needed by the starving men. After devouring their meal, the POWs were lined up against a wooden fence and were ordered by a red-headed German guard to march out into the countryside. They could hear the rumble of battle in the distance as the men marched out of town. It turned out they were setting out on a frozen hellish journey, headed for Stalag III A, in the town of Luckenwalde near Frankfurt on the Main, Germany. From Kustrine to Luckenwalde was almost two hundred miles, and none of the American POWs was prepared for such a prolonged, frigid march. But as they marched westward down the frozen country road, they hoped and prayed they would not get caught in another battle between the two armies.

The first night on the road was a preview of just how unbearable the journey would be. The red-headed German guard set a fast pace, and the men were quickly becoming fatigued. As night fell, they were herded into a frozen plowed field and told to bed down. They had no shelter or blankets and most were clothed in standard army issue clothing. Sleep was impossible as they lay together in the fetal position in an attempt to keep from freezing to death. As the long, miserable night gradually turned into a cold, crisp dawn, the men arose like zombies and were given a slice of rancid black bread with nothing at all to drink. Following that "breakfast," the POWs prepared to continue their hellish parade. However, the lack of food was causing terrible stomach pains for everyone. With each break in their march the men would dig rotten and frozen carrots and potatoes from nearby fields. Those meager morsels were the mainstay of their menu during their migration to Luckenwalde.

The next morning, the marchers passed by a small German airfield where German Stuka dive bombers were taking off. One of the planes roared down the runway and rose unsteadily into the frosty morning air. As the plane gained a few hundred feet of altitude, it suddenly shook violently, rolled over on its back and crashed in a ball of fire. The men cheered loudly as the plane crashed, knowing that it was one more plane that would not be able to bomb the Allies. As the men cheered, the red-headed German guard cursed loudly and fired a machine gun blast over their heads. But they kept on cheering until he said, "The next burst will not be over your head." That silenced the men, but it did not dampen their joy at seeing the plane go down in flames.

Few Finish March

During the march across the cold, bleak German countryside, many of the American POWs, suffering from disease, starvation, and exposure, dropped out and no doubt died along the frozen roadside. Those that were able to march were ordered to continue, leaving their fallen comrades to an unknown fate. Sgt. Hall recalled that on one overnight stop they were quartered in a barn. That cold, barren barn seemed to them like a grand hotel. That night they scrounged around and found a large iron kettle, and some of the men contributed frozen carrots, potatoes, green weeds, or anything else that might be eaten and dumped them all together into a boiling pot of water. The result was a passable soup that the men gulped down. At another overnight stop, some of the men ventured into a farmhouse where their guards had taken refuge. They found a pitcher of cold milk that they carried back and divided with the men. They assumed the farm woman knew what was going on and said nothing, which reflected another act of kindness in a world gone mad.

Weather Worse, Conditions Horrific

As the march continued, the conditions became much worse. The weather became much colder, and there was a blanket of new snow on the ground. One evening as the men bedded down in another barn for the night, the red-headed guard said he was going into the nearby town where his father was a doctor in the local hospital. He never came back. Perhaps he deserted, or was reassigned, but in any event, the POWs didn't know and didn't care. They were then under the control of several older guards. On one occasion, one of the older guards gave Sgt. Hall and two of his friends a piece of sausage and bread. That act, the old German guard at Stalag III C, the lad and the lady at Kustrine, and the milk at the farmhouse were about the only acts of kindness ever shown the POWs.

Because of the lack of food and the rotten food they had to eat, Sgt. Hall's dysentery began to flare up again. Toilet facilities were nonexistent, and the very act of relief was painful and laborious. Also, the rash resulting from lice bites became more painful. Although many of the men had been bitten by rats in some of the barns where they slept, Sgt. Hall said, "Thankfully, I was never bitten because I think if I had been bitten by a rat, I would have gone over the edge." With all of those circumstances against him, he was about ready to lie down beside the road and give up, but something within him would not allow him to give in. He felt someone had to live to tell the story of the terrible suffering of the American POWs in the hands of their captors.

Each night it became more apparent to Sgt. Hall that their numbers were dwindling. After eight days and seven nights, those men still standing marched into Stalag III A at Luckenwalde. The survivors only hoped that some of those who didn't make it all the way may have been befriended by some kindly German. But the reality probably was that dozens of American POWs frozen to death along the roadside or had just wandered off in the woods and died somewhere between Kustrine and Luckenwalde. Sgt. Bill Hall was grateful the march was over, thankful he had survived, and hopeful that he could start regaining his strength.

CHAPTER 6
Stalag III A: Almost Free

Let my people go.
Exodus 5:1

Stalag III A was a holding camp for thousands of Allied POWs that were marched west across Germany ahead of the Russian army. As Sgt. Hall and those weakened men staggered through the prison gates at Stalag III A, they were first given their barracks assignment. Their barrack buildings were slightly larger than Stalag III C but just as cold, depressing and uncomfortable. Their bunks were three high along each side of the room and consisted of the familiar planks covered with a mattress of rough canvas ticking stuffed with lice infested straw. The lice at the new camp were just as hungry as the lice at the old camp, and they continued to make life miserable for the POWs. After weeks of marching west in the winter weather, the POWs were starving and in need of nourishment and medical care. They received no medical care, but were given one fourth of a loaf of black bread and a bowl of that old familiar "garbage soup" delivered to their barracks. At least the soup was hot and the meal tasted like a steak dinner to the starving men. Sgt. Hall "wolfed" down that sour bread and hot soup with relish and even licked the bowl. Following the meal, he was issued a blanket, assigned a lower bunk where he wrapped himself in the blanket, collapsed, and fell into a deep sleep. Even the lice could not keep him awake.

At Stalag III A, the men began receiving some Red Cross parcels every other week. In one of the parcels was a deck of cards which meant poker games continued almost day and night with clothing, candy, and cigarettes as the medium of exchange. Sgt. Hall recalled winning a tanker's jacket in one of those games. It was much warmer than his standard field jacket. He recalled that he even wore that tattered tanker's jacket to bed and did not play poker any more for fear of losing his precious Red Cross supplies.

The American, British, and Russian prisoners were separated in three different sections of the compound. Many of the guards were older men and veterans of WW I and showed some compassion toward the POWs. Occasionally, late in the evenings when the men would approach the barbed-wire fences separating the compounds, the guards would pull back the wire and allow the Americans and British to cross from one area to another. The men would then usually reward them with a couple of cigarettes.

On one occasion during Bill Hall's visit to the British compound, he met a "Brit" wearing one of their battle jackets similar in style to the American Eisenhower jacket. The two men agreed to trade jackets, but Bill was to receive twenty "fags" (British term for cigarettes) to boot. Although he hated to give up his cherished tanker's jacket, the weather was beginning to get warmer and even under those hellish conditions, the young sergeant recalled that vanity probably played a part in the trade. The "Brit" did not have the "fags" with him, but they exchanged jackets and the "Brit" agreed to bring him the "fags" the next evening. He gave Sgt. Hall his name, barracks number, and bunk number. However, after four evenings the "Brit" did not show up with the "fags." Then on the fifth night, Bill Hall and his good friend, Bill Shortall, decided to "invade" the British compound. In his healthier days, Sgt. Shortall was a robust six-foot-three-inches tall and weighed 220 pounds. But even in his weak, emaciated condition, he still made an intimidating figure as the two men approached the

"Brit" lying in his bunk. Needless to say, the "Brit" gave Sgt. Hall the promised cigarettes.

For the first time since his capture by the Germans, Sgt. Hall was permitted to attend mass. In Stalag III A, a French priest had erected a makeshift chapel in a shed near the barracks. One Sunday following mass, a starving American POW was shot to death by a German guard for stealing turnips off of a horse-drawn wagon near the mess hall. The incident so incensed the POWs, that they called a meeting, and Link Ford, their camp representative, agreed to protest the killing to the camp commander. He told the commander that after the war, this matter would be reported to the Allied War Crimes Commission. The incident demonstrated two things: that the POWs were not going to accept such brutality without speaking out against it, and that the German guards were dangerous and would still take extreme measures to enforce the camp rules. After several days of heightened security and extreme tenseness in the compound, the camp settled down into a monotonous routine of trying to survive.

The prisoners' day began each morning at 6 a.m. when the men were required to line up outside their barracks for a head count. The count was taken by the old German guards and the men would do their best to confuse those old timers. After being counted, some men would step out of line and run behind the line to the end and be counted again. Sometimes the old guards would grow tired of these pranks and call one of the SS guards who would club a few men with their rifles if they chose to keep up the charade.

For the men in Stalag III A life was a daily routine of picking lice out of their clothes, trading Red Cross food and cigarettes, and creative cooking using good old American ingenuity to make a hasty tasty pudding. That was accomplished by mixing sour bread soaked in powdered milk with a sprinkle of sugar from a Red Cross parcel on top. This pudding was then cooked in a tin container on a small blower stove made from an empty powdered milk can. The blower consisted of a tin fan blade and a tin crank with a string for a pulley. A small fire would be started in the bottom of the can and the pudding mixture placed over it. The hand crank blew the heat up to the pudding and made a passable tasting hot dessert dish. Sgt. Hall recalled he was never clever enough to make one of those blower stoves, but did trade cigarettes occasionally for some of that hasty tasty pudding.

Soviet Russia never became a part of the Geneva Convention that attempted to require humane treatment of POWs among member nations. As a result, the Russian POWs suffered the cruelest kind of treatment at the hands of the Germans. Of course, they never received any Red Cross parcels and had nothing of value to trade. But the Americans would, from time to time, throw a few cigarettes and food over the fence to those starving Russians. Since both men and women fought together in the Russian army, the Russian camp contained both men and women housed together. There seemed to be no sense of modesty among those starving men and women. However, since they were all near death from starvation, survival was the only thing on their minds.

Late one evening, the German guards opened up with machine gun fire on the Russian latrine, killing and wounding several POWs. Following the deadly shooting, the Germans left the dead bodies of their victims lying outside until the stench became almost unbearable throughout the whole compound. Several days later, they finally removed the rotting bodies.

The massacre of the Russians made everyone in the American and British compound more anxious and unsettled. Unknown to many of the men, there was an escape committee in camp attempting to dig a tunnel to freedom. They maintained a tight security over the secrecy of the plan, and even Sgt. Bill Hall had no knowledge of the plan until the guards discovered the half-completed tunnel. Apparently someone in camp had tipped the guards as to the tunnel location.

The escape committee interrogated everyone in camp in an attempt to locate the traitor.

The Germans always housed air corps POWs and infantry POWs in separate camps. The air corps POWs were placed in camps called "Dulag Luft" camps. But just before the secret tunnel was discovered, a new prisoner had arrived in camp. He claimed he was a member of the Eighth Air Force from Indiana who had recently been shot down. He arrived in Sgt. Hall's barracks wearing a new leather flying jacket and fleece-lined boots. The escape committee also strongly interrogated the new "Air Corps" POW. Following his interrogation, he was never seen again in the compound and had obviously been planted by the Germans. He had accomplished his assignment and discovered their plans to escape and the location of the tunnel. He had been tripped up when he did not know that the Indiana University basketball team was called "Hoosiers."

In mid-April, 1945, the American POWs at Stalag III A heard on the underground radio that President Franklin D. Roosevelt had died of a massive stroke. The men were devastated and grief stricken. At noon the next day, every American POW assembled as a group in the courtyard in honor of their fallen leader. They stood silently at attention with eyes closed and heads bowed for five minutes. It seemed to confuse their guards, and their German captors never did know why or what they were doing.

When Bill Hall entered the Army in 1942, he weighed 145 pounds. However, after several months of living on sour bread, garbage, and Red Cross parcels, his weight dropped to 95 pounds. His ribs stuck out of the sides of his rib cage like railroad ties. He had not shaved for two months, making him appear much older than his 21 years. He still suffered a severe red rash on his upper body and thighs because of the lice. But Sgt. Hall wrote in his memoirs, "My stomach must have been getting used to the rancid food because my dysentery was more under control than it had been in quite some time."

One morning in late March, the men of Stalag III A awoke to the sound of distant artillery fire. Their underground radio reported the Russians had crossed the Oder River and were racing across Germany. Although no one knew how far the Russians had penetrated into Germany, rumors were rampant, the POWs feared that once again they would be caught between the Russian and German armies.

Each day the sounds of battle grew louder as artillery and mortar fire drew closer to camp. Then early one morning the roar of aircraft engines could be clearly heard overhead. Rushing outside, Sgt. Hall looked up and saw the blue German sky was black with American bombers, and all of the men stood outside cheering them on. Even the guards seemed to be awed by the sight of hundreds of heavy bombers overhead being escorted by dozens of fighter planes. The flight stretched for miles across the morning sky. Sgt. Hall said, "We knew then the end was surely in sight." Also, every night the British heavy Lancaster bombers and Mosquito fighter bombers were dropping their deadly load of bombs on the retreating Germans. It did not appear that the German army could resist much longer.

At night, Sgt. Hall, recalled one of the most fascinating sights he had ever seen were the "Christmas Tree" flares, which were dropped in clusters shaped like a Christmas tree and were a colorful red, white, blue and green. The sky was illuminated by white phosphus flares while the German search lights looked like long blue-white fingers reaching out for enemy planes overhead. Occasionally, a beam would light up a bomber, and the German anti-aircraft guns would zero in on it. But the men cheered the bombers repeatedly, knowing they were pounding the German industry and armies.

Even though Stalag III A was located several miles outside of Frankfurt on the Main, the ground shuddered as the impact of thousands of pounds of bombs struck railroads and factories. As the bombings became more intense over the next few days, sounds of automatic small arms fire soon became audible, and it was apparent that a battle was taking place only a few miles away. But the men had no way of knowing if it was between Germans and Americans or Germans and Russians.

The next evening with the sounds of battle only a few miles away, a German SS colonel entered Sgt. Hall's barracks. He wore a long, black leather coat with the infamous skull and crossbones insignia on his collar. He spoke English with a crisp British accent. His message was, "The Russian army is near the compound and if anyone attempts to leave the camp they will be shot." He also told the POWs that if they remained in camp, they should be relatively safe because both the Russians and Germans knew it was a POW camp and neither side would destroy it. But both German and Russian combat troops were in the area and would certainly fire on anyone seen outside the camp. With that warning, the German colonel promptly left the compound and the silence in the camp meant the men were seriously considering his warning.

After the German colonel left, the men held a meeting and decided for the present they would remain in camp. Later that evening one of the old WW I German guards in charge of Sgt. Hall's barracks came in and asked the prisoners to give him shelter. He was convinced he would be shot on sight if taken by the Russians. Barracks leader, Link Ford, took his rifle and gave him some old GI clothing and a blanket. He then instructed him to get into one of their empty bunks and keep his mouth shut. Unlike the Germans, the American showed some compassion on their enemies. After they were liberated, Sgt. Hall never did find out what happened to the old German WW I guard.

William Hall in the year 2000 still suffers trauma from his POW experience.

CHAPTER 7
Liberty at Last

Take heed lest this liberty of yours becomes a stumbling block.
I Colossians 8:9

A few days after the SS colonel had warned the men to remain in camp, they were awakened by the thunderous roar and rumble of tanks. Sgt. Hall jumped out of his bunk and rushed outside in time to see a huge, low-slung noisy Russian tank come crashing through the barbed wire gate into the compound. Sgt. Hall said, "To my utter amazement, a smiling Russian woman wearing a tanker's helmet was standing up in the turret." She was smiling and waving at everyone, and, no doubt was the most welcome sight the men had seen since their capture.

As she brought her tank to an abrupt halt, some of the men climbed up on the tank treads. Still smiling she handed out cigars and bottles of potato vodka that tasted like re-run gasoline and burned like iodine. Some other tanks came crashing into the compound followed by armored cars and foot troops. The troops handed out biscuits, cigars, strong Russian cigarettes, and more vodka. The men were now liberated—or were they?

The guards were gone and the Russian combat troops were busy chasing the Germans toward Berlin. Very few other Russians ever entered the compound and the POWs were left on their own. The prisoners now had the run of the camp, and they raided the food stores and personnel files. Sgt. Hall found his POW data sheet with his fingerprints and confinement records. Bill Hall still has those documents in his possession, which serve as a grim reminder of the suffering and sacrifice he made for his country.

After further searching throughout the camp, the men found a large cache of Red Cross parcels, and they were soon distributed to the POWs by those now in charge of the camp. Now the starving men had instant coffee, powdered milk, chocolate "D" bars, and candy to add to their diet. Also, they now had more cigarettes to trade for other things. After more "scrounging" around inside the compound, they discovered a small warehouse full of turnips and black sour bread. As a result the men were able to improve their diet slightly over their previous rations. The addition of some real food did much to improve the morale of the starving prisoners, but did little to better their appearance.

Sgt. Hall recalled he received the shock of his life when he confiscated a small mirror and was able to see himself for the first time in months. His face was gaunt, and his eyes, sunk deep in their sockets, were weak and watery. His teeth were full of cavities, and he had long since gotten used to the daily pain they caused him. His hair was filthy, matted and turning grey. He had not shaved for weeks. His ribs could be counted from ten feet away as they protruded through the sides of his chest. With the camp empty of guards, the men took over the former officers' quarters which contained showers and soap. Although there was no hot water, the men could take daily showers. Oh, what a relief that was!

After waiting several days in camp, the prisoners ventured into the town of Luckenwalde on numerous occasions. The town was occupied by Russian soldiers who paid little attention to the wondering POWs. Sgt. Hall said, "I think I saluted every Russian soldier I met which must have surprised a lot of buck privates." While in town they raided several abandoned houses and found such treasures as unspoiled potatoes, carrots, and turnips. On one such trip they went to a Russian food depot, and, after a long delay, they were rewarded with loaves of white bread. It was really a treat for the men, and they marveled at the soft texture and golden crusts. The men were also given more vodka which Sgt. Hall said still "tasted like gasoline."

At one point, sections of the American army entered Luckenwalde and an American colonel took command of Stalag III A. He announced to the men they were being moved into a former Hitler Youth camp on the outskirts of Luckenwalde. The men marched out of the prison camp to their new home with high hopes. Their new quarters were like a luxury hotel compared to Stalag III A. The bunks had real mattresses with warm heavy blankets.

Their new quarters were filled with souvenirs of the once mighty Third Reich. There were full military uniforms, swastikas, arm bands, flags, pistols, helmets, boots, daggers, swords, and military equipment of every description. As it turned out their new quarters were too good to be true. Luckenwalde was under Russian control, and the Americans were soon moved back to the American lines. The Russians then ordered the POWs back to Stalag III A because they wanted the Hitler Youth camp as quarters for their own troops. Just as the American POWs were getting comfortable, they were ordered back into the filthy squalor of Stalag III A.

As the American POWs tried to settle back into their lice-infested quarters again, they were literally "itching" to get back to their own lines. A few days later, the men packed their meager belongings and attempted to walk out the gate toward the American lines, only to find the road blocked by the Russians. For some unknown reason, they would not allow the Americas to pass and ordered them back into the prison compound. Now they were prisoners of the Russians instead of the Germans, with an equally unsure future. But Sgt. Hall and three of his friends, Bill Shortall, Jim Jordon, and Mike Vacca, were determined to take their fate into their own hands and make a break for the American lines across the Elbe River.

Early the next morning the four men packed food, blankets, extra socks and underwear and sneaked out the gate, headed for home. They walked through the woods which was in itself a dangerous decision, because they might have been shot by either Russians, Germans, or Americans. During that period of the war, Germans, Russians, and Americans were shooting first and asking questions later.

After walking several miles through the woods, the four men fortunately reached the main road. Each time they heard a vehicle coming, they would dive into the brush beside the road. On one occasion, a small, three-wheeled, rickety old German truck came belching smoke and wobbling down the road. For some unknown reason, it stopped near where the four men were hiding. Two Russian soldiers, who had "liberated" the truck, got out and were examining their vehicle. Then for some unknown reason, perhaps motivated by a "Higher Power," the four Americans stood up and raised their hands and shouted "Amerikanskis" to the Russians. The soldiers grabbed their weapons and ordered the men to approach them. It was evident that they were friendly drunk and feeling no pain. They laughed, hugged the Americans, and gave them a kiss on each cheek and a friendly slap on the back and told then to get into the truck bed.

As the truck lurched forward belching blue smoke behind it, the four Americans crawled under a tarpaulin in the truck bed only to find they had to share it with two recently slaughtered pigs. After driving perhaps 15 miles, they ran into a Russian road block. Sgt. Hall and his friends feared the worst, that they would be caught again and be sent back to Stalag II A. But as they approached the road block, they crawled under the tarp with the two dead pigs. After much loud talking and laughing between the Russians, they were waved along. Evidently the men knew each other and were good friends so they allowed them through the roadblock without searching the truck. Happily again they were on their way headed west toward the American lines.

After driving another 20 miles, the Russians brought the rickety, three-wheeled truck to a halt in a rural area. They motioned for the men to get out of the truck, and as they untangled themselves from under the tarp, they were glad to get away from those smelly pigs. Without a word, the Russians sped off down the road leaving the men out in the middle of nowhere. They had no idea where they were, but they could hear sporadic small arms fire in the distance and they knew they were still in the middle of a war.

The four pilgrim POWs held a brief parlay in the middle of that lonely road and decided Jim Jordon, as the ranking non-com, would be the one to make the decision. Jim decided the four should go on walking west, keeping their eyes and ears open for both German and Russian troops. The four continued walking the rest of the day, hiding beside the road as vehicles passed them by. That evening, they moved from the road and followed a railroad into a small village that had several derailed passenger cars on a siding. One of those passenger cars looked like a good place to spend the night so they went inside and made themselves comfortable.

Sgt. Hall found a shattered piece of steel and built a fire to warm the interior of a battered boxcar. They had brought some bread with them which they shared equally. Also, they had brought blankets and managed to keep fairly comfortable during the night. They went to sleep talking about what their next move might be and what would be the best way to reach the American lines.

The next morning the weary pilgrims resumed their trek toward what they hoped would be the Elbe river and the American lines. Later that day, they came upon a farmhouse with a topless Russian command car parked in the front yard. Sitting inside was a Russian soldier armed with a submachine gun and smoking a pipe. As they approached with their hands raised, they shouted "Amerikanskis."

The soldier was so startled he dropped his pipe out of his mouth and raised his machine gun menacingly toward the men. It took a lot of shouting "Amerikanskis" before he realized what and who the men were. After recognizing them as American POWs, he flashed a toothless smile and waved the four men into the house.

As the men entered the farmhouse, they were greeted by an elderly farm couple. The woman immediately set the kitchen table and invited the weary men to sit down. She placed two boiled potatoes on each plate along with a bowl of watery soup. At least for a change, the soup was hot and worm free. Then the starving POWs were served a glass of cold milk and two slices of fresh dark bread. It was not the sour bread they had been used to and was delicious.

After their scrumptious feast, the old farmer took the men to the barn where he motioned they could sleep for the night on the dry straw. He also provided each man with another blanket. That night they slept undisturbed except for an occasional burst of machine gun fire. Although they had no idea what was going on outside, it did serve to remind them they were still in a war zone.

The next morning, the Russian soldier was no where to be seen. After eating a slice of bread, the four POWs said thanks and goodbye to the farm couple who had fed them and put them up in their barn. They continued walking westward toward the Elbe River, though forced many times to take cover from several small fire fights in the fields around them. But after three dangerous days, the four rag-tag POWs reached the Elbe River.

As the POWs walked down the street of a small village on the east side of the Elbe, they were stopped by a middle-aged German man on a bicycle. He had a medical identification badge attached to his bicycle and spoke excellent English. He was concerned that the Russians had occupied his town and would probably be there for a long time. The four told him their only concern was getting across the Elbe River. He directed them to a bridge that had been heavily bombed.

Although the bridge was only partially destroyed, crossing it even on foot looked dangerous, for they would have to cross by scaling the narrow beams. Since the weary POWs could see the Americans across the river, suddenly the danger became secondary. Luckily the Russians offered no resistance, and the men began the slow, tedious task of crossing. At the midpoint of the river, they had to traverse a one-foot-wide beam about a distance of seventy-five feet. Sgts. Hall, Shortall, and Jordon straddled the beam and inched their way across the swirling muddy river fifty feet below them. But Sgt. Mike Vacca stood up and walked the steel beam like a skilled iron worker.

Scaling the muddy banks of the Elbe River, the POWs came face to face with a group of American soldiers. Other than their fellow prisoners and one American captain at Stalag III A, the men had not seen another American for seven months. There was several minutes of hand shaking and back slapping. One of the soldiers had a camera and snapped several photographs. Sgt. Hall asked him to send him copies after they were developed, and even though he said he would, he never did. By the grace of God and their own fierce determination, the weary prisoners were free at last.

The GIs delivered the POWs to their officers. Then, they were immediately escorted to the mess tent, but before they had eaten anything, two doctors came rushing into the mess tent and instructed the cooks to prepare hot oatmeal, toast, jelly, and coffee. To this day, Sgt. Hall says, "Words cannot describe how wonderful that breakfast tasted to our starving stomachs."

Following breakfast, the four men were placed under quarantine in the camp's makeshift hospital. There they were given complete physical exams and checked for malnutrition and communicable diseases. After a week of rest, tests, and nourishing food, the four freed POWs were airlifted in an Army C-47 to Bristol, England. There the men were placed in a regional U.S. Army hospital for more rest and tests.

After several weeks of rehabilitation, Sgt. Hall and his three friends were permitted to leave the hospital and go into the British city of Bristol. It was the first time they felt really free, and they thoroughly enjoyed their visit into town. Bill Hall said, "It was great to be human again after so many months of inhuman treatment at the hands of the Nazis." With their bellies full and their bodies clean, the former POWs' morale was at an all-time high.

As soon as the men began to regain their strength, they were loaded aboard the hospital ship, USS *Blanch S. Sigman* (named for an Army nurse in WW I). After eight days the ship landed in Charleston, South Carolina, and the four friends were placed in Stark General Hospital. There the four friends were separated when Sgt. Hall was shipped to Gardner General Hospital in Chicago. After being treated for a week he was sent to Hot Springs, Arkansas, for more rest and relaxation in an old resort hotel with lots of hot water baths. After more rehabilitation, Bill Hall was given a 30-day leave and went home for the first time in over a year.

Following his furlough, Sgt. Hall reported back for duty at Camp Crowder, Missouri, where he was assigned to the Signal Corps. When the Japanese surrendered in August, 1945, he was discharged. All the young sergeant could say was *"Thank God, it was over"* and he had survived. The suffering, sights, and sounds he had experienced would remain with him as long as he lived.

All of the POWs trapped by the advancing Russian army and the retreating German army in late January, 1945, had to make a decision. Their choice was to: (1) remain in Stalag III C and risk being shelled by both armies, (2) walk out the prison gates and walk east toward Poland as did Phil Hardin and friends, or (3) walk out of Stalag III C and walk west as did Bill Hall and friends. The men who took one road always wondered what happened to those men who chose the other road. Their question was, would they have been better off on the other road?

Only now, over a half a century later, are some of these questions being answered. Even as late as March, 1998, Leonard Borneman, a former POW at Stalag III C during those perilous times, was still wondering what happened to those who chose to take the other route. This war time saga shows dramatically that during Sgt. Phil Hardin's walk east toward Warsaw, Poland, and Sgt. Bill Hall's walk west toward Luckenwalde, Germany, both suffered terrible hardships, inhumane treatment, starvation and exposure to the winter weather. But each one can now have an idea of what would have happened to them if they had taken the other road.

Photo: Dwayne Price

Pfc. Franklin Sousley, one of the Iwo Jima flag raisers made famous by Joe Rosenthall's photograph taken on top of Mt. Suribachi. Pfc. Sousley was killed before the island was secured.

PART III

IWO JIMA: THE FLAG, FIGHT, AND PHOTO

Private Franklin Sousley's Story

This monument, located at the grave of Franklin Sousley in Fleming County, Kentucky, is a replica of the famous photo taken by Joe Rosenthall in February, 1944. (Sousley is second from left).

CHAPTER 1
From Kentucky Home to the Battlefield

We have done that which was our duty to do.
Luke 17:10

Franklin Runyon Sousley was born in the beautiful, rolling hill country near Elizaville in Fleming County, Kentucky, on September 19, 1925. He was the second of three sons born to Goldie (Mitchell) and Merle Duke Sousley, who were married November 15, 1922, in Maysville, Kentucky. Malcolm, the oldest son, died when Franklin was two years old. Their youngest son, Julian, who was always a sickly child, died in 1951 at the age of 18.

Young Franklin's father died when he was nine years of age. Because of the devastating loss of his father, he was extremely close to his mother and always felt a keen responsibility to help her with the work around the farm. The red-haired lad attended Elizaville Elementary School and graduated from Flemingsburg High School. He was average among the 65 students who graduated from the high school on May 28, 1943. While in high school the five-foot-eleven-inch, 170-pound, athletic farm lad played both basketball and baseball and was active in the Glee Club and FFA (Future Farmers of America). His ambition in high school was to own a dairy farm someday.

During his junior year of high school, his mother married James Henley Price. The wedding took place in neighboring Maysville, Kentucky, on January 29, 1942. Two children were born to that union, James, Jr., and Janice.

Following high school graduation in 1943, the 18-year-old farm lad realized he would soon enter the armed forces. Like so many young Kentuckians at that time, while awaiting his call to the Army, he crossed the Ohio River and went to work, in his case at the Frigidaire Division of General Motors in Dayton, Ohio. He worked on an assembly line for 60 cents per hour. While he was in Dayton, he wrote regularly to his mother in Kentucky and sent money home, hoping that it would help her and she would not have to work so hard. Since he had no automobile, he did not get to come home often.

It was during his time in Dayton, Ohio, that young Franklin wrote a friend that he was, "dating, but was not serious; however, there is one girl that I really like but she doesn't know I exist." But later on he became more serious and hoped someday to marry.

Volunteered for the Marine Corps

During the fall of 1943 when Franklin turned 18 years old, it became apparent that he would soon be called to military service. Rather than be drafted, he elected to enter the Marine Corps and was ordered to report for duty on January 5, 1944. Franklin knew his mother needed help, and he worked as long as he could in order to help make her life easier. He wrote his mother on December 29, 1943, "I will be home for a couple of days before I enter the Marine Corps Reserves on January 5, 1944." While there he said to his mother what would turn out to be a very prophetic statement, "I hope I can do something that will make you proud of me while I'm a Marine."

The young Kentucky lad was sent across country to the San Diego, California, Marine Base for "Boot Camp." Following his basic training, he was assigned to Company E, 2nd Battalion, 28th Marines,

5th Marine Division. Pfc. Sousley was an automatic rifleman with that unit during his entire career. From California, he wrote his mother saying, "It was a three day train trip through the west and southwest, but I was not impressed with Colorado, New Mexico or Arizona. I will take Kentucky over those states anytime." He wrote his mother at least once a week during his basic training giving her a detailed report of the rigors of Marine life. He told her of the required discipline, forced marches with full combat gear, target practice on the firing line, going on maneuvers, and practice beach landings. As every Marine knows, the basic training required to build Marines is intense, rigorous, and difficult, but Franklin passed every test required to become a combat Marine. By the end of 1944, his division was given a furlough before being sent to the South Pacific, and he was able to see his mother one last time.

Pfc. Sousley and the 5th Marine Division embarked from California on January 7, 1945, aboard the USS *Tallega*. After landing at Hilo and Honolulu, they disembarked at Maui on January 13, 1945. While on Maui the division participated in practice amphibious landings. The men of the 5th Marine Division embarked from Hawaii on January 27, 1945. They crossed the international date line on January 31. Following stops at places the men had never even heard of, e.g., Eniwetok and Saipan, they sailed from Saipan on February 14, 1945, prepared for the assault on Iwo Jima. That was just another island they had never heard of, but one that soon would become a part of America's vocabulary.

Bloody Beach Battle Begins

Iwo Jima is a volcanic island five miles long and two miles wide. It was a place of rock, sand, tuft grass, and stinking sulphur pits. But that pile of rock and sand was of great strategic importance to the American war in the Pacific. Exactly halfway between the American-held island of Saipan and Tokyo—700 miles in each direction—it was the perfect base for fighter support for the B-29s based in the Mariana Islands on their bombing raids on Japan. It would also be a haven for crippled B-29 bombers drained of gas by strong head winds on the 3,000 mile round trip to Japan. Thus Iwo Jima had been on the American planning board since September, 1944. Its code name was operation "Detachment."

The Japanese also recognized the strategic importance of Iwo Jima and had occupied the island for a year. Lt. General Tadamichi Kuribagashi had 21,000 troops waiting for a year working feverishly transforming that barren island into an underground fortress of caves, tunnels, and underground gun emplacements, so cleverly concealed that they did not show up in photo reconnaissance. The Japanese had also constructed two airfields and were in the process of building another one. Their fighter planes were taking a heavy toll on the B-29 bombing raids. Therefore, the American high command believed the island had to be taken. The task of leading the assault on Iwo Jima was assigned to the 3rd, 4th, and 5th Marine Divisions.

Successfully assaulting the island presented several tactical problems. The only feasible landing beach was narrow and steep—3,500 feet wide and 300 feet deep. Code named "Green Beach," it was anything *but* green and consisted of powdery, soft, shifting black volcanic sand that would be difficult to cross with heavy equipment. At the north end of the narrow beach was Mt. Suribachi, and at the south end was a high cliff. It was the worst possible site for an invader and the best possible one for a defender, high ground at either end where the enemy could pour deadly fire down on an invader.

D-Day on Iwo Jima was February 19, 1945. H hour was 9:00 a.m. The success of the invasion lay in the hands of the 3rd Marine Division commanded by Major General Graves B. Erskine, 4th Marine Division commanded by Major General Clifton B. Cates, and the 5th Marine Division commanded by Major General Kelley B. Rockey. Those troops and other ancillary units totaled 70,000 men of the 5th

Amphibious Corps. It was the largest Marine force up to that time ever committed to one battle. The 5th Amphibious Corps was under the overall command of Major General Harry Schmidt, and the landing went off like clockwork. The first troops struck the beach at exactly 9:00 a.m. The second wave landed in perfect precision three minutes later, and right behind them came another and another. From the sea the landing boats kicked little white plumes of wake that looked like the largest water ballet ever staged. Ashore, it was anything but pretty.

On Monday morning February 19, 1945, General Kuribagashi was as ready as he could be for the assault. He had written his wife time and again that no Japanese troops would leave the island alive. In an earlier letter to his wife he reflected the fanaticism of the Japanese in battle when he wrote, "Please stop hoping you will ever see me alive or that I will ever return to you again."

The heavily entrenched Japanese defenders had been stunned by the final shelling from the battleships and bombing by aircraft. But even as the first troops landed, the gunfire began to rain down on them from Mt. Suribachi, slowly at first like the patter of a soft summer rain then rising steadily to the crescendo of a mountain storm. The shelling, air bombardment, and early battle fire had been so intense that Tokyo radio reported that the extinct volcano Mt. Suribachi had erupted.

Within an hour after the troops hit "Green Beach" it was stained red, littered with bodies and parts of bodies twisted grotesquely in the sand. Also littered about were guns, medicine, K-ration cans, bits of torn letters, burning jeeps, floundering landing craft, a toothbrush, and even a beer can. In the first nine hours that the Marines were pinned down on the beach at Iwo Jima they suffered 2,400 casualties, including 600 dead.

Mt. Suribachi was the well fortified high ground that dominated the beach landing area. Although Green Beach was the code name given the beach landing area, to the men of the 5th Marine Division who landed there, the volcanic sand appeared more like the dregs of used coffee grounds on Monday morning, and they referred to it as "Coffee Grounds Beach."

The black sand was both friend and enemy. It was easy to dig a fox hole, but it was difficult to deal with that fine sifting stuff. The sand got in their eyes and caked around their eyelashes. It became mixed in their hair like gritty dandruff. It invaded their small cans of K-ration ham and eggs as soon as they were opened. It crept over the tops of their leggings and worked its way down in their shoes. The men had to be particularly careful to keep the sand from clogging their weapons. But the sand was only a minor distraction.

Marine Casualties Mount

For two days the men were pinned to the ground by deadly machine gun and rifle fire from the line of pill boxes hidden in the shrubbery at the base of Mt. Suribachi 400 yards away. Even if one head showed above a fox hole, it brought deadly fire immediately. The men had to lie on their sides to eat, drink from their canteens, or urinate. An errand between fox holes became a dash between life and death. Green clad bodies of dead and wounded Marines who lost their race littered the landscape. Hundreds of men hugged the beach spread out in a scattered pattern; they were cut up and disorganized by the heavy fire when they landed. Their supplies were ruined. Many of their wounded lay where they had fallen despite the heroic efforts of the Medical Corps. But after two days being pinned down on the beach, the Marines began to move slowly forward.

Japanese Entrenched Under Suribachi

On D-Day plus 2, aided by tank reinforcements, the troops moved painfully forward foot by foot. They slowly cleared the area from the beach to the mountain. But there were still many of the enemy everywhere. With the tanks lobbing shells into the stone and concrete bunkers, the Marines began to secure their positions. But, after the soldiers had passed, the enemy would emerge behind them from their camouflaged bunkers and fire at the rear of the troops. When the Japanese were driven from one pill box, they would retreat through underground tunnels and appear in another emplacement.

As those gallant Marines moved toward the foot of Mt. Suribachi, for the first time they began to see dead Japanese soldiers. There were dead enemy soldiers in every conceivable contortion of men who had met death violently. Their arms and legs were wrenched about their bodies and fists were closed in frozen defiance. There were dead Marines also. Some platoons had lost all their officers and non-coms. Some had lost 75 percent of their men since landing two days earlier. The terrible carnage of human lives lost in war was evident everywhere. But the Marines, had fought their way under the heavy gun emplacements to the base of Mt. Suribachi. However, there were still many more Japanese pill boxes and hidden snipers that had to be cleared at the base of the mountain before any attack could be launched to assault the mountain.

The third day after landing, one Marine detachment fought its way around one side of the base of Mt. Suribachi. Another detachment did the same thing on the other side of the mountain. There they dug in for the night. About 1:00 a.m., the enemy launched a heavy counterattack and kept coming until daybreak. Although the Marines suffered heavy casualties, they successfully beat back the attack. All day the next day the Americans were busy cleaning out tunnels, caves, and concrete emplacements around the base of the mountain.

Later that night Sgt. Ernest R. Thomas of Tallahassee, Florida, led a platoon in a final drive to the top of the mountain. They were accompanied by their executive officer, Lt. Harold G. Shriver, of Richmond, Missouri. Slowly they inched their way upward amid heavy resistance. They were fighting for each square foot of ground and the going was slow and casualties were heavy. When darkness came, they dug in for the night along a torturous path that led to the mountain top. It was a bad night! The rain came down in torrents and the small rivulets of water trickled down the mountainside through their fox holes, into their clothes, washing the fine sand across their bodies. The cold wind made them shiver as they huddled in their fox holes trying to keep their weapons dry under their ponchos. But the rain stopped just before daybreak.

Marines Reach Top of Suribachi

At 8:00 a.m. on D-Day plus 4, the orders were given to take the hill, and Pfc. Sousley and the men of the 28th Marines began their final ascent. The volcanic sand on the steep path offered poor footing and men would take two steps forward and slip back one step. Stubby plants would break off in their hands or come out by their roots as the men tried to pull themselves upward. But the only resistance they encountered was the occasional ping of a sniper's bullet that sometimes found an unfortunate Marine. As the men reached the top, they located several more gun emplacements manned by live Japanese. Those were soon cleaned out with flame throwers, BARs (automatic rifles) and satchel charges (explosives in packages thrown into the pill boxes).

By 11:30 on February 23, 1945, the Marines were in undisputed control of the top of Mt. Suribachi. As soon as the Americans had wrested control of the mountain top, Green Beach far below began taking on the appearance of any other beachhead since they were no longer under fire from the mountain. The volcanic sand was littered with abandoned equipment and the shore was lined with boats delivering more supplies and evacuating the wounded.

CHAPTER 2
Flag Raised as Battle Rages

Lift up a banner upon a high mountain.
Isaiah 12:2

At 11:37 a.m. on Friday, after the 5th Division Marines gained undisputed control of the top of the volcano, Sgt. Henry O'Hanson of Somerville, Massachusetts, looked around for a pole and found a 15-foot section of Japanese lead pipe on the ground. Lt. Schriver pulled a small American flag from his pack, and he and other men of the 5th Division attached the flag to the Japanese pipe and stuck it into the ground at the highest point on the top of the mountain. Lt. Schriver ordered the men to hurry because they were still in danger and Iwo Jima was far from secured. A few miles to the north, Marines were still fighting the battle of Motoyama Airfield No. 2. With the raising of the flag at Mt. Suribachi, however, the Marines felt they had avenged what they considered a humiliating experience when the enemy on that mountain made them wallow in the sand on the Green Beach for two days.

It was about noon, just 23 minutes after the small flag was raised over Mt. Suribachi, that a flag twice as large was brought to the mountain top. Pfc. Franklin Runyon Sousley and several other men of Company E of the 28th Marines were still making sure the area was secure when a sergeant handed them the larger flag and ordered them to take the small flag down and replace it with the larger flag. In raising that flag, Pfc. Franklin R. Sousely and five of his comrades would forever be enshrined in hearts and minds of Americans because of a photograph of that event.

Photo Taken of Larger Flag Raising

As the six men raised the second flag, they hardly noticed the bespectacled civilian combat photographer, Joe Rosenthal, who had been ruled unfit for military service by his draft board. He snapped the picture as the flag went up. Joe Rosenthal later described the moment and circumstances that surrounded the famous photograph.

"There were a number of Marines on top of Mt. Suribachi . . . perhaps 50 that were digging into the rubble of the Japanese gun positions and checking those gun positions and making sure there were no more live Japanese left. The men didn't talk much. The six who raised the flag were working on the foundation for the pole ... finally the Marine in charge said, 'OK, let's go!' There was almost no conversation as the flag went up. Somebody said 'Let's swing it up fast.'"

He continued: "I was standing back about 40 feet. I had never seen these men before and, while they presumably knew I was there, they paid no special attention to me. If there was any drama in the flag raising it was pretty silent drama. There wasn't any whooping or hurrahing about it. I don't recall ever seeing any of those men again on Iwo Jima."

Those Marines had been told by their Lieutenant as they fastened the flag to that 15-foot section of Japanese pipe, to hurry it up because there was plenty of work to be done. They were ordered on to the northern Iwo Jima front where three of the six men were eventually killed and one was wounded. Pfc. Sousley wrote to his mother before he was killed, "Mother, a photographer took my picture and you may be seeing it in the paper." The young Marine was killed shortly before the photo shot was released.

A Moment That Will Live Forever

The first person to see the photograph was Marine Photo Specialist, Pfc. Joseph W. Fleck, stationed on the South Pacific island of Guam. Rosenthal's film was flown from Iwo Jima to Guam where it was handled routinely in the Third Marine Division Photographic Laboratory. Pfc Fleck said, "We processed a good deal of this type of film. Naturally I looked at it when we made the first print after developing the negative. To me, and others in the laboratory, the print was of good quality, but was just another picture." Later when word filtered back to Guam about the picture's impact in the United States, Pfc. Fleck and the others re-inspected the negative. Admiral Chester W. Nimitz, commander of all naval forces in the Pacific, summed up the picture's impact on the nation when he wrote to Joseph Rosenthal, "You have caught a moment in the lives of six of our valorous Marines which will live forever in the hearts and minds of their countrymen."

The Immortal Six

The six men who raised the flag on Mt. Suribachi were symbols of the cultural diversity of America and her citizen army of World War II. Those six identified in the photograph included a full-blooded Pima Indian, a Wisconsin wrestler with a trick knee, a former member of the Merchant Marine, a man who first had been rejected for military service, the son of an immigrant coal miner, and a rural Kentucky farm lad. They ranged in age from 19 to 25 and had been in service from 18 months to 6 years. Their personalities ranged from what was described as one of the quietest and nicest boys in town to a wild daredevil who wanted more action. All had been eager to enlist and do their part for their country. Three of them would die on Iwo Jima, an indication of the terrible price paid to capture that island. One man of the six would also be wounded before the bitter fighting ended on the northern part of the island.

Pfc. Franklin Sousley

The first man in the photo, looking left to right, with his hand raised higher on the flag pole than anyone else, was Fleming County native Franklin Runyon Sousley. The Kentucky farm lad's name was first listed as unidentified because he was killed a few days after the photo was snapped. His name was withheld until his mother had been notified that he had been killed in action. Pfc. Sousley was the youngest of the group and had been in the Marines only 18 months. He was typical of the thousands of America's finest men killed at the beginning of their life during WW II.

After the family moved away from the house where he was born, it remained empty for many years and was used as a storage building for hay, corn, and tobacco. Twenty-five years after the death of the young Marine, an unsuccessful attempt was made to purchase the old house with one acre of land to be used as a historical landmark.

Pfc. Ira Hayes

The second man in the photograph is Pfc. Ira H. Hayes, age 22. He has his rifle slung over his shoulder and was then a combat-hardened veteran who always kept his rifle close at hand. His parents, Mr. and Mrs. Job Hayes, lived in the Indian Village of Bapchula, Arizona. Ira Hayes attended the Pima Indian Reservation Elementary School at Scaton, Arizona. He later attended the Indian High School in Phoenix where he starred in football and basketball. His teachers remembered him "as always being in the thick of things, and always staying with anything he started."

Pfc. Hayes was a qualified parachute jumper and received two bronze stars for gallantry under fire during the landings at Vella Levella and Bouginville. He had one nineteen-year-old brother in military service and two younger brothers at home. Pfc. Ira Hayes survived the war and returned home to see his family again.

Sgt. Michael Strank

The third man in the photo, just barely visible to the right of Ira Hayes, is Sgt. Michael Strank. Sgt. Strank's parents emigrated to America from Czechoslovakia and settled in the coal mining area of Cambric County, Pennsylvania. Michael was born in Cambric County and attended elementary and high school at Franklin Borough. He was a member of the high school orchestra and played on the basketball team.

Michael Strank had served in the Civilian Conservation Corps for 18 months before joining the Marines. He enlisted in 1939 and planned to make the Marine Corps a career. He had one brother in the Navy and one brother and one sister at home in Pennsylvania. Sgt. Michael Strank was killed a few days later in the bitter fighting north of Green Beach.

Ph. Mate John Bradley

The fourth man in the photo is U.S. Navy Pharmacist Mate 2nd Class John H. Bradley, 21. He was the only non-Marine in the group. He had been assigned to E Company, 2nd Battalion, 28th Marines as a medic on Iwo Jima. John attended elementary and high school in Appleton, Wisconsin. He graduated from Appleton High School in 1941. While in high school he was on the wrestling team, and as a result of wrestling came out of high school with a trick knee. In January, 1944, he managed to hide the trick knee from medical examiners when he enlisted. Since his dad was a veteran of WW I, John had always planned to enlist in military service. Before entering the Navy, Pharmacist Mate Bradley had been an undertaker's assistant. Although he suffered a serious leg wound in his first major engagement at Iwo Jima, the young sailor survived to return home.

Pfc. Rene A. Gagnon

The fifth man in the photo, the one whose helmet is barely visible, is Pfc. Rene A. Gagnon. He was the son of Mrs. Irene Gagnon of

Manchester, New Hampshire, and was engaged to Miss Pauline Harris. The 20-year-old Marine carried his fiancee's picture inside his helmet throughout the war. The young couple had met when they worked together in the same room at the Chicopee Mills factory. They planned to be married following the war.

Rene Gagnon tried to enlist in the Navy at age 17 and was rejected because of high blood pressure. But he was determined to get into the military service so he carefully followed his physician's instructions for a year, and was then able to pass the Marine Corps physical the next time. Pfc. Gagnon wanted to become a policeman in his native New Hampshire after the war. He once told New Hampshire Governor Charles M. Dule, "This war is making some tough fighters and it will take some tough men with training to keep them in line after the war." Pfc. Gagnon was one of the three men in the photograph to survive the war and he returned to Manchester to pursue his dream.

Sgt. Henry Hansen

The sixth man at the base of the flag in the photo is Sgt. Henry O. Hansen, 25. He was the son of Mrs. Madelene Evelley of Somerville, Massachusetts, and the oldest of the six men pictured in the photograph. According to his mother, her son was always the daredevil in the group. As a child he was always climbing the highest tree, jumping from the highest point, or swimming across the widest stream. He joined the Merchant Marine at age 17, but finding life aboard a transport ship too boring, he enlisted in the Marine Corps in 1938.

After serving as a gunnery instructor for much of the war, Henry volunteered for overseas duty because he wanted to get into combat. Sgt. Henry O. Hansen had three brothers in military service and a sister who was a Navy nurse. The young Marine got his wish for combat on the bloody island of Iwo Jima. He was killed in the final days of the fighting to capture the island.

Marine using a flame thrower to smoke Japanese out of caves on Mt. Suribachi (Yank)

D-Day Plus 8

While the battle for Iwo Jima was still raging to the north, the southeastern part of the island had settled down to an almost garrison-like atmosphere. The invasion beach that had run red with American blood one week earlier had been cleared of enemy machine gun and sniper fire. But two miles north of the beach the Marines were still advancing in the face of deadly bombardment and artillery fire. On the beach, the Military Police ordered the Marines to clean up around their foxholes because the higher brass was coming. Some junior officers were even snapping peacetime stateside salutes at their superior officers. A brand new, open-air 18 holer had replaced the slit trench used as a bathroom by the enlisted men. The officers had a bathroom covered by a tent. Many of the rear echelon troops were sneaking up Mt. Suribachi looking for souvenirs in the caves.

The beach bristled with what could be called organized confusion. Amphibious vehicles such as "Ducks" and "Weasles" huffed and puffed among the Amtracks, bulldozers, and trucks creating huge clouds of dust as they clanged their way from one area to another. The vital supply line to the advancing Marines was now operational as bare chested men sweated, cursed, and argued as they tried to push their freight ahead of someone else. An officers' sedan looked as out of place on the beach as an old maid in a bawdy house. But the scope and grisly reality of the bloody conflict was just beginning to take shape.

Grave Diggers Busy

The Seabees were busy "buzzing" on the beach. Above their camp some of their bulldozers had cleared and leveled a strip of land. There were a dozen men with shovels quietly digging graves. A surveying crew took careful measurements to fix the exact grave for each body. Behind the line of freshly dug graves there were several rows of freshly filled graves. Above each grave there was a dog tag hung on a pointed stick. Later those sticks would be replaced with white crosses. Several Marines moved slowly and reverently between the graves, being careful not to step on a grave, as they examined the dog tags looking for fallen friends.

Pallbearers slowly carried bodies shrouded in Marine green broadcloth to the empty graves and carefully lowered them into their resting places. Then they returned for more bodies. This continued for hours because the losses were terrible. One of the pallbearers asked Pvt. John W. Conley of LeRoy, New York, in charge of the pallbearer detail, for a receipt for each body they buried. Conley handed him a slip of paper identifying each body buried and said, "It's too bad you can't even be buried without a receipt."

To the northeast near the battle line was an artillery post. The men there had landed at 3:00 a.m. on D-Day plus 1, and each man had fired an average of 350 rounds a day since landing. The men were resting while Sgt. Walter T. Edwards of Lakeland, Florida, received telephone instructions from the fire leader. Reporting back to his men he said, "The first patrol is moving into a new village." "That must be where all those geisha girls are," said Cpl. George T. Delta from Berkley Springs, WV, one of the crew members. "I heard they have 400 of them." As the men talked about the geisha girls, the phone rang again, and the Sgt. listened intently on his earphones for a few seconds. Hanging up the phone quickly, he shouted, "OK. Let's go!" The crewmen jumped to their positions as their sergeant barked out, "Change the deflection, right one-three-four. Fire." The men's rest period was over, and they were back in the war.

Battle Rages on

Across from the artillery post was a supply dump, piled high with boxes of K and C rations. Cpl. Floyd M. Barton from Sarasota, Florida, sat on a crate of Spam marking figures on a pad. He had no helmet and his face was twisted in a frown of concentration. He appeared undisturbed by the booming of guns around him. His job was distributing rations, and he thought Iwo Jima was a better place to distribute rations than either Guam or Saipan where he had been before. "It's cooler and there are not as many insects," he said.

Further north there were many people and activities that indicated the front line was not far away. Pfc. Steve A. Trochek of Clarion, Pennsylvania, lay close to the ground on his back beside the crude airstrip taken from the Japanese two days earlier. He was repairing a communications line between the airstrip and the front lines. Trochek had been in the front line for five days and was sent back for a rest and less hazardous duty. He expected to return to the front line the next day.

Marines begin the bloody assault on Mt. Suribachi. (Yank)

Just two days earlier the front line had been right down the middle of the airstrip. But bitter fighting by the Marines had driven the enemy back from the airfield. There were ruins of Japanese fighter planes and bombers strewn across the runways and in the hard-ground storage areas. A grader worked at one end of the field filling bomb craters preparing a base for our own bombers to land. Pfc. Darrel J. Farmer of Broken Bow, Nebraska, ran a grader he had brought in before the Japanese were driven out. He started his work while under sniper and mortar fire. "We'll have the field ready in two days," he told a captain anxiously standing by. Five bulldozers and four tractors were also working feverishly to insure the strip would be ready to receive

American bombers. Farther toward the front, Pvt. John R. Dober of Milwaukee, Wisconsin, operated a magnetic mine detector. He was as careful with it as a new bride with a new vacuum cleaner, covering every foot of the road to make sure it was safe for the tanks and bulldozers that followed. In a small clearing just past where Pfc. Dober was sweeping the area for mines was a battalion aid station. There, under a small white tent with no sides, corpsmen were giving blood plasma to two wounded Marines. It had been less than one hour since they had been wounded, and in another 30 minutes they would be aboard a waiting hospital ship. Medical Officer Captain Floyd T. Jenkins had just returned from the front lines and ordered the corpsmen to prepare to move the aid station forward. The captain said, "They've been going like hell today and are moving forward again in one hour."

Moving on toward the front lines, the road topped a ridge and disappeared into a sandy field. Fighting had been vicious there, and the tragic evidence was everywhere. An American heavy tank lay grotesquely twisted on its side. Its turret had been blown 30 yards away by a land mine. The tank gunner carried away by the turret had been butchered by the jagged pieces of iron. Arms, legs and bodies of other members of that tank crew had been twisted as badly as their tank.

In another corner of the sandy field lay the bodies of six more American Marines. They were covered with ponchos and shelter halves, and extending from beneath those covers was a defiant clinched fist. Other American dead lay where they had fallen. The battlefield was so new and fighting still so intense there was no time to clear it.

Beyond the next ridge were the front line reserve troops. They crouched in their foxholes and talked quietly. They inspected their weapons and occasionally fired them to make sure they were in working order. A Marine's worst enemy under those conditions would be a jammed rifle. As they waited quietly for orders to move up, they chewed on fig bars, smoked cigarettes and pawed the dirt restlessly with their feet. Beyond them were the front lines of war. Then their sergeant barked the order, "Saddle up and move out!"

Compared to the noise, cursing, and confusion going on at the supposedly peaceful southern end of the secured beach, the front lines were relatively quiet on D-Day plus 10. However, that soon changed. The Marines were now just in front of Airfield No. 2 about 700 yards from Sandy Ridge, the last major objective on Iwo Jima. The battlefield was a flat desert-like plain with no hills, shrubbery, or trees for protection. It was dominated by Japanese machine guns, snipers, and mortars from a high ridge overlooking the plain. But the Marines were slowly advancing forward in the face of deadly fire.

Foxhole To Foxhole Fighting

Every yard forward was an individual problem. It involved one Marine at a time charging across the sand from one foxhole to another. A man would silently hunker down in a covered position and look across the open sand to the foxhole ahead. He would watch the man ahead of him try to reach that foxhole and try to figure the angle of machine gun and rifle fire that sputtered in trying to stop him. After watching the man in front of him make it successfully, then the next man would try to reach the next foxhole himself. When one Marine failed it was a psychological barrier for everyone else. There were too many failures. There were too many Marines sprawled in the sand with dried blood caked into their olive drab fatigues. It was a foxhole hopping war!

Surprisingly that area was a field of silence. There was no conversation about the war or horrors of battle. There was no cursing or bickering. When a man stumbled into a foxhole that was occupied, the men who were already there automatically made room for him. When someone decided to leave there was no back slapping or melodramatic well-wishing. When enemy bullets dropped a man, he went down like a character in a silent movie. There were no groans or calls for help as you see in so many Hollywood war movies. That bloody battlefield was a hushed pantomime of war which the sounds from machine guns, rifles, and mortar fire seemed to accentuate.

Cpl. I.D. Mason, a rifleman from Lincoln Park, Michigan, watched from behind a sand dune at the edge of the killing field. Since early morning he had been moving slowly ahead of the riflemen. He was a reconnaissance man, and it was his job to see that there were no unnecessary gaps between his regiment and the one on their flank. For 10 days he had been moving forward yard by yard one foxhole at a time. He would carefully calculate every move before dashing from one foxhole to another. So far he had figured right. Now the vanguard patrols were beyond his vision and it was time to dash again.

Mason studied the next foxhole carefully and then studied the ridge from which a machine gun and two snipers consistently fired at anyone who tried to reach that hole. Dirt had spluttered danger-

Franklin Sousley's birthplace in Fleming County, Kentucky. Attempts failed to restore this birthplace of Franklin Sousley, Kentucky's most famous WW II hero.

ously close to the feet of two corpsmen as they slid into the foxhole a moment before. One dead Marine who made the wrong calculation lay four feet to the right of the hole.

Mason chewed nervously on his tongue as he mulled over the chances of his making it safely. Counting down to what he believed was the right time he grabbed his rifle and as he dashed madly across the open field his feet pounded the dirt, creating a wake of dust and ashes. As he approached his objective, the rat-tat-tat of the machine gun spoke sharply kicking dust up around his feet and the sniper bullet pinged over his head. Then he crashed into the hole head first. A moment later he crawled carefully down the other side. He had made the correct calculation once more.

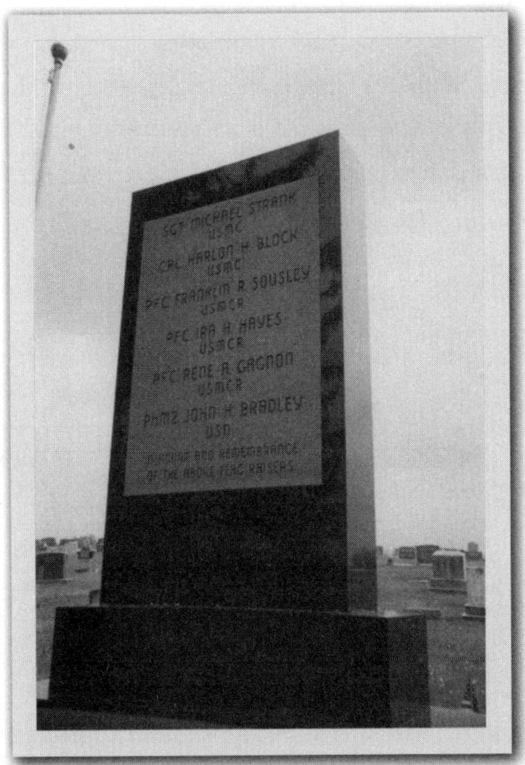

All six flag raisers are listed on the Franklin Sousley Monument in Fleming County, Kentucky.

CHAPTER 3
Pfc. Sousley Died on Iwo Jima

Greater love hath no man than this, that he lay down his life for his friends. John 15:13

The successful assault on Iwo Jima by the 5th Amphibious Corps against an almost impregnable defense was costly. Although Japanese were still surrendering for many months, the island was declared "Secured" on March 26, 1945. The victory required 36 days and cost the lives of 5,931 Americans who were either killed or later died of their wounds received on that battlefield. Also 17,372 men were listed as wounded but survived. In addition, 21,000 Japanese troops perished in defense of the island. But it was later pointed out that 2,251 crippled heavy bombers carrying 24,761 American flyers found refuge at Iwo Jima on their return from bombing Japan. The bitter fighting and bravery of the men was confirmed by the 34 Medals of Honor awarded during that campaign, and the assault troops received the following Presidential Citation:

THE SECRETARY OF THE NAVY
WASHINGTON

The President of the United States takes pleasure in presenting the
PRESIDENTIAL UNIT CITATION to
ASSAULT TROOPS OF THE FIFTH AMPHIBIOUS CORPS, REINFORCED
UNITED STATES FLEET MARINE FORCE
for service as set forth in the following

CITATION:

"For extraordinary heroism in action during the seizure of enemy Japanese-held Iwo Jima, Volcano Islands, February 19 to 28, 1945. Landing against resistance which rapidly increased in fury as the Japanese pounded the beaches with artillery, rocket and mortar fire, the Assault Troops of the FIFTH Amphibious corps inched ahead through shifting black volcanic sands, over heavily mined terrain, toward a garrison of jagged cliffs barricaded by an interlocking system of caves, pillboxes and blockhouses commanding all approaches. Often driven back with terrific losses in fierce hand-to-hand combat, the Assault Troops repeatedly hurled back the enemy's counterattacks to regain and hold lost positions, and continued the unrelenting drive to high ground and Motoyama Airfield No. 1, captured by the end of the second day. By their individual acts of heroism and their unfailing teamwork, these gallant officers and men fought against their own battle-fatigue and shock to advance in the face of the enemy's fanatical resistance; they charged each strong point, one by one, blasting out the hidden Japanese troops or sealing them in; within four days they had occupied the southern part of Motoyama Airfield No. 2; simultaneously they stormed the steep slopes of Mount Suribachi to raise the United States Flag; and they seized the strongly defended hills to silence guns commanding the beaches and insure the conquest of Iwo Jima, a vital inner defense of the Japanese Empire."

The following Assault Troops of the FIFTH Amphibious Corps, United States Fleet Marine Force, participated in the Iwo Jima Operation from February 19 to 28, 1945:

9th Marines; 21st Marines; 3rd Engineer Battalion (less detachment); 3rd Tank Battalion; 3rd Joint Assault Signal Company (less detachment); Reconnaissance company, Headquarters Battalion, THIRD Marine Division; Liaison and Forward Observer Parties, 12 Marines; Pilots and Air Observers, marine Observation Squadron 1; 23rd Marines; 24th Marines; 25th Marines; Companies A, B, and C. 4th Tank Battalion; Companies A, B, and C. 4th Engineer Battalion; 1st Joint Assault Signal Company; lst, 2nd, and 3rd Platoons, Military Police Company, Headquarters Battalion, FOURTH Marine Division;Companies A, B, and C. 4th Pioneer Battalion; 10th Amphibian Tractor Battalion; 5th Amphibian Tractor Battalion; Reconnaissance Company, Headquarters Battalion, FOURTH Marine Division; Companies A and B and Detachment, Headquarters Company, 2nd Armored Amphibian Battalion; 7th Marine War Dog Platoon; Pilots and Air Observers, Marine Observation Squadron 4; Liaison and forward Observer parties, 14th Marines; 1st Provisional Rocket Detachment; 26th marines; 27th Marines; 28th Marines; 5th Engineer Battalion; 5th Tank Battalion; 6th War Dog Platoon; 5th Joint Assault Signal Company; 3rd Amphibian Tractor Battalion; 11th Amphibian Tractor Battalion; Companies A, B, and C, 5th Pioneer Battalion; Reconnaissance Company, Headquarters Battalion, FIFTH Marine Division; lst, 2nd, and 3rd Platoons, Military Police Company, Headquarters Battalion, FIFTH Marine Division; 3rd Provisional Rocket Detachment; Pilots and Air Observers, Marine Observation Squadron 5; Liaison and Forward Observers Parties, 13th Marines; Companies C. D, and Detachment, Headquarters Company, 2nd Armored Amphibian Battalion.

For the President,

John L. Sullivan
Secretary of the Navy

942297
DGP-mp

20 September 1948

My Dear Mrs. Price:

I am directed by the Commandant of the Marine Corps to forward to you the following posthumous awards to which you are entitled as the next of kin of the late Private First Class Franklin R. Sousley, U.S. Marine Corps Reserve:

Copy of Presidential Unit Citation with ribbon bar and one star awarded the Assault Troops of the Fifth Amphibious Corps, Reinforced, - service on Iwo Jima, Volcano Islands.

Asiatic-Pacific Campaign Medal Victory Medal World War II.

Sincerely yours,
L.S. HAMEL
Colonel, U.S. Marine Corps

Enclosures: 4

Mrs. Goldie Price,
Ewing, Kentucky

The Kentucky farm lad wrote often to his mother, no matter how difficult his situation. In a letter shortly after landing he wrote, "Mother, there are at least four Japanese soldiers who will not see Tokyo again." In the last letter she received from him written shortly before his death he said, "I never knew anyone could come so close to being killed so many times and still not receive a scratch. I've had bullets fly over my head, hit all around me and even go through some of my clothing and equipment. But so far I've escaped without a scratch." But on March 21, 1945, five days before the island was declared secured, and one month and two days after landing with the first invasion forces on Iwo Jima, Pfc. Franklin Sousley from Fleming County, Kentucky, was killed during the final fighting on the northern tip of the island near Kitano Point. (He was originally reported killed on March the 12, but that was later changed to March 21.) His comrades said a sniper's bullet struck him and he fell quietly and never knew what hit him. His body was recovered, and he was one of more than 5,000 temporarily buried in the military cemetery on Iwo Jima.

Photo Used in Bond Drive

On May 15, 1945, the seventh bond drive of the war was launched from New York City. Since the flag raising photo and the six men who had triumphantly raised the flag on that mountain top had become such a symbol of triumph at home, it was decided to use the photo as the theme of the bond drive. Therefore, the three mothers who had lost their sons were invited to come to New York by the War Finance Committee to help launch the bond drive. Those mothers were Mrs. Madeline E. Evelley, Somerville, Massachusetts; Mrs. Charles Strank, Johnstown, Pennsylvania; and Mrs. Goldie Price, Ewing, Kentucky.

While at the bond rally, the mothers met the three Marines who survived. Those surviving Marines were Ph. Mate John H. Bradley, Pfc. Rene A. Gagnon, and Pfc. Ira H. Hayes. As they all were intro-

Pvt. Sousley's platoon at the completion of their training at San Diego, California. (Franklin Sousley is in the second row down from top and the second man over from the left.) (Photo: Dwayne Price)

duced, the three surviving Marines hugged the mothers of the three who did not come back. It was at that point that the 10,000 wildly cheering onlookers became strangely silent. Many looked downward and could be seen rubbing tears from their eyes. Everyone could imagine what those three mothers were asking those three Marines, "Can you tell us what happened to our sons, or how they died, or did they suffer, or did they have any last words?"

As the enlarged photograph of the flag raising was unveiled, neither the mothers nor the survivors looked at it, perhaps because the photograph brought too many painful memories for the mothers of those killed as well as for those Marine survivors. Later on, Mrs. Price, the mother of Pfc. Sousley, said her son told her when he entered the Marine Corps, "I want to do something to make you proud of me. I don't think he could have done anything greater than to help raise that flag over Mt. Suribachi."

Fleming County, Kentucky, Honors War Hero

Until 1982, the grave of Fleming County's most famous war hero had gone practically unnoticed except for the usual military marker. It was in July of that year that Marine Master Sergeant Shirley T. White of Cynthania, Kentucky, made several attempts to locate the grave. It was then that Sgt. White decided to do something about honoring Sousley. Therefore, on November 4, 1982, in Lexington, Kentucky, the Franklin Runyon Sousley Foundation, Inc., was founded. It was a nonprofit organization whose members included Robert D. Ross, Louisville, Kentucky; Donald D. Francis, Mousie, Kentucky; Jackie L. Murphy, Stamping Ground, Kentucky; David A. Palmisano, Cincinnati, Ohio; Edward E. Anderson, Winchester, Kentucky; Larry R. Napier, Lancaster, Kentucky; Gary James Movinsky, Blue River, Kentucky; and Shirley T. White, Cynthania, Kentucky. That group supported by the Franklin Runyon Sousley V.F.W. Post 1834 and the American Legion Post 5 were determined not to rest until a suitable monument was erected at Sousley's grave.

Thanks to their efforts, there is now an impressive monument above the grave site. The black granite monument is about six feet high and eight feet wide, and sits on a two-tier tapered base. A replica of the flag raising photograph is carved on the front of the monument with Franklin Sousley highlighted as the dominant figure. On the back of the monument are the names and ranks of each member of the group. Also, the base of the monument is inlaid with 100 pounds of soil and rock from the summit of Mount Suribachi.

There is also a statue of the Iwo Jima flag raising in Washington, D.C, and a stamp depicts the photograph of those brave Marines. These memorials recognize not just Kentucky's Franklin Runyon Sousley and his five companions but all the 5,931 other Marines who died on that remote Pacific Island.

Captain J.T. Daugherty (L) and wing man at El Toro, California, on their way to the Pacific War.

PART IV

KENTUCKY'S FLYING LEATHERNECK: IN WAR AND PEACE

Colonel J.T. "Big Dog" Daugherty's Story

Captain J.T. "Big Dog" Daugherty's Marine Flight Division, credited with destroying seven Japanese ships on a bombing run at Rabaul in the South Pacific in 1944. (Front L-R) Lt. Walter W. Powers, Escalon, CA; Captain J.T. Daugherty, Morehead, KY; Lt. T.T. Gentry, Carrollton, GA. (Rear L-R) Lt. Paul L. Fullop, Mt. Carmel, IL; Lt. George Stamets, Dallas, TX

CHAPTER 1
From Citizen to Soldier

A Sound of battle is in the land, and of great destruction. Jeremiah 50:22

Throughout the 200-year history of the U.S. Marine Corps, they have been called "Leathernecks." It is a name they have gladly worn as an indication of their determination, dedication and toughness. One of Morehead's most famous heroes of WW II was flying Marine Leatherneck Lt. Colonel John Thomas, J.T., Jack, "Big Dog," Daugherty (all one person). J.T., as he was known growing up in Morehead, was born in neighboring Bath County, Kentucky, on January 18, 1919. He was the only child of Carroll ("Cap") Browning and Hazel Tackett Daugherty. In the 1920s, Cap Daugherty believed there was a brighter future for him and his family in the neighboring Morehead, Rowan County, Kentucky. Therefore, in 1927, he moved with his family to that small college town where he soon became successful in the coal and ice business. He also was one of the founders of the new Citizens Bank in 1928. It is still a successful independently-owned bank in Kentucky.

Growing up in Kentucky

J.T. enrolled in the third grade at Breckinridge Training School at Morehead State Teachers College. During his first year in Morehead, J.T. met classmate and neighbor Walter Winston Carr. The two boys formed an immediate friendship that was to last a lifetime. They spent many happy hours together, swimming and fishing, in Triplett Creek that ran through the valley and hunting in the hills surrounding the town.

Basketball was the major sport in Kentucky, and J.T. and Walter were outstanding members of the Breckinridge High School basketball team. But the school did not have a baseball team, and the two young boys loved to play baseball. During the summer many of the local boys would play baseball all day on a vacant lot near Wilson Avenue and Second Street, or until they lost their last baseball in the weeds surrounding the empty lot. Walter said, "J.T. always had to do his chores such as mow the lawn, carry in coal or pump water before he could play baseball." Young J.T. learned responsibility at a young age.

With no organized youth baseball in the small college town, J.T. and Walter organized their own team. They asked dozens of businesses and individuals to support the local youth baseball team. The two boys kept a record of who gave and how much they gave. That was J.T.'s first experience at raising money for a good cause. Records that are still available today show those that supported the first youth baseball team in Morehead were: The Big Store, $0.50; Mutts Café, $0.25; Doc Nickell, $0.50; Regal Store, $0.50; A.B. McKinney, $1.00; Eagles Nest, $1.00; Midland Trail Garage, $0.50; J.A. Allen, $0.50; F.M. Calvert, $0.50; Model Laundry, $0.50; Morehead Independent, $0.50; Morehead Ice and Coal Company, $1.00 (owned by J.T.'s father); and Morehead College Dean Vaughn, $0.50. Those two young boys kept a detailed record of who gave what and how much. Therefore it was apparent that J.T. learned to raise money at an early age. That was a good indication of his future success in banking.

With the money they collected, J.T. and Walter purchased baseballs, Louisville Slugger bats, and a catcher's mitt and mask. Then they let it be known around town that a baseball team was being organized. Among those that showed up for their first practice were: James Johnson, Lloyd Brown, Murvell Caudill, Bob Fraley, Ligon Kessler, Ralph Holbrook, P.J. Reynolds, and Leo Oppenheimer. J.T. and Walter were the managers, and the two boys had to learn to keep a baseball score book and read a box score. They scheduled games with surrounding towns, such as Flemingsburg, Bethel, Mt. Sterling and Owingsville. J.T. was a pitcher and outfielder. Even though he loved baseball, tennis was his most successful sport. He won the Kentucky Junior Tennis championship at age 16.

As a young boy, J.T. was required to work in the family ice and coal business. Even though he was from an upper middle class family, his father insisted that he learn responsibility, dependability and the value of a dollar earned through hard work. Wallace Fannin was the regular delivery man for the Morehead Ice and Coal Company. At first he delivered ice and coal in a wagon pulled by two mules. J.T. would help carry those 25- or 50-pound blocks of ice into the customer's home or unload a wagon load of coal, one shovelful at a time. Later on, by the time J.T. was age 16, his dad purchased an ice truck, and J.T. would drive the truck and deliver ice to surrounding communities such as Haldeman, Clearfield, and Farmers.

During his first two years at Morehead State College's Breckinridge High School, young J.T. was known as an energetic, mischievous, practical joker. He sometimes turned the firehose on the basketball team in the locker room. He also raised some local eyebrows when, dressed in his tennis uniform, he led his school tennis team prancing and high stepping down the middle of Main Street using his tennis racket as a band leader uses a baton tossing and twirling it into the air, while the rest of the tennis team followed behind using their tennis rackets as trombones, trumpets, and drums. He was never mean or destructive, but his parents thought he needed more firm discipline than the university high school at Breckinridge offered.

Preparing for the Military

Following his sophomore year at Breckinridge, his parents decided to send J.T. to a military school. They believed a school that offered a military atmosphere, firm discipline, and insistence upon academic excellence was what he needed at that time in his life. After examining the programs of several military schools, they enrolled him at Riverside Military Academy located high above the banks of the Chattahoochee River in Gainesville, Georgia, about forty miles northeast of Atlanta. The exclusive military school had a winter campus located in Hollywood, Florida.

The 1938 Riverside yearbook listed John Thomas ("Briarhopper") Daugherty of Morehead, Kentucky, as a cadet in Company E. He earned letters in basketball, football, and tennis and was also a member of the Glee Club. Following graduation in 1938 from Riverside Military Academy, he attended Morehead State College, the University of North Carolina at Chapel Hill, and Centre College in Danville, Kentucky.

In July, 1941, J.T. Daugherty joined the U.S. Marine Corps and took his basic training at Webster Field in St. Louis, Missouri. Ironically it was on December 7, 1941, the day Pearl Harbor was bombed, that Cadet Daugherty was assigned to the Naval Air Station in Pensacola, Florida. In July, 1942, the young Air Cadet completed his flight training, received his wings , and was commissioned a second lieutenant.

Following his commission, he was given a much deserved furlough and returned to Morehead. On August 12, 1942, he married his college sweetheart Katherine (Kay) Palmer in an elaborate ceremony at the Morehead Methodist Church. The bride was given away by her father, John M. Palmer and her only attendant was her sister, Mary Palmer Northcutt. The best man was the groom's father C.B. "Cap" Daugherty. J.T.'s uncle, the Reverend John Moss, officiated. After a brief honeymoon, Lt. Daugherty (with his young bride) had to report to his next assignment in Texas.

During World War II, the fledgling U.S. commercial airlines had an agreement with the U.S. military services that allowed military pilots to train and fly as co-pilots on the commercial airlines. Therefore, Lt. Daugherty was placed on temporary duty and sent to the American Airlines Multi-Engine Pilot Training Program in Ft. Worth, Texas. There he learned to fly the twin engine DC-3, which was the same as the military C-47. After completing the multi-engine school, J.T. and his young bride were sent to Minneapolis where he continued multi-engine pilot training with Northwest Airlines.

In mid-January, 1943, the young Marine and his bride were transferred to North Island in San Diego, California, where he was scheduled to fly Marine transport planes. But the need for torpedo-bomber pilots was more critical at that time, and once again J.T. was transferred this time to El Toro Marine Corps Base outside Laguana Beach, California. For the next six months he received advanced training on single engine dive bombing and low-level torpedo bombing as well as navigation. Upon completion of his dive bombing training, Jack Daugherty was assigned to the VMTB Red Devil Squadron 232. According to Ken Everson, one of Jack's Marine wing men, "The "V" stood for heavier than air; the "M" stood for Marine; and "T" meant Torpedo and "B" meant bomber." In July 1943, their squadron boarded the Dutch merchant transport ship called the *Japari* headed for the South Pacific Theater of War. The *Japari* was loaded with a total of 4,000 troops on what was a small merchant vessel converted to a troop ship. The senior officers lived in the 12 staterooms on the ship. The Junior officers were quartered on the deck in temporary small covered quarters. The enlisted men were all packed below deck in metal "racks" (folding cots) stacked five high with little room to breathe.

South Pacific Landing

On July 31, 1943, Marine Flying Leatherneck Jack Daugherty along with the rest of the 232nd Red Devil Squadron landed on the American-held Island of Espiritu Santo and found their planes were already there waiting for them. Espiritus Santo (Spanish for "Holy Ghost") is a beautiful South Sea island in the New Hebridesa. At that time there was not much on the island except sand, coral, and coconut palms.

The first thing that was built upon the island by the American "Seabees" was a crude airplane runway. It was paved with crushed coral that soon hardened into a concrete-like surface. Ken Everson told this writer that he and Jack "re-visited the island 40 years later and the landing strip was still as hard as concrete and black as coal."

The men were housed in "Dallas Huts" which were small, square, prefabricated huts with metal roofs. There were very few screens to keep out insects, and they constantly battled mosquitoes, took atabrine tablets to prevent malaria, and slept under mosquito netting. Before even beginning war on the Japanese at Espiritu, the American forces declared war on the mosquitoes. It was a constant battle and those insects were never eliminated. Many of the men contracted malaria as a result of their assignment on the island. Espiritu Santo soon became an armed camp filled with men, planes, bombs, torpedoes, and all types of armament. There were no hangers for the planes and they sat outside covered with camouflage netting. Among those stationed on the island was a young naval lieutenant by the name of James A. Michener. The island may or may not have been used by Michener as the setting for his first book *Tales of the South Pacific*, but it was used by the Flying Leathernecks of the 232nd Squadron to bomb many enemy bases, supply lines, and fortifications before moving north to Guadalcanal and the other Solomon Islands. There Jack Daugherty was soon promoted to captain and given command of a Marine Flight Division that consisted of six Grumman "Avenger" torpedo bombers and their crews. Early in Jack Daugherty's Marine Corps experience, one of his commanding officers constantly mispronounced his name by calling him "Dogerty." Therefore, the men began to call him "Dog" for short. After he was promoted to captain and given command of a Marine flight division, he was called "Big Dog" Daugherty. It was a term of affection and respect like Admiral Halsey's "Bull" or General George Patton's "Blood and Guts." In the 232nd Red Devil Marine Air Squadron, it was "Big Dog" Daugherty, the six-foot three-inch Kentuckian, that led their D (Dog) Flight Division as the pack hunted for prey.

The plane flown by Captain Daugherty throughout the South Pacific campaign was a Grumman "Avenger" torpedo bomber. It had a wingspan of 54 feet and was 41 feet long. It could carry a 21-inch torpedo, or a 2,000-pound bomb, or four 500-pound bombs. It could also be modified to carry mines that could be dropped into shipping lanes from the air. The Avenger carried a crew of three. In the rear seat behind the pilot was the turret gunner, who operated a fifty-caliber machine gun. Underneath the bottom of the aircraft was the radio operator-gunner. He fired a thirty-caliber machine gun from what was called the "stinger." The Avenger was a highly successful torpedo bomber that was also used as a dive bomber. The sturdy aircraft had a range of five hours and could be land based as well as carrier based. Captain Daugherty and the 232nd Marine Squadron were entirely land based and flew from many small islands during the Pacific military campaign.

Following the attack on Pearl Harbor on December 7, 1941, the Japanese soon occupied the town of Rabaul, the major port town on New Britain Island, northeast of New Guinea, and the Japanese quickly established a major naval and air base there. The island was also used as a staging area for troops to be used in attacking New Guinea, Guadalcanal, and other islands in the Solomon chain and was also considered critical in the defense of a planned Japanese attack on the coast of Australia. Therefore, it became a constant target for Allied bombing attacks during 1943 and 1944.

An Avenger torpedo bomber flown by
Captain Daugherty in the raid on Rabaul

CHAPTER 2
Battle of Rabaul and Bougainville

Let us go up at once and possess it; for we are able to overcome it. Numbers 13:30

The flying Marines on Espiritu Santo were assigned to fly combat missions every other day for six weeks. They would then be relieved for rest and recuperation (R&R) usually in Australia for six weeks. In late February 1944, Naval Intelligence reported a large buildup of troops and ships in Rabaul harbor. It was believed they were preparing a counterattack on Guadalcanal now occupied by the Americans or an attack on New Guinea. Captain Daugherty and other Marine flyers were immediately ordered to begin a bombing attack on Rabaul. The operation took advantage of the fact that Simpson Harbor at Rabaul was shaped like a horseshoe. If the ships were caught anchored in the harbor, it could be mined and they could not easily escape a bombing attack. On Tuesday, March 2, 1944, Naval Intelligence reported the ships were anchored in the harbor.

Four flying Marine divisions of six planes each were selected for the attack. The first two six-plane divisions of Avengers were equipped to carry mines to be dropped in the mouth of the harbor. At daybreak on Wednesday morning, March 3, 1944, the twelve Avengers approached their target. They were met with fierce enemy resistance by fighter planes and anti-aircraft fire. That group of flying leathernecks lost 6 planes that day, but they successfully mined the harbor. Captain Daugherty told this writer, "The sacrifice made by those men assured the ultimate success of the bombing attack by preventing the enemy ships from escaping out to sea."

On Thursday, March 4, Captain Daugherty and his six plane, 18 member combat flight division met before dawn to go over their preflight check of the target, weather, plans, men, and equipment. Their target was to bomb the ships trapped in Simpson Harbor at Rabaul. "Big Dog" Daugherty was a stickler for details and on their day to fly, every man had better be prepared to do his job. Between missions the men were all one big happy family, but on their day to fly, Captain J.T. was a strictly "Chicken _____ GI by the book Marine."

At daybreak, "Big Dog" Daugherty revved up the engine of his Avenger loaded with four 500 pound bombs with delayed fuses. His plane rumbled slowly down the hard coral-based runway and seemed to shudder as it grudgingly became airborne. "Big Dog" was followed by Lt. Paul L. Fullop, known as the "Pride of Mt. Carmel, Illinois." Next came Lt. George Stamets from Dallas, "Big D," Texas. George hummed the song "The Eyes of Texas Are Upon You" most of his waking hours. He said it kept him from being so homesick. Lt. Stamets was a typical Texan who loved the state, and he wanted everyone to know he was a Texan. The fourth man to become airborne was Lt. Charles Metezelaars from Mattoon, Illinois. "Metz" was a skilled pilot known for his bravery and toughness. The fourth plane airborne was piloted by Lt. Walter W. Powers from Escalon, California. "Walt" was a native Californian who couldn't understand why everyone didn't love the "Golden State" the way he did. The last pilot to get his bomb-laden Avenger airborne was Lt. T.T. Gentry from Carrollton, Georgia, who was nicknamed "Gent" because of his name and his courteous slow-talking demeanor. Those six pilots and crew made up the division to attack Rabaul the day after 50 percent of the first two divisions had been shot out of the skies after they dropped their mines into the harbor at Rabaul.

As the six-plane division slipped into formation, the men were all quietly thinking of the previous day and of the men and planes that were lost mining the mouth of the harbor. But Captain Daugherty and his men had been given a target, and each man silently in his own mind was determined to carry out those orders to the best of his ability. The flight division led by Captain Daugherty approached Simpson Harbor at 5,000 feet, but could not locate the ships. He said, "The ships were so well camouflaged that only after circling the harbor several times then flying a few hundred feet above the water, were we able to distinguish where the shoreline ended and the ships began." The official Marine Corps news release datelined Guadalcanal March 8, 1944, read:

> Six marine torpedo bomber pilots who obtained permission from reluctant supervisors to break combat flight rules and participate in consecutive day aerial raids, destroyed seven Jap ships in the Rabaul area last weekend, it was announced today.
>
> The flight division, led by Capt. John T. Daugherty, Morehead, Kentucky, sank three ships Thursday, two more Saturday and then returned Sunday morning to polish off two remaining transports and strafe other ships, barges, cargo-packed wharfs and beach installations at the Jap base.
>
> Daugherty was credited with sinking one ship, Lt. Paul L. Fullop, Mount Carmel, Illinois, with three; Lt. George C. Stamets, Dallas, Texas, with two; Lt. Walter W. Powers, Escalon, California, with one; and Lt. Charles Metezelaars with two.*
>
> Powers was also credited with one damaging miss, and Lt. T.T. Gentry, Carrollton, Georgia, with two damaging misses.
>
> Daugherty said the group circled Simpson Harbor at Rabaul several times before locating the ships on the last two raids.

> "I've never seen such well camouflaged ships," he said. "Only by flying a few hundred feet above the water could we spot the difference between ship and shore." Lt. Fullop returned from the Thursday raid with more than 100 anti-aircraft shell holes in his ship, but no Jap fighters attempted to intercept the Marine pilots.
>
> The six flyers obtained permission to make the Sunday raid despite a policy of only every other day flights when Daugherty told his superior officers that "nobody else can find the other transports we spotted yesterday, but we'll guarantee to find them."
>
> *In the original Marine Corp release these ships were credited to Lt. John Dexheimer, but the men on that mission said Dexheimer did not fly that day.

That was one of the most successful military campaigns in the Pacific area in WW II. Before that bombing attack ended three days later, not only did Captain Daugherty's six-plane division sink seven Japanese ships, but the 232nd Red Devil Squadron sank 19 more for a total of 26 enemy ships sunk. J.T. Daugherty and each of his men were awarded the Distinguished Flying Cross for sinking those ships.

J.T. Daugherty modestly recalled, "It was a joint effort by everyone. Those men that mined the harbor at great sacrifice and loss of life were the key to the success of our operation. Each man showed extreme courage under strong enemy fire, and each of us simply did our duty." However, it was later pointed out by Admiral William Halsey that "attack on Simpson Harbor, Rabaul contributed greatly to the Americans regaining control of Rabaul with much less loss of life." Admiral Halsey also pointed out that those Marine Flying Leathernecks helped shorten the Pacific island-hopping campaign of WW II.

Captain Daugherty received the Distinguished Flying Cross for sinking two Japanese ships in the raid on Rabaul.

Mission at Bougainville

Captain Daugherty and the members of the 232nd Red Devil Squadron, under the general command of Admiral William F. "Bull" Halsey, also took part in the attack and occupation of Bougainville in November, 1943. Bougainville, the largest island of the Solomons group in the southwest Pacific Ocean, is 127 miles long, 49 miles wide, and has mountains up to 10,246 feet high. During WW II it was of strategic importance in the American plans for island hopping to Japan.

As soon as American forces landed in Bougainville, they immediately established three airfields, one for fighter planes, one for heavy bombers, and one for torpedo bombers. Ken Everson, wing man of J.T. Daugherty, said, "Our landing strip was a dirt strip covered with steel marston matting surrounded by high mountains. The Japanese still controlled some of the mountainous area surrounding our airstrip, and each morning as we were loaded with bombs and sitting at the end of the airstrip, the Japanese would drop artillery shells in the middle of the runway. They must have thought they were stopping us from taking off. But as soon as they stopped shelling us, the Seabees would rush out and fill the craters and quickly replace the steel matting and we would take off with only about a 15-minute delay. Many times, as we took to the air, the Japanese guns would be shooting down at us from the mountains surrounding the airfield. Even after we were airborne and several thousand feet up, they would still be shooting down at us because they were on the high mountains surrounding the airstrip."

Captain Everson said, "On one mission over Bougainville, our six-plane division lost three planes. I personally witnessed the three planes spinning into the ocean—one in front of me and one on each side of me. There were no parachutes from either of those planes. My plane was full of bullet holes but it continued to fly and I returned safely to base. It was not until later on when the Chaplain came around to our living quarters and collected the personal effects of the lost airmen to send home to their families, that it really hit us. They were gone. Perhaps subconsciously up to that point we believed they would by some miracle be rescued and returned to base. They did not, and became a tragic consequence of war."

Also Captain Everson recalled the Japanese would shell the mess hall every morning. Prevented from eating breakfast, the men would doggy-bag some food from the night before to be their breakfast. Ken Everson remembered that, "During our six weeks in Bougainville, we were constantly harassed by Japanese bombing and strafing attacks. It was so bad that J.T. Daugherty and I had to move out of our 'Dallas Huts' and live in very deep foxholes for the remainder of our time on Bougainville."

In a special commendation signed by Admiral "Bull" Halsey, Captain Daugherty and the 232nd Red Devil Squadron were commended for their efforts in paving the way for American landings on Bougainville. The citation read, "For personal heroism in blasting Japanese shore installations in the face of fierce enemy fighter opposition, you helped reduce the number of men that would have died in the invasion."

One of the greatest losses suffered by the 232nd Red Devil Squadron in WW II was the crash of a transport plane that killed 18 of their men. In each six-plane division there were 18 men, just enough to fill a twin engine C-47 transport plane. On one occasion, when the men of a division were returning from R&R in New Guinea, their plane crashed, killing all 18 passengers plus the crew. Losing an entire Marine flight division in one crash was a traumatic experience for the men of the squadron. Even though that was the worst, it was only one of many losses suffered by their squadron.

Captains Daugherty, Metzelaars, and Everson were three of the gallant "flying leathernecks" in the 232nd Red Devil Marine Squadron. They, like their fellow flyers, did much to distinguish themselves in the South Pacific during WW II. Even though they received the Distinguished Flying Cross for sinking Japanese ships, they would never accept the term "hero." Captain Daugherty, who later attained the rank of Lt. Colonel, said just a few days before his death, "It was a team effort. Every man had a job to do and did it to the best of his ability. We were men in the right place at the right time with the right skills and training to best serve our country."

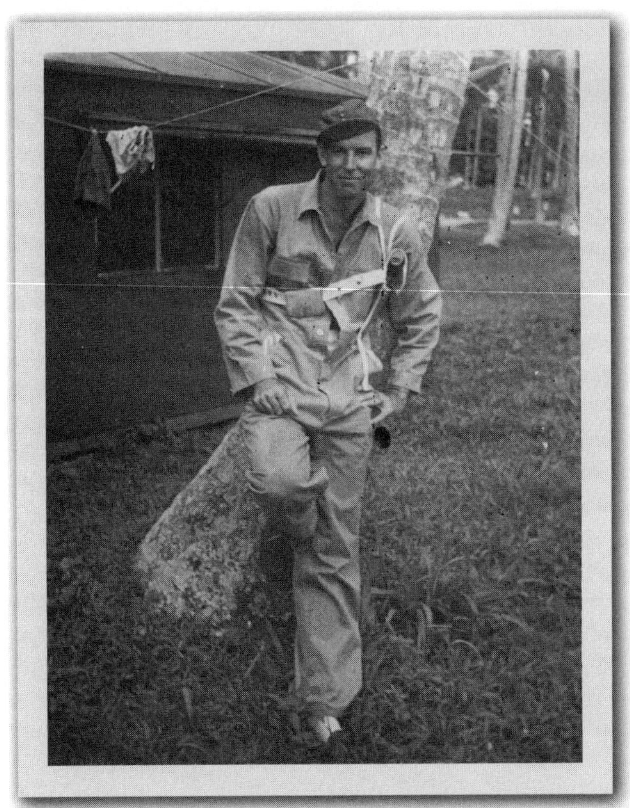

Captain Daugherty relaxes on Espiritos Santos Island in the South Pacific.

CHAPTER 3
From Soldier to Citizen

They shall beat their swords into plowshares and their spears into pruning hooks. Isaiah 2:4

In April, 1944, Captain Daugherty rotated back to the U.S. after flying 44 combat missions in the South Pacific. He was immediately given a 30-day furlough and returned quietly to his hometown of Morehead, Kentucky, to await orders for his next assignment. Even though he was recognized as a hero in the national press, he was not recognized as such in his hometown.

Following a visit back home, J.T. and Kay were ordered to report to Cherry Point, North Carolina. It was May, 1944, when Captain Daugherty began advanced pilot training in some of the newer combat aircraft coming off the nation's wartime assembly lines.

Leatherneck Test Pilot

In September, 1944, Captain Daugherty (and Kay) were transferred to the Patuxent River Naval Air Station in southern Maryland. It was located in a rural area called Cedar Point that later became known as Lexington Park. At the Patuxent base, Daugherty was assigned the job of testing new military aircraft coming off the nation's wartime assembly lines.

Commander F.M. Trapnell was the officer in charge of the Navy's first test pilot program. At that time there were only five or six Navy test pilots. The first testing method used required each pilot to test one assigned system in the plane, e.g., armament, electrical, hydraulic, or aerodynamics. Each test pilot would then write his report separately and then they would meet together and report their results. After testing all systems, the pilots would write a comprehensive syllabus together that included their test results, e.g., the plane's responses and its limits, weaknesses, and strengths.

In order to meet the need for more test pilots, the Navy assigned a few of their most experienced and best Marine combat pilots to the program. When those new pilots arrived, the Marine Corps changed the method of testing the new planes. The new test pilots were called Service Test Pilots, and their job was to test every system in the new aircraft. Captain Daugherty was among the very first pilots in that new program. As a Service Test Pilot, his job was to take those untried aircraft into the air and push them to the limits of altitude, speed, climbing, and diving ratios. Test pilots were the ones who really "pushed the envelopes" on those new planes. Their jobs were dangerous since one never knew when a plane might stall or fail to pull out of dive. Many of those early test pilots became America's first astronauts with such household names as John Glenn, Scott Carpenter, and Alan Shepard. J.T. Daugherty said, "All of those early astronauts were in the Navy Test Pilot Program in Maryland. I knew all of them, but was especially close to John Glenn because we were both Marine Corps Pilots. Those were the glory days and romance of Naval aviation when we had propellor planes instead of jets. We were just a happy go lucky group of Naval aviators doing what we dearly loved—flying." He was always proud that he was a member of the first class to graduate from the Test Pilot Program. He remained in the Marine Corps at that base until 1947 and retired with the rank of Lt. Colonel.

Kay Daugherty said in an interview "Jack and I never had any plans except to return to Morehead after the war. In 1945 during his tour of duty at the new Naval Base Test Pilot School, we lived in Lexington Park and I taught school. It was at that time my husband recognized the potential for future growth in the area."

When the naval base was built in 1942, there was a critical housing shortage. The population had increased rapidly in the small community, and many people were literally forced to live out of tents. Most of them found that living conditions in Lexington Park were aggravating and stressful. Many of those early residents looked forward to the time they could shake the Maryland dust off their feet and leave that "Godforsaken place."

Leatherneck & Entrepreneur

In 1945 Lexington Park, Maryland, was a small crossroads community with one restaurant, one service station, one blinking stop light, and less than a dozen businesses in the whole community. The first housing development, known as the "Flat Tops," had just been completed. But Jack Daugherty believed in the future of the tiny hamlet and convinced his wife Kay that they should remain in Lexington Park instead of going back to Morehead.

In 1946, the former Marine combat pilot opened the first of many successful business enterprises in St. Mary's County, Maryland—a service station. That business was soon followed by an appliance store, a T.V. store, a furniture business, and a moving and storage company. The latter was extremely successful because of the many Navy families moving in and out of the naval base. One of Daugherty's contemporaries described him as being "extraordinarily intelligent at tactical business," which meant he recognized an opportunity when he saw one and quickly reacted.

The former pilot once brought his father "Cap" Daugherty, a successful banker from Morehead, Kentucky, to Lexington Park, Maryland, to advise him whether it was a good idea to remain there and go into business. He met the elder Daugherty at the train station and drove him around the area and showed him some of the investments he planned to make. J.T. said his father looked the place over and didn't say a word until he took him back to the station to return home. Then he said, "It will be fine for you to stay here but when buying property pay as little down and as little per month as possible. Also you should have the owner hold the note on the balance ... that way you would save some interest." The land records of St. Mary's County, leaves no doubt that J.T. took his father's advice.

Daugherty recognized the power of the press, and, in 1950, there was no newspaper in that community. He talked to the owner and publisher of the *Weekly Enterprise* located in the St. Mary's County seat of Leonardtown. He offered the publisher a "deal" to move to Lexington Park. In order to get the newspaper publisher to move, Daugherty agreed to put him on the payroll at $125 per week. He also agreed to guarantee the owner one full page of advertisement every week for as long as he remained in business. The editor agreed and that guarantee lasted for almost 40 years and resulted in an estimated $1,000,000 worth of advertising over those 40 years.

Every few years there were rumors that the Patuxent River Naval Base would close. Since the economy of Lexington Park was based primarily on the naval base, business loans were considered poor risks by the regional banks. On the contrary, Jack Daugherty and other local leaders were convinced that the base would remain in Lexington Park. They were also convinced that, if the town was to grow, it had to have a local bank. In 1959, those local leaders opened the Citizens Bank in Lexington Park. That was the first new bank chartered in Maryland since 1912. Later the name was changed to Maryland Bank & Trust Company, and Jack Daugherty was the first president, a job he held for 35 years.

Establishing a bank required a lot of capital and J.T. once recalled, "I borrowed money from a banker in Leonardtown and the day the note was due, there was a raging snowstorm. I called the banker and told him it was snowing hard and could I bring him the money the next day. He told me the snow would not stop me if I was coming to borrow the money. He was right and I drove through a foot of snow to pay the note."

Establishes Leatherneck Bank

Many of Jack Daugherty's former flyers in the Marine Corps invested in the new bank. Ken Everson said, "Jack contacted me and asked if I wanted to invest in a new bank he was planning. I was flying commercially in South America at that time and had saved a few thousand dollars. I said, 'Sure, I'm with you, old buddy,' and I loaned him several thousand dollars on a handshake deal. A few years later after I came back to California and I wanted to build a house, I called Jack and said I needed the money. He promptly sent a check along with all accrued interest. We have been lifetime friends and I've made other profitable investments in some of his business ventures."

Today the Maryland Bank and Trust Company is the oldest and largest independently owned bank in Maryland. It includes branch banks in Calvert, Prince George, Charles, and St. Mary's counties in Maryland for a total of eight locations. It has always called itself the bank that cares about people. The advertisement and billboards have always proclaimed, "Where others have their branches, we have our roots and we are the Yes bank." The billboards in the area proclaimed it was a bank founded by naval aviators.

In 1960, following the opening of the new bank, the community seemed to just explode with growth. Real estate loans were one of the bank's most prosperous investments. Soon J.T. and others helped start a 200-lot subdivision and a shopping center. Merchants from Baltimore and Washington, D.C., soon opened businesses in the area. Jack said that his real estate investments had proved successful over the years, and waterfront property was one of the best investments that could be made in St. Mary's County. His philosophy of entrepreneurship was that if you invested in enough businesses, the number of successes would eventually far outweigh the number of failures. It was a philosophy that served him well throughout his lifetime.

J.T. Daugherty founded or co-founded many successful enterprises, e.g., Esso Service Station, Locker Club, Sports Center, Baby Land, Merchandise Mart, Radio Station WPTX "high above the Daugherty Building," the *Weekly Enterprise* newspaper, Anchor Van Lines, Citizens Bank (Maryland Bank & Trust Company), Mayjack Real Estate Development Company and Executive Airlines. The latter company was a feeder airline that flew passengers, mail, and freight from small east coast cities to the larger airports. But, Executive Airlines was one of J.T. Daugherty and other former pilots successful business ventures. Daugherty also held business interests in Charleston, South Carolina, and in St. Croix, Virgin Islands.

People Person

Jack Daugherty was a well-liked and well-known genial, gregarious person. He was the kind of man who made everyone he met feel at ease and that he was genuinely interested in their problems. When people came to see Bank President Daugherty, they were usually asked these questions: (1) How are you? (2) What is your problem? and, (3) How can I help you? As a banker he enjoyed helping young people get started. Because of his personality, power, and prestige, he was a natural to run for political office, and he ran unsuccessfully on two separate occasions. In 1954 and 1958, he was narrowly defeated, once by only 29 votes, in a contested race for state senator. In one campaign he was traveling door to door in rural Maryland handing out yardsticks announcing his candidacy. After knocking on the door of one rural farm, house he gave the woman answering the door a yardstick. She looked at it and said, "I'm sorry I can't vote for you." Jack asked her why not and she said, "You have campaigned your way out of your district—you are now out of St. Mary's County and into

Colonel Daugherty returned from the South Pacific in 1944 and became one of the first Service Test Pilots at the Patuxent River Naval Air Station in Maryland.

Charles County." Even though he failed to get elected, he was an enthusiastic campaigner.

Mr. Daugherty's failure to win his elections only seemed to sharpen his interest in politics. He was a delegate from Maryland to several Democratic National Presidential conventions. Through his political influence, he was instrumental in bringing federal funds to St. Mary's County for sewer, water, roads, schools, and parks. He helped form a Navy Alliance that successfully stopped the navy base from closing. Although Mr. Daugherty was a strong supporter of President Kennedy, his favorite politician was Lyndon Baines Johnson. Perhaps that was because many people told him there was a striking physical resemblance between him and L.B.J. Like the former president, Jack Daugherty was a large man, but unlike L.B.J., Jack was sometimes referred to as the "Gentle Giant."

Jack and his wife, Kay, were active in many civic and charitable causes. They were both strong supporters of St. Mary's College and he was credited with heading a drive to raise the endowment funds that helped put the small private liberal arts college on a sound financial basis. Also along with the bank, Jack and Kay Daugherty endowed twelve scholarships to help young people in their educational endeavors. They both believed that the privilege of a scholarship was earned and not given, and many young people earned a college education with the help of the Daugherty's scholarships. Kay and Jack also endowed the new commons building on the campus of St. Mary's College. It was named the Daugherty-Palmer Commons in honor of their parents, C.B. and Hazel Daugherty and John and Sally Palmer. Jack was a civic leader who helped establish Lexington Park's Little League baseball teams, and he was one of the founders of St. Mary's County Chamber of Commerce. He was also a former member of the city commission and a member of the board of trustees for St. Mary's College. Kay was active in building the first public library as well as establishing a shelter for abandoned animals. Although teaching was her first love, she was always a leader and was active in her church.

With all of his business success, Jack Daugherty was known as an unpretentious family man. Despite his multi-million dollar business success, he never flaunted that success. He dressed conservatively and casually. He always wore something on his head that resembled a golf hat. Although he was big and brawny with thinning hair, he was very athletic and always looked younger than his age. He usually drove an older model Ford with a bumper sticker that showed his support for the Baltimore Colts (before they moved to Indiana). His dress and appearance belied his power and position.

One snowy day, a man and his wife were driving down the street in Lexington Park. Crossing the street from the bank to a restaurant in front of them was a large man in a ragged looking overcoat. He was holding something orange over his head as protection from the bad weather. The woman turned to her husband

and said sympathetically, "Oh, look, dear at that poor man crossing the street in front of us." He husband quickly replied, "Dear, that poor man is Jack Daugherty, one of this county's best known and most successful businessmen."

Wartime Survivor Peacetime Builder

Had Captain J.T. Daugherty not survived WW II and been just a statistic among the 258,000 Americans who were killed in that conflict, he would have been remembered only as a name on a plaque in Rowan County, Kentucky. There would have been 93 names on that plaque instead of 92 and the world around Lexington Park, Maryland, would have been much poorer.

Like so many men who returned safely home from a dangerous combat zone, perhaps J.T., deep down inside himself, often wondered why he came back and many others did not. Perhaps he, like many combat veterans, felt a sense of guilt because he survived. Therefore, many of them began their peace time life as if they themselves were on a mission to prove something—that they were trying to compensate in some way for their comrades' failure to return from the war. Sadly, the old Marine veteran passed away on his 58th wedding anniversary on August 12, 2000.

He will be greatly missed by Kay, his wife of 58 years, his daughter Katherine (Daugherty) Watts, son George T. (Tom), three grandchildren, and many, many friends. He wore many hats in his life time, and his death left a large void in the community of Lexington Park, Maryland. He left large footprints on the sands of his time that will be difficult to fill.

The ten men crew of the "Roarin' bull" with Lt. Reynolds standing 2nd from right

PART V

"ROARING BULL": THIRTY-FIVE MISSIONS OVER GERMANY

Lieutenant P.J. Reynolds' Story

Lt. Paul J. Reynolds, known as K.Y., a bombardier-navigator on the B-17 Flying Fortress "Roarin' Bull" was awarded the Distinguished Flying Cross for heroism over Nuremburg, Germany, in 1945.

CHAPTER 1
Thirty-Five Missions Over Germany

That thou by them might warest a good warfare.
I Timothy 1:18

Paul J. Reynolds was born in Morgan County, Kentucky, but moved to Morehead in the next county as a preschooler. He is the son of the late James S. and Anna Caudill Reynolds. He married his childhood sweetheart, Mabel (Carr) Reynolds, and they are the parents of three children: Ann, Roy, and Joe. He attended Breckinridge and Morehead High School, graduating from MHS in 1937.

P.J., as he was called by his friends, attended Morehead College, playing football and baseball for two years. He then dropped out and went to work in the steel mills of Detroit, where he worked until he received his call to become a citizen soldier during WWII.

He entered the Army on September 18, 1943, and was assigned to the Army Air Corps. At the time the completed basic training, there was an urgent need for bombardiers and navigators. He finished both training programs in Midland, Texas, and was commissioned a second lieutenant and awarded his wings. P.J. was immediately assigned to a B-17 heavy bomber flight crew for more advanced training. It was there P.J. was given the nickname K.Y. (So many men were given the nickname of their home city or state.)

Flying the Atlantic

In August, 1944, P.J. (now known as K.Y.) and his crew flew the B-17 from Florida to England, via Maine, Gander (Newfoundland), Iceland, Wales, and England. Upon arrival in England, the plane and its ten-man crew were assigned to the 412th Squadron in the 95th Bomb Group of the Eighth Air Force. They immediately named their beloved B-17 the "Roarin' Bull," and painted it with a picture of a mad bull snorting flames of fire. In 1944, Britain was bombing Germany by night, and the U.S. was doing daring daylight raids over the heart of Nazi Germany. At that time, if a bomber crew survived 25 missions, they were rotated out of combat, but one-fourth of the crews did not survive 25 missions. The terrible loss of men and planes gave the Eighth Air Force bomb runs the name of Death Valley. It was into Death Valley that the "Roarin' Bull" flew its first mission over the Mainz, Germany railroad yards on September 27, 1944. It was a seven-hour flight through heavy flak and fighter planes into the very heart of Germany. The plane returned safely with only minor damage. Each mission was a gamble between being shot out of the skies, parachuting into enemy hands, being wounded by flak, or returning to base for a hot meal. The stakes were high, and the odds were very unfavorable. There was always a quietness among the crew as they approached the target. The chatter over the intercom would stop, and it was as if each was silently, solemnly praying in his own way.

Mission 22—Historical

On January 14, 1945, the crew of the "Roarin' Bull" flew their 22nd mission. The target was the Derben oil storage depot deep in the heart of Germany. It was an eight-hour flight, and their fighter escort was unable to remain with them all the way to their target. They approached the target at 25,000 feet, but because of heavy cloud cover, had to drop under the clouds for their bomb run.

As the B-17s began their run they were met by a force of a dozen German fighter planes. During this attack Technical Sergeant James I. Garvey of Philadelphia, Pennsylvania, the flight engineer and top turret gunner on the the "Roarin' Bull" shot down the first jet aircraft in military history. He received credit for destroying a German ME 262 jet-propelled fighter plane.

Mission Number 25—Frankfurt, Germany

On February 17, 1945, their 25th mission was the railroad yards in Frankfurt - Mainz, Germany. The mission was a success. The railroad yards, terminals, and rolling stock were nothing but rubble, though

The "Roarin' Bull" prepared for take-off on one of its 35 missions over Germany

the world-famous brewery adjacent to the railroad yards was completely untouched. It was a seven-hour flight and the risks had been reduced slightly because their P-47 and P-51 fighter escorts were now equipped with extra gas tanks enabling the fighters to protect the bombers most of the distance to the target. For that reason 35 missions were required, instead of 25, to complete their combat assignments.

Mission 27—Almost the Last

On February 20, 1945, the crew of the "Roarin' Bull" was on their 27th mission, a massive flight of about a thousand planes. It was a nine-hour flight to destroy the railroad yards at Nuremberg. Upon reaching the target they came under heavy fighter attack and anti-aircraft fire. The air was full of planes, flak, bullets and, smoke. Just after releasing its bombs, the aircraft was hit by an exploding anti-aircraft shell. The right inboard engine was knocked out, the plane's radio and intercom were destroyed. Both the pilot and waist gunner were wounded and P.J. was hit with two jagged pieces of hot steel flak. One lodged in his flak jacket, and the other in his parachute webbing. (He still has these two wicked-looking pieces of steel that came close to ending his life.) Tail gunner Dave Durran's leg was almost blown off below his knee. He screamed for help and P.J. crawled back through the plane to try and help him. He put a tourniquet around his leg, sprinkled powdered sulpha on the wound, applied a pressure patch, and gave the wounded man a shot of morphine for the pain. With the plane crippled and the co-pilot flying the aircraft, P.J. began to man the machine guns of the wounded crew member. Although the "Roarin' Bull" had completed her mission and was headed back to England, they were still under heavy attack by enemy fighters. Just as an enemy fighter appeared in his gun sights at 9 o'clock about 100 feet from him, P.J. pulled the trigger on the twin-fifty machine guns. He recalled he could see the young man's face clearly as their eyes met for an instant, and P.J.'s machine gun jammed. He always said afterwards he was glad the gun jammed.

Fighter Planes to the Rescue

Soon the American P-51 and P-47 fighter planes came in and drove the German fighters away. By that time it was apparent that the wounded gunner was in critical condition. His broken leg was flapping around grotesquely in turbulent air. He grabbed P.J.'s arm and said, "K.Y., don't let me die." Although he had doubts, P.J. assured him they would get him back. With the co-pilot struggling to keep the aircraft flying on three engines, and one crew member critically wounded, P.J., as navigator, plotted a course to the nearest friendly airfield. The co-pilot headed the plane to Brussels, Belgium, but upon arrival, the weather would not allow a landing. P.J. then plotted a course to Lille, France, for emergency landing and medical treatment. However, they were unable to land there because of weather. Then Paul J. plotted a course back to their home base in England. Throughout the flight back P.J. applied pressure, and occasionally loosened the tourniquet on the wounded man's leg. The crippled plane finally arrived back at their home field where they were immediately met by medical personnel. Dave Durran survived. For Paul J. Reynolds' heroic action on the mission over Nuremberg, he was awarded the Distinguished Flying Cross. (This medal was awarded only for extreme bravery under fire.) He was also awarded three battle stars, and the Air Medal with four oak leaf clusters (meaning five air medals). On the Nuremberg mission 36 planes and 365 gallant men were lost—a day P.J. Reynolds has never forgotten.

During his 35 missions over enemy-occupied Europe, Lt. Reynolds flew 272 hours and 45 minutes over enemy territory. His group flew over 300 missions, and Paul J. flew 35 of those missions. He returned to the states in time to celebrate VE Day, Victory in Europe, May 7, 1945.

Kentucky had many brave and heroic soldiers during World War II. Every one of them has a story to tell. Lt. Paul J. Reynolds' story is representative of America's citizen soldiers in WW II who served gallantly and returned safely.

Lt. Reynolds and the members of the 412th Squadron, 95th bomb group, Eighth Air force ran into heavy flak over Germany after dropping their bombs.

35 MISSIONS – LT. PAUL J. REYNOLDS

First Mission: Sept. 27, 1944 Last Mission: March 1, 1945

MISSION NUMBER	DATE	TARGET (ALL IN GERMANY)	FLYING TIME IN HOURS	BOMB ALT. IN THOUSAND FT. (APPROX.)
	SEPT. 1944			
1	27	Mainz - Railroad yards	6:55	24
2	28	Merseburg - Oil plant	7:55	25
	OCT. 1944			
3	7	Leipzig - Oil Plant	8:45	26
4	12	Bremen - Aircraft plant	7:00	24
5	19	Mannheim - Oil plant	7:10	26
6	26	Hannover - Industrial plant	7:05	26
	NOV. 1944			
7	2	Merseburg - Oil plant	7:35	29
8	4	Neunkirchen - Oil plant	7:20	25
9	5	Ludwigshafen - Oil plant	7:45	27
10	26	Gutersloh (Hamm) - Railroad yards	5:50	24
11	29	Hamm - Railroad yards	6:00	24
12	30	Merseburg - Oil plant	8:05	36
	DEC. 1944			
13	2	Coblenz Recall (bad weather)	6:00	----
14	11	Giessen - Railroad yards	8:00	24
15	12	Darmstadt - Railroad yards	8:00	27
	DEC. 1944			
16	16	Stuttgart - Railroad yards	8:00	21
17	24	Biblis - Airfield	8:30	25
18	25	Bad Munster - Railroad yards	6:40	23
19	27	Fulda - Railroad yards	7:50	25
20	28	Coblenz - Railroad yards	7:00	27

	JAN. 1945			
21	7	Cologne - Bridges	7:50	25
22	14	Derben - Oil storage depot	8:00	25
	FEB. 1945			
23	1	Wesel - Bridges	6:00	25
24	3	Berlin - Railroad yards	8:30	27
25	17	Frankfurt am Main - Railroad yards	7:00	24
26	19	Osnabruck - Railroad yards	6:00	24
27	20	Nuremberg - Railroad yards	9:00	24
28	22	Bamberg - Railroad yards	9:30	21
29	24	Bremen - Railroad bridges	7:00	24
30	25	Munich - Railroad yards	9:00	26
31	26	Berlin - Railroad yards	9:00	27
	MAR. 1945			
32	1	Ulm - Industrial plant	8:15	22
33	8	Dortmund - Oil plant	7:15	24
34	9	Frankfurt am Main - Aircraft plant	7:15	24
35	10	Dortmund - Railroad yards	7:00	23

UNIT CITATION
LT. PAUL J. REYNOLDS, WW II, ENGLAND

Under the provisions of Executive Order No. 9396 (Sec I, Bull 22, D, 1943) and Sec IV, Cir 333, ..D, the 95th Bombardment Group (H) is cited for outstanding performance of duty in action in connection with the first aerial daylight attack by United States heavy bombers on Berlin, Germany, 4 March 1944.

The energies of the entire Eighth Air Force were devoted to this vital operation but only the 95th Bombardment Group and twelve aircraft from one other group got through to the primary target and bombed it.

At take-off, weather conditions were so bad that one entire Division was forced to cancel the mission. The 95th Group assembled in proper formation and departed the English Coast as scheduled, despite local snowstorms and generally adverse weather. Soon after the continental coast was crossed, all participating units of the Eighth Air Force except one wing either abandoned the operation or attacked other targets because of treacherous, towering cloud formations and dense, persistent contrails which made formation flying difficult. The one wing, led by the 95th Group, resolutely continued on to the objective. In the target area twenty to thirty single engine enemy aircraft pressed home vicious attacks, mostly in elements of two or three aircraft at a time. Friendly fighter support was inadequate and enemy ground positions fired heavy concentrations of anti-aircraft fire at the attackers. Nevertheless, the 95th Group maintained a tight defensive formation and released forty-two and a half tons of high explosives on the cloud covered German capital. Even after the target was bombed, enemy fighters continued to attack the formation until the rallypoint. The courageous crews of the 95th Group destroyed three of the hostile fighters, probably destroyed one and damaged one more.

A safe withdrawal was completed, although it was necessary to fly directly through solid clouds since the exhausted oxygen supply made it impossible to rise above them. Nine bombers were damaged by enemy action, four were lost. Forty-one officers and enlisted men were missing in action, and four were wounded.

By heroically electing to follow the more hazardous of two equally acceptable and honorable courses of action, the 95th Bombardment Group clearly distinguished itself above and beyond all other units participating in this momentous operation. The extraordinary heroism, determination, and esprit de corps displayed by the officers and enlisted men of this organization in overcoming unusually difficult and hazardous conditions brought to a successful conclusion our country's first combat operation over the capital of Germany. The fortitude, bravery and fighting spirit of the 95th Group on this historic occasion constitute a noteworthy contribution to the war effort and add notably to the cherished traditions of the Army Air Forces.

News Release

Technical Sergeant James I. Garvey, 21, of 2951 Frankford Avenue, Philadelphia, Pa., engineer and top turret gunner on a B-17 Flying Fortress of the 95th Bombardment Group, an Eighth Air Force component, has received credit for destroying an M.E. 262, jet-propelled German fighter plane, that attacked his Fortress during a bombing attack on an oil plant at Derben, Germany, in middle January.

The AAF gunner is a member of the Fortress group commanded by Colonel Jack E. Shuck of Casper, Wyo., and Monroe, Conn., which led the first American bombing attack on targets in Berlin. The 95th has been cited singly by the President for its exploits on a mission to Munster, Germany, in October, 1943, when the group fought its way through hundreds of attacking enemy planes to bomb railroad marshaling yards successfully, then rallied straggling elements of other groups and led them safely back to England. As a unit of the distinguished Third Air Division, the 95th also shared in another Presidential citation given the entire division for its historic England-Africa shuttle bombing of an important Messerschmitt fighter plane plant at Regensburg, Germany, in August of 1943.

Sgt. Garvey, son of Mr. and Mrs. Francis Garvey of 2951 Frankford Ave., Philadelphia, was formerly a machinist for the Philadelphia Gear Works.

PAUL J. REYNOLDS, 0718135, First Lieutenant, Army Air Forces, United States Army was cited for extraordinary achievement while serving as bombardier of a B-17 aircraft on a combat mission over Nuremberg, Germany, 20 February 1945. On the bombing run, a gunner was seriously wounded and Lieutenant Reynolds was knocked down by bursts of anti-aircraft fire. The plane was severely damaged and soon had to leave the flight formation. After skillfully administering first aid to the wounded gunner, which resulted in saving his life, Lieutenant Reynolds, although trained as a bombardier, navigated his plane safely out of enemy territory back to the home base despite dangerous cloud formations. The technical skill and courageous devotion to duty displayed by Lieutenant Reynolds on this occasion reflect the highest credit upon himself and the Army Air Forces.

FIRST AMERICAN DAYLIGHT BOMBING OF BERLIN 4 MARCH, 1944

For many months, at early morning briefings for 8th Air Force Missions over Europe, the announcement of targets deep into Germany were always greeted with loud groans, whistles, moans, and other signs of apprehension. Even veteran airmen dreaded the day when Berlin would become the priority target. Missions to places like Kiel, Kassel, Frankfurt, Stuttgart, the Ruhr Valley, and other industrial centers were successful, with acceptable crew/plane-loss ratios; but every flyer knew that Berlin "Big B" was heavily guarded as the nerve center of Hitler's war machine and government. More than 2500 anti-aircraft guns and hundreds of fighter aircraft surrounded the city. The first daylight attack on the major Nazi strongholds would be a test of courage and stamina. Several planned missions to Berlin were scrubbed or diverted to secondary targets because of the notoriously bad weather over England and the continent during the winter of 1943-44.

THEN CAME 4 MARCH, 1944...

Field Order #477 was received at Horham, Suffolk from 3rd Air Division headquarters on the cold, blustery night of 3 March, 1944. The teletype clacked as the message was typed on the long yellow sheet:

MAXIMUM FORCES WILL BE DISPATCHED AGAINST OBJECTIVES IN BERLIN AREA ON 4 MARCH, 1944.

Because of heavy clouds predicted over the North Sea it would be necessary to fly over the heavily defended heartland of central Europe—Belgium, Frankfurt, Leipzig, Cologne (to name a few)—in the path of thousands of defensive anti-aircraft batteries plus most of the fighters of the Luftwaffe on the Western Front. Every available B-17 and B-24 in the 8th Air Force was scheduled. More than 750 Flying Fortresses and Liberators assembled over England and headed to Berlin at 0930 hours.

Renowned British Artist John Rayson, working with personal accounts from mission leaders, captured details of the dramatic moment when American B-17's released the first bombs on Berlin, 4 March 1944, with air cover provided by American P-51's. The lead plane "I'll Be Around," and the Pathfinder aircraft showed precisely the bomb run formation. The heavy clouds, extremely cold temperature, and the combat box formation with protective

P-51 fighter cover all projected the vivid hues as seen on 4 March, 1944 to bring into perspective this important moment of history.

NOTE: The full story of the Berlin Mission of 4 March 1944 may be read in the book *Courage*Honor*Victory*—the first-person story of the 95th Bomb Group (H) in WW II, written by the men who made history with this storied Group. Published by the 95th Bomb Group (H) Association, 125 Clark Street, Clarks Green, PA 18411.

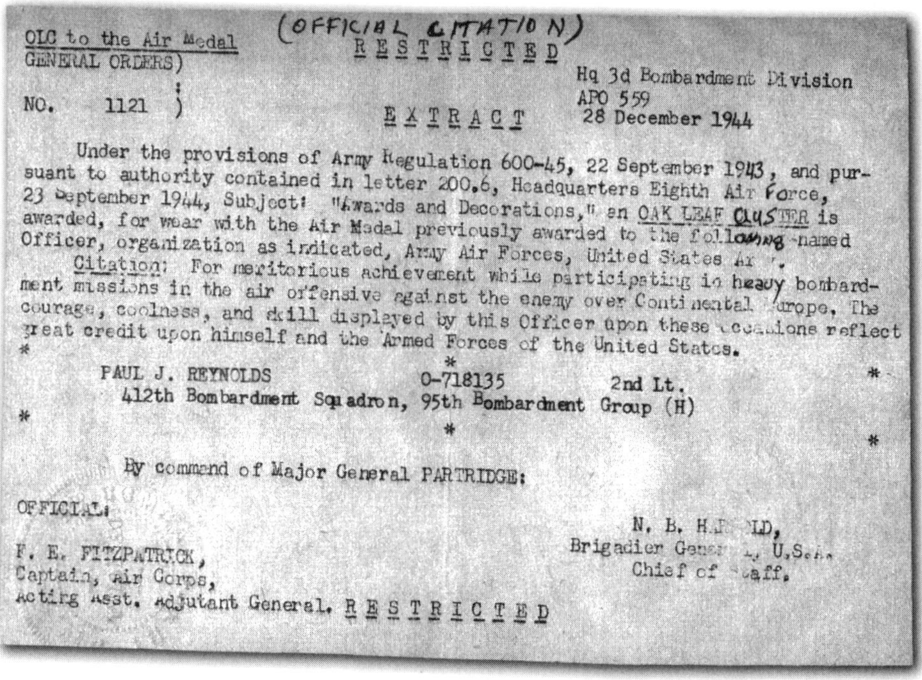

OLC to the Air Medal (OFFICIAL CITATION)
RESTRICTED

GENERAL ORDERS)
: Hq 3d Bombardment Division
NO. 1121) APO 559
EXTRACT 28 December 1944

Under the provisions of Army Regulation 600-45, 22 September 1943, and pursuant to authority contained in letter 200.6, Headquarters Eighth Air Force, 23 September 1944, Subject: "Awards and Decorations," an OAK LEAF CLUSTER is awarded, for wear with the Air Medal previously awarded to the following-named Officer, organization as indicated, Army Air Forces, United States Ar[illegible].

Citation: For meritorious achievement while participating in heavy bombardment missions in the air offensive against the enemy over Continental Europe. The courage, coolness, and skill displayed by this Officer upon these occasions reflect great credit upon himself and the Armed Forces of the United States.

* * *

PAUL J. REYNOLDS 0-718135 2nd Lt.
412th Bombardment Squadron, 95th Bombardment Group (H)

* * *

By command of Major General PARTRIDGE:

OFFICIAL:

N. B. H[illegible]LD,
Brigadier Gen[illegible], U.S.A.,
Chief of [illegible]aff.

F. E. FITZPATRICK,
Captain, Air Corps,
Acting Asst. Adjutant General. RESTRICTED

Official Citation for meritorious achievement against the enemy

A BRIEF HISTORY
95th BOMB GROUP (H)
13th COMBAT WING - 3rd AIR DIVISION - 8th AIR FORCE
HORHAM, ENGLAND - STATION 119
WORLD WAR II

Of the 41 heavy bombardment groups stationed in England during WW II, the achievements and recognition of the 95th Bomb Group are unequaled. This outstanding group was known for its dedication to mission, its pride, camaraderie and leadership in combat.

Intensive training began at Geiger Field, Washington, in October, 1942 and continued at Rapid City AFB, South Dakota. On March 18, 1943, the Group's 39 B-17's and 399 crew members were ordered to Europe. Flying from Florida through Brazil and Africa, the Group began operations at Alconbury, England on May 13, 1943. Later the Group was based temporarily at Framingham before moving to its permanent base at Horham (Station 119). From this date until beyond the end of the war, the 95th participated in every major campaign and air battle, earning honors of the highest order because of the undaunted courage of the air crews and the dedicated, faithful, professional service of the ground support units.

In brief summary, the 95th Bomb Group (H):

Flew 321 combat missions; dropped 19,769 tons of bombs.

Flew 7 "Chowhound" missions—low-level food supply to the starving Dutch Nation.

Flew 4 "Revival" repatriation missions—to return downed POW's and forced laborers from France, Belgium and Holland.

Flew a total of 8,625 credited sorties (plane missions).

PART VI

PEARL HARBOR SURVIVOR

Sgt. John D. Barker's Story

Sgt. John D. Barker, Pearl Harbor survivor, served in the Army from 1940-1945.

CHAPTER 1
Sgt. John D. Barker

Whence come wars and fightings among you?
James 4:1

In the summer of 1940, Germany's war machine was running rampant throughout Europe. Adolf Hitler's troops had launched a successful lightning attack against France, Belgium, and Holland. In June, 1940, Britain had been driven from France at what was known as the Dunkirk defeat. Germany's Chancellor Adolf Hitler had forced the French to sign a humiliating armistice in the same railroad car where Germany had been forced to sign the armistice following WW I in 1918. The Battle of Britain had begun, and Great Britain was the only nation standing in opposition to Hitler's war machine. September 1, 1940, Russia entered the war against Germany. WW II was widening.

In the summer of 1940, the Japanese army and navy had swept across Manchuria, Korea, parts of China, and Malaysia. In late November, 1941, it was obvious that Japan had ambitions to rule the Far East, and that the United States was about to become involved in another world war.

The Bombing Begins

At daybreak on Sunday, December 7, 1941, 360 Japanese war planes secretly took off from six aircraft carriers 300 miles north of Hawaii. They succeeded in reaching the U.S. naval base at Pearl Harbor undetected. The Japanese attack sunk or seriously damaged eight U.S. battleships and fourteen smaller ships and decimated the air forces. Their continuous dive-bombing and strafing left 2,400 Americans dead and 1,300 wounded. Tragically, amid burning battleships, painfully wounded soldiers, sailors, civilians, and unrecognizable corpses, America was at war. President Franklin D. Roosevelt called December 7, 1941, "A date that will live in infamy."

Survivor Describes Attack

Sixty years after that infamous attack, there are very few survivors left to tell about what happened on that fateful day. One Pearl Harbor survivor however, is very much alive and living in Morehead, Kentucky, today. His name is John D. Barker and he is a retired agent for the Commonwealth Life Insurance Company.

Sgt. Barker eating from his GI mess kit following the December 7, 1941, attack

In the year 2000, his family and just a few of his closest friends were the only ones who knew his story. Like so many veterans of WW II, he did not want to talk much about it. John Barker is a sincere, quiet, humble Christian man who would never in any manner call attention to himself. It was only in casual conversation with Harold Johnson, chairman of the Rowan County Veterans' Association, that John's wife Pearl mentioned the fact that her husband was a Pearl Harbor survivor. Harold told this writer and John D. Barker reluctantly agreed to allow me to publish his story. John Barker believed he was just serving his country in the best way he could at that time.

John D. Barker was born in the small Elliott County, Kentucky, community of Gimlet on October 14, 1917. Gimlet is located on Mauk Ridge near where Rowan, Carter, and Elliott Counties converge. John was the son of John and Margaret (Sparks) Barker. He attended the Carter County schools before moving to Montgomery, West Virginia, and going to work in the coal mines.

From One Dangerous Job to Another

Coal mining paid well but the work was dangerous, and John Barker and his friend, John H. Riddle, decided to volunteer for the Army in order to get the branch of service and station of their choice. On November 4, 1940, over one year before Pearl Harbor was attacked, John and his friend were sworn into the Army at Fort Hayes, Ohio. The two men wanted to be assigned to the Philippines but that station had no vacancies, and the two young men elected to serve in Hawaii. If the two young soldiers had been assigned to the Philippines, it would have been much worse because the Japanese conquered the Philippines shortly after the Pearl Harbor attack. On January 25, 1941, almost a year before Pearl Harbor was attacked, John and his friend were shipped out to Camp Molokai on the Island of Oahu. Looking back over his life, John said, "That was God taking care of me and I didn't know it."

Following his basic training, Pvt. Barker was assigned to the 251st Post Artillery Anti-aircraft Unit stationed at Molokai about five miles from Pearl Harbor. He later was promoted to sergeant and was in charge of an 18-man gun crew. Johns' buddy became a searchlight operator.

Gun Crews Stand Down From "Alert"

In November, 1941, tensions were mounting between the U.S. and Japan. On November 21, 1941, Sgt. Barker and his gun crew were put on "red alert." That meant there was a crew on duty at their battle station 24 hours a day. But when the newly appointed Japanese envoy Kurusu arrived in Washington, D.C., in mid-November to continue the peace talks, the possibility for peace looked better.

On December 5, 1941, two days before the attack, all the anti-aircraft gun crews were ordered to stand down from their "red alert." They were then ordered back to regular duty and to prepare for a general inspection. On Saturday, December 6, 1941, because of their recent red alert, Barker said about 90 percent of the gun crew battery were given weekend passes. Although most of those men were on leave from their post on Sunday, December 7, 1941, Sgt. John Barker said he returned to the base on Saturday night. The reason he returned was because during the week the men ate out of the standard GI aluminum trays and ate the standard GI food. But on Sunday you could either sleep in or you could go to breakfast and eat your meal in grand style. On Sunday morning, you could order whatever you wanted to eat and it was served to you on china dishes on tables covered with table clothes. That was a real treat and an added incentive for the men to return to base on Saturday night.

Breakfast and Bullets

Sgt. John D. Barker entered the flimsy wooden barracks that had been converted to a mess hall Sunday morning, December 7, 1941,

Men of the motor pool at Pearl Harbor 1941

about 7:30 a.m. He sat down at a crude table covered with a tablecloth and ordered his eggs "sunny side up," black coffee, fried potatoes, ham, biscuits, and all the trimmings. He had just started eating when he heard airplanes diving low overhead. Thinking they were U.S. planes from Hickam Field, he paid no attention until machine gun bullets came tearing through the thin wooden walls splattering his eggs and china everywhere. John said, "The bullets were hitting about six inches apart across the table in front of me." By then the shock was over, the men knew they were under attack, and they were ordered to fall out and line up. There were about a dozen Japanese Zeros strafing their barracks, killing or wounding many men as they slept. The planes continued to strafe the motor pool, mess hall, and their gun emplacements. John recalled, "With the men lined up outside, they were an easy target for the attacking planes." They quickly ran for cover and he dived under the barracks to escape the deadly machine gun fire.

BAR Man Shoots Down One Plane

It was the job of the anti-aircraft battery to protect Pearl Harbor. But most of their guns were out on the open parade grounds ready for inspection. Men were running everywhere trying to get to their battle stations. One of their men who was their BAR man (operated a Browning Automatic Rifle) bravely dashed through the machine gun fire and got his BAR and succeeded in shooting one Zero out of the sky. John said, "He watched the plane with smoke trailing behind crash into the sea."

Sgt. Barker said he could also see the swarms of torpedo bombers diving and dropping their deadly loads on the helpless ships anchored in Pearl Harbor. He could also see the black smoke as it rose up over the harbor signifying the terrible damage inflicted.

Had Men Remained on "Alert" –Results Would Have Been Different

John recalled, "Those Japanese planes strafed us for about two hours keeping us from our battle stations. It was obvious the Japanese intelligence reports had been excellent. They knew where we were and what our jobs were. They knew they had to stop our guns if they were to be successful. There were about 1,500 men in our group and we had 25 or 30 90-mm anti-aircraft batteries throughout the island. Each battery had a crew of 18 men and they could fire 40-45 shells per minute." Had those men remained on a red alert for another two days, the Pearl Harbor attack might have had a different outcome. But the U.S. Army and Navy took heavy casualties that terrible day. Mr. Barker recalled, seeing trucks "filled with bodies stacked like cord wood headed for burial." But that attack gave the U.S. forces a battle cry for the rest of WW II—"REMEMBER PEARL HARBOR."

Gun Crew Moves into Other Battles

On May 22, 1942, Sgt. Barker and his gun crew landed on the island of Fiji in the South Pacific. From Fiji they were ordered on to Guadalcanal. They boarded the USS *Leonard Wood*, which was a former oil tanker converted to a troop ship. Guadalcanal Island was the scene of intense and bloody battles between American and Japanese forces. It was the job of Sgt. Barker's gun crew to set up their anti-aircraft batteries to protect the newly taken airstrip.

In March, 1943, the 251st A.A. Battery was ordered to Bougainville in the Solomon Islands. The three-day journey to Bougainville was aboard an LST. It was a landing ship with a flat bottom that carried heavy equipment as well as troops on beach attacks. When Sgt. Barker and his gun crew landed on Bougainville, only a small section of the island was under American control.

The first thing the Americans had to do was clean a landing strip out of a jungle with bulldozers and explosives. It was the primary task of the anti-aircraft crews to protect that landing strip. But as the infantry moved forward to push the Japanese off the island, the anti-aircraft crews were converted to field artillery. Therefore as the battle line moved forward, the artillery gun crews moved just behind the front lines. They were told that if the front lines did not hold, they were to grab rifles and reinforce the infantry. While at Bougainville, the troops lived in foxholes and were under constant aerial and artillery attack. They also had to constantly battle the mosquitoes as well as the Japanese.

During the heaviest fighting on Bougainville, Sgt. Barker said, "The company commander ordered his gun crew to move up against Japanese positions located on top of a volcanic mountain called 'Blue Ridge'." It was there the young sergeant was involved in his most intense action. He said, "During one battle, their guns were fired so rapidly that the gun barrels became so hot they had to stop firing at times to allow the guns to cool." It was during that action that Sgt.

Barker received the Bronze Star for meritorious service. Portions of that citation are as follows:

10 June 1944
By Order of Major General Griswold

"A Bronze Star Medal is awarded to Sgt. John D. Barker, 150 147 83 Coast Artillery Corps, U.S. Army for meritorious service in action in Bougainville, Solomon Islands during the period of March 22, 1944 to April 4, 1944. As gun commander of a 90 mm antiaircraft gun emplacement on our frontlines he was responsible for the destruction of Japanese positions on Blue Ridge. He distinguished himself by his determination, leadership and superior ability in the face of great obstacles. He was also an inspiration to his men in the destruction of enemy artillery guns, pill boxes, and supply dumps."

The 251st Anti-Aircraft Artillery Gun Crew in Hawaii, December 7, 1941, succeeded in shooting down one enemy plane during the attack. John Barker, front left.

Many Men Gave Many Years

Sgt. John D. Barker was honorably discharged from the Army after giving four years and eight months of his life as a citizen soldier in the service of his country. Three years and nine months of that time were outside the continental U.S. and considered overseas duty. He came home and married Pearl (Lewis) Barker and they have one son, Scott.

John Barker was typical of fifteen million men and women who gave a significant part of their youth during WW II to help keep our nation free. There were over 258,000 who did not return. They gave their tomorrows that we might have our todays.

This B-24 bomber was shot down over Truk in the South Pacific March 29, 1944. All men were lost. The crew included, Front (L-R) J. Decker, D. Eastland, M. Sorrow, Adrian McKinney (Morehead, KY), J. Knaggs and A. Porvanna. Rear (L-R) W. Mara, J. Morarity, S. Peel and R. Conners.

PART VII

THEY GAVE THEIR ALL: MIAs AND KIAs

Sgt. Adrian McKinney, top turret gunner-radio operator on a B-24 Liberator bomber, missing in action since March 29, 1944, and presumed dead.

CHAPTER 1
Missing in Action
Sergeant Adrian McKinney's Story

Greater love hath no man than this: that a man lay down his life for his friend. John 15:13

There are over 40,000 veterans of WW II listed as Missing in Action after fifty years. They valiantly served our nation in defense of freedom and never returned. Hundreds of thousands laid down their lives in the global conflict known as WW II. Those are honored especially on Memorial Day as a flag is placed on each grave. But let us not forget there are thousands who died that do not even have a grave where a flag can be placed. Those are "Missing in Action and Presumed Dead."

There were over 258,000 brave young men who died for their country during WW II. But there were also over 58,000 that, after half a century, are still missing in action. Those men have no grave on which to place a flag, no monument with birth and death dates. Those were brave young men, many still teenagers, who would never know the joy of being called "Daddy," never see their children grow up, never go on a family picnic, and never come home to their own family and be greeted at the door by that special woman they hoped to grow old with. All that remains is their name on a plaque in a courthouse yard.

This is the story of one gallant young citizen soldier from Morehead, Kentucky, who could be representative of the more than 58,000 still listed as Missing in Action from WW II for over 50 years. It is the story of one young man whose name is listed on the memorial plaque at the old Rowan County Courthouse lawn. He was born Adrian Turner McKinney on July 14, 1922, in Rowan County, Kentucky. He was the son of Laban McKinney, Sr., and Molly Crosthwaite McKinney. His dad was a shoemaker by trade and operated a shoe shop on Main Street in Morehead. His mother was a homemaker.

Believed in Duty, Honor, Country

Adrian, the fourth of seven children born into the family, grew up in Morehead. He attended the local public schools and was popular among his classmates. He had a good sense of humor and a keen sense of honor and duty even as a child. His childhood was spent helping in the shoe shop, working in the garden, and helping to care for the younger children. As time allowed, he loved to roller-skate, ride bicycles, have rubber gun wars, and play marbles. As he grew older he loved to go swimming in Triplett Creek and hunt in the fields and hills surrounding his home. During the depression years of the 1930s, there was very little money and his father struggled to support the family in his shoe repair business. But Adrian had an enjoyable childhood growing up in the small town.

In May of 1941, Adrian graduated from Morehead High School. Little thought was given at that time to the terrible trauma this nation would face in the next few months, so he went up to Shelby, Ohio, and got a job working on the railroad. He was eagerly anticipating a bright future until December 7, 1941, when his life changed drastically, as did millions of other young men at that time.

Early in 1942, young Adrian returned to Rowan County to help his parents who had moved to a farm near Bangor, Kentucky. He could have been deferred to work on the farm because raising food was considered an essential occupation to the war effort. But he would have none of that because of his deep sense of honor, duty, and love of country. Without waiting to be drafted, he volunteered to serve in the Army Air Corps. As he waited for his call to report for duty, he began carrying mail on a rural mail route from Farmers to Bangor in Rowan County. During this time he began to take special notice of a

Adrian McKinney and his wife, Lucille. They were married for three days before he shipped out, never to see her again.

beautiful young girl along the route. Her name was Lucille McKenzie and they began seeing each other. By the summer of 1942, when Adrian received his call to report for duty, he was very much in love, and when he left Kentucky, theirs was a tearful good-bye as he boarded the bus to enter the Army Air Corps to become a citizen soldier.

Four Day Honeymoon

During the next year he completed basic training at Eglin Field in Florida, Radio School at Chanute Field, Illinois, and Gunnery School in Pueblo, Colorado. That was an extremely busy time and Adrian and Lucille corresponded regularly. At last, after just over a year of separation, Adrian got his first furlough, 15 days before shipping out to the South Pacific.

While home on leave, he and Lucille were married in Maysville, Kentucky, August 31, 1943. They had a honeymoon that lasted four days, because on September 4, he had to report back for duty. She never saw him again. S/Sgt. Adrian McKinney was assigned to a B-24 Liberator crew as the radio-operator and top turret gunner. The plane and crew were assigned to the 371st Bomb Sqdn., 307th Bomb Group on an island in the South Pacific. While there he wrote his wife saying: "I am on an island in the South Pacific, although I can't tell you where. It is not really a bad place here."

The long-range B-24s were assigned to bomb Truk, a strong Japanese base in the South Pacific. The Japanese had been building strong fortifications for years before the war began. In fact, there is some documentation that the famous female pilot Amelia Earheart's plane was shot down over Truk in 1937 because the Japanese thought she was spying on their base.

Final Flight

On March 28, 1944, McKinney and nine other young men took off in their B-24 Liberator for the long flight to Eten Airdrome on Truk.

Long past the range of their protective fighter planes, they were met by a swarm of Japanese Zero fighter planes as they approached their target. They successfully completed their mission, but as they returned, their plane suffered a direct hit by enemy fire and began to go down. Other members of the squadron who returned safely reported that four parachutes opened out of a crew of 10. However, five Japanese fighter planes strafed those men in their parachutes and the plane as it went down all the way to the water. There were no survivors.

The dreaded telegram arrived at his home in Kentucky in early April, 1944, saying that "S/Sgt. Adrian McKinney has been reported missing in action in the South Pacific." Another letter came in May, 1944, with a few more details. In January, 1946, another letter was received by the family stating that their son had now been declared dead. A final letter came in May, 1949, five years after he was reported missing. No other report has ever been received by the family after more than 50 years.

The sad part about the battle for Truk was that the Army and Navy decided to bypass the islands, because they believed it would be too costly in lives to invade. Therefore, with the dropping of the atomic bombs on Japan in 1945, and Japan's ultimate surrender, Truk surrendered to the U.S. without firing a shot. Those who died on those bombing raids seemingly died in vain.

There are very few friends or family who even remember Adrian. His mother died of a broken heart in 1946, after he was declared dead. His wife of three days remarried and lives in Rowan County, Kentucky. That is the tragic story of one name on a plaque in the yard of a Kentucky courthouse.

WAR DEPARTMENT
The Adjutant General's Office
Washington, 25, D.C.

IN REPLY REFER TO:
AGPC-S 201 McKinney, Adrian T.
(23 Jan 46) 35,508,069

23 January 1946

Mr. and Mrs. Labe F. McKinney
Bangor, Kentucky

Dear Mr. and Mrs. McKinney:

Since your son, Staff Sergeant Adrian T. McKinney, 35,508,069, Air Corps, was reported missing in action 29 March 1944, the War Department has entertained the hope that he survived and that information would be revealed dispelling the uncertainty surrounding his absence. However, as in many cases, the conditions of warfare deny us such information.

Public Law 490, 77th Congress, as amended, provides for a review and determination of the status of each person who has been missing in action for twelve months. Accordingly, your son's case was reviewed and he was continued in the status of missing in action as of 30 March 1945. The law further provides that a subsequent review shall be made whenever warranted. Upon such subsequent review the making of a finding of death is authorized.

All available records and reports concerning the absence of your son have been carefully investigated and are deemed to warrant a subsequent review of his case. Information in the hands of the War

Department indicates that your son was a crew member of a B-24 (Liberator) bomber which participated in a mission to Eten Airdrome, Truk Island, on 29 March 1944. The planes encountered enemy aircraft after leaving the target and in the ensuing engagement your son's plane sustained damage. Four parachutes were seen leaving the plane and they, as well as the plane, were strafed continuously by five enemy fighters until they landed in the water. Intensive searches were made with negative results.

Since no information has been received which would support a presumption of his continued survival the War Department must now terminate your son's absence by a presumptive finding of death. Accordingly, an official finding of death has been recorded. The finding does not establish an actual or probable date of death for the purpose of termination of pay and allowances, settlement of accounts and payment of death gratuities. In the case of your son this date has been set as 23 January 1946.

I regret the necessity for this message but trust that the ending of a long period of uncertainty may give at least some small measure of consolation. An appraisal of the sacrifice made by your son in the service of his country compels in us feelings of humility and respect. May Providence grant a measure of relief from the anguish and anxiety you have experienced during these many months.

Sincerely,

EDWARD F. WITSELL
Major General
Acting The Adjutant General of the Army

1 Encl.

LUSTER MC KEE HARGIS
Date of entrance in service: June 26, 1942.
Branch of service: Army.
Trained at: Fort Eustis, Virginia; North Africa.
Date of embarkation: November, 1942.
Theater of operations: North Africa.
Rank: Private First Class.
Remarks: Killed March 12, 1943. Mother was Mrs. Eunice Hargis, Morehead, Kentucky.

WALTER G. HARGIS
Date of entrance in service: November 10, 1941.
Branch of service: Army.
Trained at: Camp Wheeler, Virginia; Panama Canal.
Date of embarkation: 1942.
Theater of operations: Panama Canal.
Rank: Corporal.
Remarks: Killed in Action August 1, 1943. Mother was Eunice Hargis, 301 Elizabeth Avenue, Morehead, Kentucky.

CHAPTER 2
Killed In Action
The Hargis Brothers' Story

Yea though I walk through the valley of the shadow of death I will fear no evil. Psalms 23:4

The practice of hanging a small 4-inch by 6-inch solid blue flag in the window of a home with a man or woman in the military service began in this nation soon after the bombing of Pearl Harbor on December 7, 1941. There were two different styles of those small blue flags. Both were the same size, but one had a silver star and the other had a gold star. Each flag had a one-inch tassel on the bottom and gold braid all the way around the flag. There was a gold silken cord at the top and a small round pointed stick about half the size of a pencil upon which the flag was draped. Most mothers or wives with men in the military service had one proudly displayed in their window for all to see.

Silver Stars or Gold Stars

Those families with two or more members in service had the appropriate number of silver stars on their flags. However, if someone in that family had been killed, there was a flag with a gold star signifying that a member of the Armed Forces from that family had been killed in the war. During WW II there was one family by the name of Sullivan from northern Illinois, that was a five gold-star family. Their five boys were in the Navy, and all five were on the same ship (contrary to general Navy regulations). However, because they all wanted to be together on the same ship, the Navy bent the regulations. Their ship was sunk, and all five brothers were lost. That mother was the only five gold-star mother in WW II. Following that tragedy, Congress enacted legislation prohibiting brothers from serving in combat in the same unit. Also, a service man was not required to serve in combat if one member of his family had been killed in combat. That was called the "Sullivan Law." Later, a ship named "The Fighting Sullivans" was commissioned in honor of those five brothers.

This nation is a ceremonial nation, whether it be sacred or secular. When our loved ones die we gather in a ceremonial fashion to acknowledge the reality of that loss. One beautiful ceremony that the Navy observes on Memorial Day is to set afloat tiny boats filled with flowers, in memory of those who have died at sea. The Navy observes that ceremony in major ports throughout the world to insure they do not forget those brave heroes who went down at sea in defense of their country.

Double Gold-Star Mother

There were no five gold-star mothers in Rowan County, Kentucky, during WW II. However, the Hargis family in Morehead was a double gold-star family. Mrs. Eunice Hargis had two sons killed in WW II about five months apart. The Hargis family lived at 301 Elizabeth Avenue at the east end of Second Street in an old wooden, weatherboarded house with a screened-in back porch. Eunice Hargis was a widow struggling to raise a large family, when on December 7, 1941, this nation was plunged into a war. In only a short time there were two Hargis boys in the Army.

Brothers Killed a Few Months Apart

Walter G. Hargis entered the Army on November 10, 1941. Walter and his family knew that when war came he would most certainly be among the first sent overseas. Following basic and advanced training at Camp Wheeler, Virginia, he was shipped to the Panama Canal Zone to help guard that strategic part of the world. Walter was an excellent soldier, and soon gained the rank of corporal. However, he was killed in action on August 1, 1942.

Luster McKee Hargis was anxious to get into the Army and help do his share in the fight for freedom. On June 26, 1942, about two months after his brother Walter was shipped overseas, Luster joined the U.S. Army. He completed his training at Fort Eustes, Virginia, in November, 1942, and after a ten-day furlough, returned to Fort Dix, New Jersey. There, he was immediately shipped out to North Africa. During that bloody campaign he was among those who fought bitterly against the German General Rommel's crack desert troops. On March 12, 1943, after three months of heavy fighting, Private Luster Hargis was killed in action. Although the U.S. finally succeeded in driving Rommel and the German troops out of North Africa, it was at the expense of the lives of many brave American boys.

Mrs. Eunice Hargis of 301 Elizabeth Avenue, became the only Rowan County, Kentucky, mother to lose two sons during World War II. She received the first dreaded telegram from the War Department in the middle of August, 1942, saying her son, Walter, was killed in action. She received the second telegram eight months later, repeating the same words that her son, Luster, had also been killed. Luster M. Hargis and Walter G. Hargis were two of sixty Rowan County service men killed in action during WW II.

Rollie R. Poston

CHAPTER 3
Killed in Action
Pfc. Rollie Ray Poston's Story

The last enemy that shall be destroyed is death.
I Corinthians 15:26

Rollie R. Poston was the youngest son of the late Samuel and Mary D. Poston. Samuel was an excellent horseman who broke and trained horses for farm work and in the log woods. Rollie grew up on the family farm in the Bluestone section of Rowan County. Rollie Ray, was a well-liked, easy-going young man. One of the popular pastimes for the young people was getting together each Saturday night at a different home to play cards. They usually played Pedro, Pitch, or Pinochle. When it was Rollie Rays's turn to host the card game, he always took personal pride in serving his guests something he had prepared. Among the "Bluestone Card Sharks" were Vernon Howard, Willard Warren, Elmer Ward, Sam Poston, Johnny Poston, Rufus and Woodrow Flannery. They always enjoyed going to Rollie's house because they knew they would get some special dish he had prepared.

Drafted into the Army

Rollie Ray reported for military service on December 1, 1942, at Camp Atterbury, Indiana. He was then assigned to Company E, 47th Infantry Battalion, and did most of his training at Long Island, New York. On May 1, 1944, he embarked from New York on a troop ship heading for a staging area in England. Ten days later the troop ship landed in Southampton, England, just two weeks before D-Day, June 6, 1944. Pfc. Poston, along with thousands of his comrades, began intensive training for the invasion of fortress Europe. His unit landed in France just five days after the initial invasion and was in the thick of the battle to free France.

Rollie Wrote Home Often

After six weeks of bitter fighting, sleeping in foxholes, eating C rations, drinking water out of his canteen, and shaving in cold water out of his helmet, Pfc. Poston was killed in action. A letter written to his mother four days before he was killed, reflected his unselfishness and concern for his family, even though he was the one suffering. Among other things the letter says:

> "Dear Mother, I was glad to hear from you and glad you're OK. As for myself I am OK. Tell all at home hello and I would like to be there to help you eat your green beans. I'm glad to hear you had a good crop. You don't need to send me anymore cigarettes we can get them here. Also, keep one of the watches I sent you and give it to Charlie. Have the other one fixed and mail back to me. I'm glad you're praying for me, and, yes, I go to church. Just don't worry about me."
>
> Love Rollie

After the war in Europe ended, Rollie Ray Poston's body was returned to his beloved Bluestone in Rowan County. It was a hot and humid September day in 1946 when he was buried in his beloved Kentucky hills. His childhood friends carried his casket to the top of Bluestone Hill to its final resting place.

PART VIII

HUMOR IN THE MILITARY: KILROY, WILLIE AND JOE

A familiar sight to every veteran was the "Kilroy was here" sign. He seemed to be everywhere.

CHAPTER 1
Kilroy Was Here

Even in laughter the heart is sorrowful, and the end of that mirth is heaviness. Proverbs 14:13

As this nation moves into a new millennium, there is one veteran who served in WW II that especially should be remembered. He is perhaps the most well-known veteran of that conflict. He first appeared in WW II and is fondly remembered by almost everyone who served in that conflict. He was the elusive, ever-present, irrepressible "Kilroy," whose impudent image was seen in every theater of that war.

Kilroy Was Everywhere

Wherever American military men were sent during WW II, it seemed that "Kilroy" had already been there. His presence was announced with a sketch on a wall or at the top of a fence with head, large nose, and two eyes showing. The large nose extended over the wall and the message, "Kilroy was here" was scrawled under the art work. (The legend was that Kilroy was always everywhere before anyone else.) Everywhere Americans landed they were greeted with that and its impudent message. When the first U.S. Marines stormed the beaches at the South Pacific, they were greeted by the mysterious notice, "Kilroy was here." When U.S.soldiers stormed the beaches at Normandy, there was the famous sign, "Kilroy was here." Even when the U.S. 8th Army captured Hitler's "Eagle's Nest" at lofty Berchtesgaden deep in southern Germany, there was scrawled on the wall, "Kilroy was here."

One American soldier rappelled several hundred feet down the sheer inside walled pit of an extinct volcano near the Kilauea Volcano in Hawaii. Upon landing at the bottom of the pit he found "Kilroy was here" eloquently spelled out with smooth stones on the polished lava floor of that crater. Following the Japanese surrender in WW II, the first American occupation troops (claiming to be first) landed on the Island of Japan. Yes, they were met by Kilroy's latest rhyming repose: "Sorry to spoil your little joke, I was here but my pencil broke." Signed "Kilroy"

During WW II the Kilroy legend lightened the load of U.S. fighting men around the world. "Kilroyisms" were also found at home. They were seen on the Capitol Dome in Washington, on the Statue of Liberty's torch in New York harbor, and San Francisco's Golden Gate Bridge. Kilroy was at home in endless variations during WW II and eventually became a part of the permanent American language.

How Did Kilroy Begin?

How did this redoubtable Kilroy get his start? Where did the legend begin? Was there a Kilroy or was he the figment of a fertile GI imagination? The explanations are almost as varied as the tales of that mystery warrior's exploits. The saga, some say, began in the Air Transport Command of the U.S. Army Air Corps. There was a real Francis J. Kilroy stationed at a Florida airfield. He was a star on the airfield baseball team, and he contracted the flu and it was rumored Kilroy would not be able to play the next game. However, when his condition improved, a friend posted a note on the bulletin board, "Kilroy will be here." Another Air Corps version was that Kilroy was a frequently absent-without-leave enlisted man. His irate commanding officer would continually send the

Military Police out looking for him. All they ever found, was where he had been at one time, and a note saying "Kilroy was here." Still another account was that the original Kilroy was a spit-and-polish, go-by-the-book-strictly GI sergeant at a base in Kansas. That Kilroy was marked absent without leave from a special detail and his name placed on the company bulletin board. When that Kilroy saw his name on the bulletin board as AWOL, he took a heavy red pen and wrote KILROY WAS HERE beside his name.

Military and Civilian Kilroy

Another attempt at solving the Kilroy controversy came from the girlfriend of an Irish-American named Kilroy who served in the British Royal Air Force. During the British defeat and evacuation at Dunkirk, he was shot down over France. He was later rescued by the French and smuggled out of the country, but his name lingered on as a symbol of the promise of future liberation. Also, there was one civilian account of the beginning of the legend of Kilroy. That account was called in on a radio talk show in Massachusetts during WW II. It seemed that a civilian shipyard inspector named Kilroy claimed that after he inspected and approved certain parts of a ship under construction, he would write Kilroy was here. That was done he said to avoid losing time by someone else inspecting the same part.

Another possible explanation of how the legend of Kilroy began is offered by this writer. There was a man named Kilroy McKenzie who lived near the Licking River in Rowan County, Kentucky. Before WW II began, he left Kentucky and went to work in a shipyard somewhere on the East Coast. He could have been the original Kilroy. That is one possible explanation, especially since it was well known that wherever American ships sailed around the world during WW II, the rascal Kilroy went with them or had already been there.

Every GI in WW II has a story about an unusual place where he discovered a "Kilroy was here" sign. This writer remembers clearly when he landed in Le Havre, France, at the end of WW II, our troop ship was towed into the harbor on the high tide about dusk one evening. We did not disembark until early the next morning. By that time the tide had gone out, revealing the twisted sunken wreckage of several German ships. I remember seeing the bow of a ship that extended above the low tide with the sign clearly painted for all to see, "Kilroy was here."

Kilroy in Space?

That "shady rascal" Kilroy was rumored to have even been involved in the American race for space program following WW II. Although it cannot be verified, it was whispered throughout NASA that during Neil Armstrong's moon landing, he had to step over a "Kilroy was here" sign as he made "that first small step for a man and a giant leap for mankind." No doubt that if NASA ever does get a safe Mars landing they will find that "Kilroy" has already been there and left his image.

It will probably never be determined just how the legend of Kilroy first began. However, Kilroy's levity lightened the burden of war and separation. It also kept the GIs humble, for no matter where they landed, they usually found "Kilroy" had already been there. Whatever the source of the "Kilroyisms," they have spread throughout the world (and maybe the universe). "Kilroy" is now a part of this nation's culture and language.

CHAPTER 2
Willie and Joe Were There

A time to weep and a time to laugh.
Ecclesiastes 3:4

Most every veteran of WW II remembers "Willie and Joe." They were two dogfaces, infantry soldiers, the creation of Sgt. Bill Mauldin. They appeared regularly in cartoon form in Yank magazine and Stars and Stripes, U.S. Army publications. (Bill Mauldin won a Pulitzer prize for one of his military cartoons.)

Citizen soldiers Willie and Joe were constantly fighting hunger, fatigue, weather, and the enemy as they slogged across Europe. They often as not came into conflict with the military tradition that gave officers certain privileges not enjoyed by the enlisted man. On an army base, officers usually ate in separate mess halls, slept in separate quarters, used separate bathrooms, and attended separate social functions. Officers were thought of as gentlemen. Unfortunately, that tradition sometimes carried over into combat. For instance, as they slogged across Europe through the rain, mud, and snow, the officers usually rode in jeeps. In cities the best bars and restaurants were usually set aside for officers only. Although Bill Mauldin always pointed out there were many good officers whom he respected deeply, there were many he did not. His cartoons reflected those views as they recorded in cartoon form the plight of the infantry soldier in combat.

Sgt. Bill Mauldin sketches the Willie and Joe characters so familiar to American soldiers and saliors. (Yank)

General Patton Threatened Court Martial

Sgt. Bill Mauldin wrote in Yank magazine "that a good officer was not supposed to sleep until his men were bedded down. He was not supposed to eat until his men were fed." He said a good officer was like a prize fighter's manager. It was his job to keep his fighter in top condition. Sgt. Mauldin said, "I have the greatest respect for good officers, and the greatest disrespect for poor ones." Therefore, he sometimes riled the officers with the biting wit of his cartoons. Most officers accepted his cartoons all in good fun. However, legendary General George S. Patton once threatened to court martial cartoonist Mauldin for lack of respect for officers.

Many of the old-time regular army officers were shocked by the spirit of rebellion that showed itself in the citizen army of WW II. Sergeant Mauldin impressed upon the brass that the citizen army was made up of men who were not accustomed to being directed to the backdoor. There were many peace-time regular army cooks who were suddenly elevated to wartime captains and colonels, and they were determined to make the most of their moment of glory. They were the ones who made life miserable for the WW II GIs, and they were the ones who took whatever privilege rank offered. But to the combat infantry soldier, rank meant very little, and officers had to earn their respect as they moved into combat.

Combat Soldiers Respected Each Other

Men in combat outfits kidded each other a lot, but they had a kind of family atmosphere between them. They were allowed to kid around with each other, but no one outside that family was permitted that luxury. There was deep mutual respect for every soldier who held a dangerous job in combat. Bomber crews, paratroopers, and the combat infantry squads were about equal in that respect. They held the highest regard for each other even though they were in different jobs. Usually the infantry soldiers would call the bomber crews "fly boys," while the airmen called the infantry "ground pounders." But each held a healthy respect for the other. The paratroopers held the greatest respect for those crews of the unarmed C47s that dropped them in combat zones. Also, at the same time, you could see the respect in the eyes of those C47 crews as those gallant paratroopers "hit the silk."

Sgt. Bill Mauldin, the GI cartoonist in WW II, eventually became a best selling author. He was awarded a Pulitzer prize for his work in creating Willie and Joe. They represented every soldier who could find humor under stressful conditions as well as every citizen soldier who deeply resented the irony of the "officers and men" regulations that carried special privilege under combat conditions.

In their foxhole during a rainstorm, Willie says, “Now that you mention it Joe, it does sound like the pitter-patter of rain on a tin roof.” (Yank)

Hunkering down in a foxhole, Willie tells Joe, “I feel like a fugitive from the law of averages.” (Yank)

Hiding behind a hedgerow, Willie tells Joe, “I wish I could stand up and get some sleep.” (Yank)

Two officers admiring the view of the mountains. The caption was: "Beautiful view. Is there one for the enlisted men?" (Yank)

Willie and Joe standing in front of a strictly off limits offi cers club. The caption was: "Them buttons was shot o sir, when I took this town." (Yank)

The Veterans Club was one of the largest and most active clubs on college campuses following WW II. This was the Veterans Club at Morehead (Ky.) State College in the 1950s.

PART IX

REDEPLOYMENT:
RETURN TO CIVILIAN LIFE AT MOREHEAD STATE COLLEGE

Sgt. Norman Roberts WW II European Veteran.

CHAPTER I
Norman Roberts, John Collis, and the "GI Bill"

They shall beat their swords into plowshares, and their spears into pruning hooks...neither shall they learn of war anymore. *Isaiah 2:4*

Following WW II, the men began to return home to their families, homes, jobs, and education, never once thinking of themselves as heroes. Those men mostly thought of themselves as being in the right place at the right time, or the wrong place at the wrong time (depending on your point of view). They believed they were called upon to do a job, and they did it to the best of their ability. However, looking back at the WW II generation through the telescope of time, they were an extraordinary generation.

On August 14, 1945, three years, eight months, and seven days after the sneak attack on Pearl Harbor, the war ended. The last Axis enemy had gone down to defeat. In this nation, there was a tremendous mood swing between December 7, 1941, and August 14, 1945. It was a contrast between an attitude of shock, dread, and, near defeat and one of relief, happiness, thanksgiving, and unqualified victory. This poorly prepared nation and its army of citizen soldiers had risen from the ashes of defeat to achieve total victory against a totalitarian enemy that had been preparing for war for two decades. The war had smashed one of the greatest military machines in history and saved this nation from one of the greatest threats its freedom had ever faced. Now this nation had the problem of returning 15,000,000 men, conditioned to kill, back into a peaceful civilian life.

Redeployment of Personnel to Civilian Life

The system of returning 15,000,000 men from the military world to civilian life was called "redeployment," or "re-adjusting of personnel." Redeployment decided who came home first, and in what order. Of course the wounded were moved back to the states first. For others a system of "point value" and a procedure called a "critical score" were used to determine priorities of being discharged.

An "Adjusted Service Rating Card" was issued to each enlisted man and woman. Point totals were entered on this card covering four factors that determined who would be discharged first:

(1) <u>Service Credit</u>—One point for each month of service between September 16, 1940, and August 15, 1945.

(2) <u>Overseas Service</u>—One point for each month served overseas between September 16, 1940, and August 15, 1945.

(3) <u>Combat Service</u>—Five points for each additional award for service (Distinguished Service Cross, Silver Star, Distinguished Flying Cross, Legion of Merit, Air Medal, Purple Heart, Bronze Star and Battle Campaign Ribbons; also, Navy Cross, Marine Corps Medal, and other corresponding medals). Credit was also given for medals from a foreign country according to War Department Regulations.

(4) <u>Parenthood Credit</u>—Twelve points for each child under 18 years of age.

<u>CRITICAL SCORE</u>—At first a total of 85 points for men, and 44 points for women was necessary for discharge. The critical point score necessary for discharge quickly was lowered as men and women were discharged. But that system insured a fair and somewhat gradual method of returning 15,000,000 military personnel to civilian life.

GI Bill Opened New World for Vets

Late in 1944 the U.S. Congress passed P.L. 367 referred to as the GI Bill of Rights. It provided, among other things, that returning servicemen must be hired at their prewar job. Also, they were guaranteed home and business loans and certain unemployment benefits, such as the 52-20 Club. This writer drew $20 a week for about 15 weeks and went to Florida on vacation. I always felt guilty about that but it was a benefit. Also the GI Bill provided one year of college tuition and a stipend for every year spent in military service.

The GI Bill provided that all tuition (up to $500 per year), books, and equipment be paid for by the government. Also each GI student received a $50 a month subsistence stipend ($75 if you were married). That $500 a year total allowance would get you into most colleges in this country at that time. In 1944, the tuition at Morehead (Kentucky) State College was $3 per credit hour per semester. A normal load was 18 hours per semester. Tuition then was $54 per semester, or $108 per year. I'm sure you could have enrolled in many Ivy League Schools then for $500 per year. But if the $500 did not cover costs, the GI student had to pay the additional expenses.

When the GI Bill was passed in 1944 it was met with a great deal of controversy. On one side was Robert Hutchins, the unorthodox president of the University of Chicago, who said it "would wreck American education and convert a frightening number of veterans into educational hobos." Dr. Hutchins complained that many veterans would be wasting their time, and he advocated a national aptitude testing program to determine if veterans were capable of learning in college. He said most would be better off getting jobs. He also maintained that "money hungry, greedy colleges would take advantage of the taxpayers' money." But cooler heads prevailed, and although there was some truth to Dr. Hutchins' statements, by and large, veterans were better students than the non-veterans. They were more serious and focused.

Veterans Gradually Enroll in Colleges

With only a small fraction of men discharged by June 1945, and 15,000,000 yet to be released, there were 23,478 veterans already enrolled in the nation's colleges. That represented only a tiny fraction of those who would later be enrolled in higher education. It was in 1945 that Elwood C. Kastner, the registrar of New York University, speaking for that institution said, "We will admit every returning veteran who left this University to enter military service. Over and above that we will admit all other veterans who qualify insofar as our space and staff will allow. We will hold classes six days and nights a week, and we don't need students. But we feel an obligation to all veterans." One wonders if that University is one Dr. Hutchins's was talking about when he said, "Some would take advantage of the government."

As veterans were discharged they began enrolling in the nation's colleges. The process for entering college under the GI Bill was:

(1) The veteran filled out Form 1950 available at all colleges and V.A. Centers.

(2) The Vet sent the form to the nearest Veterans Center.

(3) The V.A. investigated the vet's service record to make sure that each had an honorable discharge.

(4) The Vet took the certificate of eligibility to any approved college in the U.S. or abroad. The vet was then admitted to the college.

(5) Eventually the veterans subsistence check ($75 monthly) for single veterans arrived. (Married veterans received $90 monthly).

Could Men Conditioned to Kill Return to a Peaceful Life?

With so many men trained and conditioned to kill returning to civilian life, there were those who feared that violence would erupt in the streets and on campuses. Many psychiatrists maintained that veterans involved in sports might become violent in a dispute over an official's ruling and that might trigger an episode of violent behavior. Also, there was fear that a veteran receiving a failing grade might kill the professor. All of those fears were entirely unfounded and nothing like that ever happened. On the contrary, the veterans were more peaceful, settled, serious, and determined. They were a generation of students with families who realized the importance of a college education, and with "Uncle Sam's" help intended to better themselves.

College Vets Partied Peacefully

That was not to say there was not a great deal of drinking and partying among those single veterans on campus. John Collis, a star football player and one of the student veterans on the campus of Morehead (Kentucky) State College recalled that in 1946 Dean Warren Lappin called him into his office one day. John said, "When you were called into Dean Lappin's Office, you were in trouble." He was nervous as he arrived at the Dean's Office and was ushered into his presence. Dean Lappin sat behind an imposing desk with a stern look on his face and said, "John, what can we do to stop this on-campus drinking by these veterans?" John responded, "Dean, those men are battle hardened veterans who fought a war and they are not easily intimidated." Dean Lappin said, "That's exactly what I thought—how's the football team doing this year?"

The GI Bill infused new life into this nation's colleges. Morehead State College located in the Appalachian hills of eastern Kentucky had a prewar high enrollment of 1,000 in 1938. During the years of WW II its enrollment plummeted. On October 13, 1945, Registrar Mary Page Milton announced the fall on-campus enrollment was 222. That included 145 women and 77 men. Also there were 84 enrolled at the Morehead Ashland Center. Clearly the College was struggling because of the lack of students. However, there was hope for the future, because in those 222 there were 20 veterans enrolled under the GI Bill, and the war had just ended.

By 1947 Over Half at Morehead [Kentucky] College Were Vets

When the winter quarter of 1946 opened, the registrar at Morehead State College announced a 76% increase in total enrollment over the previous quarter, and there were 70 veterans registered. By January, 1947, when, because of political reasons, Morehead State College had been dropped by the Southern Association of Colleges and Schools accredited list, it did not seem to slow down the veterans enrollment. In January, 1947, there was a total on-campus enrollment of 567 with almost 274 veterans enrolled under the GI Bill, including four women.

By 1947 Morehead State Teachers College had become a cosmopolitan institution. That year the enrollment included 102 out -of-state students from seven states. That out-of-state enrollment was estimated at 16 percent and was mostly veterans. Many of those students were athletes recruited by Coaches Ellis Johnson and Stan Radjunas. Others returned to Morehead after being stationed there in the Navy. Still others came to Morehead because colleges in their own states were so crowded with veterans returning to college that even though they had been accepted, they had to wait one or two years just to enroll. One such student that came to Morehead and remained was Norman Roberts.

Housing a Problem for Vets

In 1946 this nation experienced its greatest housing shortage since the Pilgrims landed at Plymouth Rock. For five years there had been no civilian construction of homes or apartments. So when the veterans began enrolling in colleges, there was very little housing available. Of course, the nation's colleges and the government recognized that, and, cooperatively, they set about to remedy that situation as quickly as possible.

For five years there had been many military barracks constructed on this nation's military camps and air fields. Now they were empty.

One of the dismal Army barracks moved from Ft. Campbell, Kentucky to Morehead, Kentucky State College and converted to housing for married veterans. This building was destroyed in the 1960s.

So the government began to disassemble many of those barracks, donate, and ship them to college campuses throughout the country. That provided a great deal of work for many men who had been out of work since the end of the war. Many carpenters, plumbers, electricians, laborers and returning veterans were employed in both the dismantling and re-assembling of those old barracks.

Vet Village Springs up on Campus

One returning veteran to find his way to Morehead State Teachers College was Wisconsin native Norman Roberts. Following four years of military service, Norman was discharged and returned to his native Wisconsin, and enrolled at the University of Wisconsin. Although he was accepted, he was told it would be another year before he could enroll because of the large enrollment of veterans. Since he could not enter college there, he decided to visit his uncle Mort Roberts in Morehead, Kentucky. While in Morehead he got a job as a timekeeper (after the previous timekeeper got drunk and was fired) on the construction of the campus married housing units that became known as Vet Village.

The Morehead State College Vet Village was constructed from old Army barracks from Fort Campbell, Kentucky. There were six two-story barracks buildings on campus. Each barracks was divided into eight separate apartment units. There were also two one-story quonset huts with two apartments each. In addition, 20 small single-family houses were built on campus. They had all been disassembled and shipped to Morehead on railroad cars. They were then reassembled and divided into one and two-bedroom apartments. They were poorly constructed with cracks in the walls, floors, and ceilings that you could see through.

While building Morehead's Vet Village, Norman Roberts recalled that the laborers all went on strike. Norman and his cousin Bill Roberts were the instigators of the strike because they were convinced they were over-worked and underpaid. When unloading material from a railroad car, it was decided that the group would sit down at 12:00 noon and refuse to work.

About an hour before the men were to go on strike, Norman was called to go from the railroad cars back to the campus building site. While he was there, the men struck. When the construction boss did not get the materials needed, he went to the railroad unloading area and found the men sitting down. They were all fired on the spot, and Norman would have been fired had he been there.

While Norman Roberts was helping to build those campus married housing units, he had no idea he would ever be living in one of them. After his marriage to Margie Stewart, they lived in Vet Village for five years. He later taught industrial education at Breckinridge High School and Morehead State University.

On January 4, 1946, a regional veterans center was established on the campus of Morehead State Teachers College by the Veterans Administration, and W.M. Wesley was the director. The center was designed not only to assist the oncampus veterans, but was intended to assist the 75,000 veterans in 25 northeastern Kentucky counties. It helped the disabled, handicapped, on-the-job training and GI loan applicants, as well as those with pension claims. That regional center was of great help to the students at the college in obtaining more housing for veterans.

Campus Housing a Recruiting Tool

Because of the acute shortage of dormitory space and off-campus housing following World War II, adequate married housing became a powerful recruiting tool for athletes as well as students. That was especially true in the case of John and Dot (Cunyus) Collis. Both were veterans and both planned to attend college.

John Collis was an outstanding football player at Oak Hill High School in Ohio. Following high school graduation, he enrolled at Ohio State on a partial football scholarship and played one year before entering the U.S. Navy. Following basic training at Great Lakes Naval Base, he wanted to become a pilot. However, he was sent to radio school at Memphis, Tennessee. Following graduation as a radio operator, he was assigned to a PB-2Y four-engine flying boat in the Navy Transport Command. They flew men, materials, and critical supplies such as blood to Pearl Harbor and throughout the South Pacific.

Sailor Married Marine

John Collis returned to San Diego after two and one-half years in the South Pacific where he attained the rank of Petty Officer 2/C. While he was stationed at the San Diego California Naval Base, still pursuing his dream of becoming a navy pilot, he began playing basketball on the base basketball team. One day the team went up to play the Galeta Marine Air Force Base (now University of California at Santa Barbara). While there he met a young Marine enlisted woman.

The Sailor married the Marine and they both returned to college following WW II.

Her name was Dot Cunyus and a faint spark of love was ignited. Dot was a Marine architectural drafting specialist that somehow the Marine Air Corps and fate, had placed in the recreation department at Galeta. That was where the two met.

The courtship between the sailor boy and the Marine girl continued mostly through long distance phone calls and the U.S. mail. It was even more long distance when it appeared John was on his way to becoming a navy pilot, and was transferred to Iowa State for pre-flight training. The Iowa State pre-flight football team was one of the best in the nation that year. Their football schedule included Ohio State, Kansas, California, Notre Dame, and some Southeastern Conference teams. The quarterback on that team was a player-coach named Ellis T. Johnson. Ellis was a former All-American football and basketball player at the University of Kentucky. He was also the pre-war coach at Morehead [Kentucky] State College.

John Collis soon became a member of that football team where Coach Ellis Johnson began to talk to him about coming to Morehead after the war. But the young sailor had his heart set on becoming a pilot, and when the war ended in 1945, he intended to make the Navy his career. In the meantime, John and his Marine fiancee were planning to marry. After a long distance romance and only five actual dates, the couple were married on August 2, 1946.

When the war ended there was less demand for pilots and John's pilot training was delayed. While awaiting assignment to advanced training, the Navy kept John and several other potential pilots busy mowing the gigantic parade grounds. That was not so bad since they were driving large tractors and mowing. But John said, "The straw that broke the camel's back and drove him out of the Navy, was when one day a 'chicken' (strictly military) captain stopped them and 'chewed' them out for not mowing in formation." Following that incident, he elected to leave the service and was sent to a separation center at Camp Wallace, Texas, for discharge.

John and Dot Move to Vet Village

Following his discharge John hitchhiked to the University of Arkansas where he had been offered a football scholarship. Knowing he would need married housing the first question he asked was if they had married housing for veterans. The answer was no, so John remembered Ellis Johnson's offer to come to Morehead. Since Ellis had already been discharged and was back in Morehead, John called him and found out that Morehead did have housing for veterans. That was what brought him and his new bride of one month to Morehead in time for the 1946 football season. Both Dot and John enrolled at Morehead in the fall of 1946 under the GI Bill. However, Dot soon became pregnant with their son Rick and had to withdraw from college.

Their first "apartment" was one room in Fields Hall. Then they moved to a small apartment in Mays Hall near the Army Barracks that had been moved from Fort Campbell, Kentucky, and converted into apartments. John's wife had maintained she would never live in one of those "monstrosities" but she changed her mind when one became available.

Move to Vet Village

Those first barracks apartments were located on a white gravel road that was dusty in dry weather and muddy in wet weather. They were hot in summer and cold in the winter. The gas pressure in Morehead was so low that the pilot light would sometimes go out in their stove. John recalled one cold winter night after the pilot light went out, he bent one of his "dog tags" (metal military name tag), and put it over the pilot light to keep it from going out. Soon every one of the veterans had another use for their "dog tags." Also, many times the electricity would go off and blow a fuse which made life equally miserable. When that happened the men would sometimes put pennies behind the fuse to restore power to the apartment (a very dangerous fire hazard).

The apartments were unfurnished except for one refrigerator for eight apartments. Those students living there brought their own furniture or rented from local furniture dealer, Parnell Martindale. Parnell was himself a graduate of Morehead and he furnished many of those apartments on a rental basis.

Later on several quonset huts (one-story buildings with rounded metal roofs) were moved from the atomic energy plant in southern Ohio to the campus. Those were converted into 20 apartments located farther up the hollow behind the Music Building. That collection of apartments was called "Riceville" in honor of the College's Maintenance Superintendent "Hony" Rice. Also during that time, the men's dormitories also housed married students. Therefore early in

1946, Morehead State College had successfully reached out to this nation's veterans by providing living space in order for them to attend college under the GI Bill.

Family Atmosphere among Veterans

The students who occupied Vet Village were like one big family. They all were struggling to get by on what the GI Bill provided. Much of their social life consisted of inexpensive events such as playing cards, going on picnics and cookouts together with an occasional movie. No one had any money and they were all in the same boat. Everyone was poor but didn't know it. Their goal was to get their college degree, and most of them focused on that goal. Statistics released by colleges throughout this nation in May, 1947, showed veterans' average grades were higher than non-veterans. That statistic was surely true at Morehead State College where the grade point average of non-veterans was 1.38, and the veterans GPA was 1.55 (on a 3.0 scale).

John and Dot Collis came to Morehead because housing was available through the Vet Village. In 1950, John graduated from MSTC. During his college years he was an outstanding football player (center) during the college's most successful sports era. Following his graduation, Collis was appointed the director of the bookstore and post office (then located in the basement of Rader Hall). He also was the supervisor of Vet Village where he and Dot lived for 13 years. John and Dot chose to remain in Morehead where they have been active in church and civic organizations. He retired as director of the University Bookstore in 1988. They still live in Morehead and have no desire to move.

GI Bill Successful Legislation

In retrospect, the GI Bill was one of the most important pieces of legislation in the history of this nation. It not only provided for advanced education and training for our veterans, but it also helped colleges to provide housing for those veterans. Both were essential to the success of that legislation.

The veterans proved worthy of this investment. Many went on to become leaders in almost every area of business, education, clergy, social work, professions, industry, and technology. Actuaries tell us that WW II veterans are dying at the rate of 1,000 per day. Economists tell us that with their death comes the greatest transfer of wealth from one generation to another that this nation has ever seen. Historians tell us that those veterans were the ones that kept this nation free. They were the citizen soldiers and freedom fighters of their generation. Those who survived WW II and received their education under the GI Bill, were forever grateful for the educational and housing opportunities it provided. That unselfish, extraordinary generation is fast passing from the scene; but their sacrifice and service will forever be remembered by a grateful nation.

Norman Roberts married Margie Stewart while both were in college in 1947. They moved into Veterans housing on the campus of Morehead (Ky.) College.

BIBLIOGRAPHY OF SOURCES

Interviews
Barker, John D., and Pearl
Carr, Walter
Collis, John, and Dot
Daugherty, J.T., and Kay
Everson, Ken
Flannery, Rufus
Hargis, John
Hall, William
Hardin, Phil, and Margena
McKinney, Hazel, and Phyllis
Northcutt, Denny, and Helen
Price, Dwayne, and Geneva
Reynolds, Paul J., and Mabel
Roberts, Norman, and Margie
Wilhoit, Lucille

Libraries
Fleming County Public Library
Kentucky Department of Libraries
Morehead State University Library
Riverside Military Academy Library (GA)
Rowan County Court Clerk's Office
Rowan County Public Library

Periodicals
Fleming County (KY) *Gazette*
Fleming County (KY) *Times-Democrat*
Lexington (KY) *Herald-Leader*
Louisville (KY) *Courier-Journal*
Morehead (KY) *News*
Patuxent (MD) *Tester*
Rowan County (KY) *News*
St. Mary's (MD) *Tide*
Yank Magazine

Government Documents and Letters
American Legion Post 126 Records
Citations of Commanding Officers
Discharges on File in Rowan Courthouse
Letters of Commendation
Personal Letters and Documents
U.S. House and Journal Records

Books for More Information
Albee, Parker B. *Shadow of Suribachi*. Praeger, 1995.

Bird, Tom. *American POWs of WW II*: *"Forgotten Men Tell Their Stories."* Praeger, 1992.

Bogart, Charles H. *The Military Post at Fort Thomas, Ky*. Bogart, 1985.

Boggs, Charles W. Jr. "*Red Devils*"*: Marine Aviation in the Philippines*. U.S. Marine Corps Historical Division, 1951.

Cooke, David C. *Famous U.S. Air Force Bombers*. Dodd-Mead, 1998.

Costello, John. *Days of Infamy*. Pocket Books, 1994.

Cross, Roy. *Military Aircraft, 1939-1945*. Graphic Society, 1971.

Dastrup, Boyd L. *King of Battle: A Branch History of the U.S. Army's Field Artillery*. Office of Command Historian, Ft. Monroe, Virginia, 1992.

Ethell, Jeffrey L. *B-17 Flying Fortress*. Arms and Armour, 1986.

Ethell, Jeffrey L. *The German Jets in Combat*. Jones, 1978.

Freeman, Roger A. *B-17, Fortress at War*. Scribner, 1977.

Gailey, Harry A. *Bougainville, 1943-1945: The Forgotten Campaign*. The University Press of Kentucky, 1991.

Goolrick, Williams K. *Battle of the Bulge*. Time-Life, 1998.

Green, William. *Famous Fighters of World War II*. Hanover House, 1957.

Holmes, Harry. *The U.S. Eighth Airforce at Wharton, 1942-1945*. Motorbooks International, 1998.

Hoyt, Edwin P. *Iwo Jima*. Avon, 1992.

101 Airborne Division: Screaming Eagles. Turner, 1995.

Parker, Danny S. *Battle of the Bulge*. Combined Books, 1991.

Raymond, Henri. *The U.S. Marines on Iwo Jima*. Dial, 1945.

Roberts, Robert B. *Encyclopedia of Historic Forts*. Macmillian, 1988.

Smith, Osprey. *Pearl Harbor, 1941: The Days of Infamy*. Osprey Military, 1999. (contains a Kentucky chapter).

Thomey, Tedd. *A Personal History of Two Photographers and the Flag Raising on Iwo Jima*. Naval Institute Press, 1996.

Tillman, Barrett. *Avengers at War*. Scribner, 1979.

Rowan County, Kentucky Honored Dead in All Wars (1900-2,001)

WWI

April 2, 1917-November 11, 1918

1. Andrew Alfrey
2. Elisha Conn
3. Earl Cornett
4. William Cundiff
5. Thomas Duncan
6. Corbie Ellington
7. George A. Jones
8. Thomas Jones
9. William Jordan
10. Clarence Ratliff
11. Emitt Reynolds
12. Thomas Rigsby
13. Robert L. Royce
14. Troy Mullins
15. Roy Mcleese

WW II

December 7, 1941-August 11, 1945

1. Tommie F. Armstrong
2. Benjamin A. Black
3. George D. Black
4. Leslie R. Brown
5. Charles L. Bumgardner
6. Herbert O. Catron
7. Lloyd V. Caudill
8. Murvel E. Caudill
9. Clifton L. Clark
10. Raymond L. Conn Sr.
11. Arthur T. Cooper
12. Virgil Crisp
13. James C. Dailey
14. William E. Dean
15. Ernest E. Epperhart
16. Claudie Evans
17. Arnold Fyffe
18. Austin R. Gregory
19. Sam E. Gregory
20. Cecil M. Hall
21. Jesse Hamilton
22. Luster M. Hargis
23. Walter G. Hargis
24. Charles E. Harmon
25. Floyd (Tay) Honaker
26. Harold V. Ingram
27. Ray James
28. Luther Jones
29. Willard H. Hones
30. Delbert Kidd
31. Grant Kissick
32. Roy Litton Jr.
33. Arnold Martin
34. Chester A. McClurg
35. Orville K. McClurg
36. George L. McCullough
37. William E. McKenzie
38. Adrian T. McKinney
39. Robert McKinney
40. Cleo Moore
41. Kennith Owens
42. Paul J. Petitt
43. Arthur Phillips
44. Rollie R. Poston
45. Arthur E. Profit
46. Jake Profit Jr.
47. Charles W. Puckett
48. Raymond K. Purvis
49. Burl Reynolds
50. Earl Richardson
51. Ora Richardson
52. Curtis R. Royse
53. Ashley E. Smith
54. Leonard D. Stevens
55. Major Stevens
56. Rufus Stevens
57. Bascom H. Tabor
58. Ernest C. Toler
59. George H. Turner
60. Joseph R. Williams

Korean War

June 25, 1950–July 28, 1953

1. Henry E. Beasley
2. William E. Beasley
3. James T. Brammer
4. Andrew J. Christian
5. Hayward Davis
6. John Finley
7. Arb Hicks, Jr.
8. Henry C. McKinney
9. Walter Toler
10. Charles Simpson

Vietnam War

August 1958–August 1973

1. Donald R. Butler
2. Kenneth A. Hardin
3. Dwight D. Jones
4. Delbert O. Lewis
5. Bruce E. Thomas
6. Fredrick B. Skaggs
7. Lionel Workman

Attack on America

September 11, 2001

1. Edward Earhart

Lonely grave of Rowan County, Kentucky soldier
Tommie Armstrong buried in Belgium.

VETERANS MEMORIAL WALL

Morehead-Rowan County, Kentucky
Dec. 31, 2001

This Memorial Wall, located on the lawn of the Old Rowan County Courthouse on Main Street in Morehead lists the names of over 2,800 men and women who served their country in war and peace in the past 100 years. It includes 1,400 who served their country during WWII. It also includes a total of 93 who were killed in action in this nation's wars during the past 100 years, including 60 killed in WWII and one from Rowan County killed in the Attack on America September 11, 2001. All are veterans who have lived in Morehead or Rowan County and have filed their honorable discharge in the Rowan County Courthouse, or were killed or missing in action. This Memorial Wall was the community's way of thanking them and of remembering their service.

The Rowan County Veterans Memorial Wall had its beginning in 1998 when County Judge Clyde Thomas appointed local veterans and interested citizens to serve as members of a Rowan County Veterans Committee. Their first meeting was held on October 7, 1998, and Judge Thomas was elected to chair the meeting. Veterans in attendance at that first meeting included: Gary Adkins, Sgt. Davis (National Guard), Jack Ellis, Scott Erdo (R.O.T.C.), Rodney Gordon, Victor Healey, Harold Johnson, Cephas Littleton, and Claude Meade (American Legion). Also in attendance at that first meeting were Rodney Hitch, Sheree Nichols, State Representative John Will Stacey, and Tracey Williams. Later on many other interested citizens and veterans joined the group.

The week of November 7-14, 1998, was proclaimed "Veterans Week" by Judge Clyde Thomas and Morehead Mayor Bradley Collins.

Rowan County Veterans Claude Meade, Freeman Hamilton, and Harold Johnson, inspecting the Morehead, Kentucky Veterans Wall under construction. The wall containing over 2,500 names was completed and dedicated July 4, 2002.

Many activities were planned that week in schools and businesses, including a Veterans Day Parade with over 200 entries.

On February 12, 2001, Attorney Willie Roberts completed articles of incorporation for the Rowan County Veterans, Inc. The initial Board of Directors included: Harold Johnson, President; Gerald McDanie, Vice President; Kenneth Vencill II, Treasurer; Jack Ellis; Rodney Gordon, and Claude Meade. Ex-officio members included: The Rowan County Judge Executive, Superintendent of Schools, Director of Tourism, Director of the Chamber of Commerce, Morehead Mayor and a representative from Morehead State University. Over $100,000 was raised by private donations through the generous support of over 425 individuals and businesses. This hallowed wall of memory was dedicated July 4, 2002. But the listing in this appendix includes only those veterans who filed their discharge before January 1, 2002. Additional names will be added to the wall at a later date.

Carl	M.J.	Aagaard	CPT	USA	1946	1948
David	Francis	Abner	SKV1	USNR	1943	1946
John	H.	Acree	PVT	USA	1940	1944
Mose	W.	Acree	PVT	USA	1943	1945
Worthy		Acres	PVT	USA	1918	1919
James	Charles	Adams	PVT	USA	1953	1953
James	E.	Adams	SGT	USA	1942	1945
John	H.	Adams		USA		
Luther		Adams	A1C	USAF	1953	1956
Robert	Gene	Adams	PFC	USAR	1957	1959
Walter	P.	Adams	SGT	USA	1943	1946
Addie	Earl	Adkins	SN 1C	USNR	1945	1946
Beecher	Hearman	Adkins	SN 2C	USNR	1945	1945
Burl	I.	Adkins	T5	USA	1939	1945

Rozella L. Abner, Pvt., Army Air Corps (WAC) 1944-45; David F. Abner, SKV 1, Navy, 1943-46.

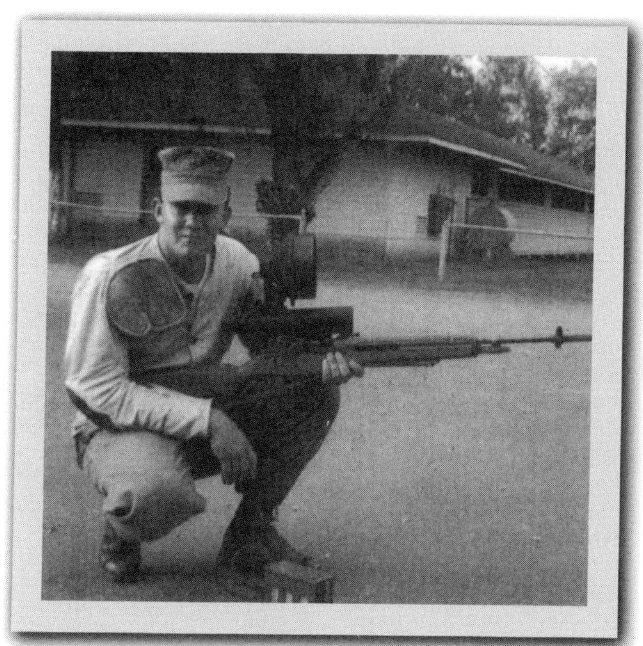

Palmer R. Adkins, Sgt. Marine Corps, 1965-1968.

Chester	R.	Adkins	PFC	USA	1941	1945
Curt		Adkins	PFC	USA	1946	1947
Danny	Dale	Adkins	SP5	USA	1968	1970
David	Gregory	Adkins	SP4	USA	1972	1974
Della	A.	Adkins	SGT	USA	1940	1945
Dennis	Lee	Adkins	SP4	USA	1972	1975
Elvin	Radson	Adkins	PFC	USA	1956	1958
Everett		Adkins	Tech. 5	USA	1943	1946
Ezra	Lee	Adkins	CSC	USN	1942	1962
Gary	William	Adkins	CPT	USA	1974	1986
Howard	L.	Adkins	SSGT	USAFR		1959
James		Adkins	PFC	USA	1941	1945
John	Paul	Adkins	SSGT	USAF	1952	1956
Kenneth	Dale	Adkins	SGT	USAF	1971	1975
Lovel	Blaine	Adkins	SA	USNR	1944	1944
Martin	Ray	Adkins	PFC	USA	1988	1992

Nicholas	Eugene	Adkins	A2C	USAF	1953	1954
Noah	C.	Adkins	Tech. 5	USA	1942	1945
Otis		Adkins	Tech. 5	USA	1943	1945
Paul		Adkins	PVT	USA	1943	1943
Silas		Adkins	CPL	USA	1945	1950
Verl		Adkins	Tech. 5	USA	1945	1946
Virgil		Adkins	PVT	USA	1943	1945
Wilburn		Adkins	SN2C	USN	1943	1945
Willard		Adkins	A1C	USAF	1954	1957
Winford		Adkins	CPL	USMC	1953	1955
Carl		Adkins, Jr.	PFC	USA	1942	1945
Chauncey		Adkins, Jr.	CPL	USA	1952	1954
Earl	Howard	Alderman	SGT	USA	1952	1954
Edward		Alderman	A1C	USAF	1952	1956
Gabriel	Isham	Alderman	CPL	USMC	1943	1946
Moody	T.	Alderman	PVT	USA	1917	1919
Posie	Q.	Alderman	CPL	USA	1942	1945
Robert	E.	Alderman	Tech. 5	USA	1942	1945
Carrol	A.	Alderson	SGT	USA		1960
John	D.	Alexander	LT	USN	1943	1956
Andrew	Jackson	Alfrey	PFC	USA	1953	1955
Corbie		Alfrey	GM1	USNR	1942	1946
Gene	Austin	Alfrey	A2C	USAF	1955	1959
Harold		Alfrey	PFC	USAR	1952	1960
James	A.	Alfrey	PFC	USA	1944	1946
Willard	Franklin	Alfrey	SN	USN	1952	1960
Andy		Alfrey, Jr.	SN1C	USNR	1943	1945
George	Lewey	Alfrey, Jr.	1LT	USAF	1953	1956
Hubert	L.	Allen	CPL	AAF	1943	1946
James	H.	Allen	SGT	USAAC	1942	1945
Robert	C.	Allen	PFC	USA	1946	1947
John	Edward	Allen, Jr.	A/1C	USAF	1951	1953
Samuel	E.	Allen, Jr.	SSGT	AAF	1942	1945

George Alfrey, Jr., Lt., Air Force, 1951-55.

Charles	Cyrus	Alley	SP3	USA	1954	1956
Bradley	Reed	Allion	SP4	USA	1985	1989
Roberet	Clement	Allison	CDR	USN	1968	1991
Edward	Lee	Amburgey	AM3	USNR	1944	1946
Elijah		Amburgey	PVT	CSA	Civil War	
Homer	B.	Amburgey	Tech 4	USA	1942	1946
Johny	R.	Amburgey	Tech 5	USA	1943	1947
Robert	T.	Amburgey	PVT	AAF	1946	1946
Wilford	W.	Amburgey	PFC	USA	1940	1945
William	Maxwell	Amburgey	SGT	USA	1953	1955
Lowell	M.	Amburgy	PFC	USA	1941	1945
Orville		Amburgy	PFC	USA	1942	1943
Clester	Clark	Anderson	PFC	USA	1957	1959
Earl		Anderson	PFC	USA	1944	1947

Jessie	T.	Anderson	LCPL	USMC	1968	1969
Roy		Anderson	SP3	USA	1954	1956
Fred		Angel III	SP4	USA	1988	1994
Francis	Earl	Apel	SP3	USA	1954	1956
Frank	E.	Archer	PVT	USA	1941	1945
Clyde	E.	Armstrong	SGT	USA	1942	1945
Leslie	P.	Armstrong	PVT	USA	1942	1946
Paul	Michael	Armstrong	SP 4	ARNG	1970	1976
Willard	R.	Armstrong	CPL	AAF	1942	1945
William	O.	Armstrong	PFC	USA	1942	1945
Rollo	W.	Arnett	SGT	USA	1942	1946
Lawrence		Arnett, Jr.	CPL	USAR		1961
Clella		Arnold	PVT	USA	1943	1946
Robert		Arnold	SGT	USA	1948	1953
Lillian	Tackett	Arrand	AK3	USN	1944	1946
Michael	Calvey	Arrand	CPL	USMC	1941	1945
Robert	Edward	Bach	SGT	USA	1948	1952
Darrel	Dean	Baer	ENCS	USN	1975	1981
Jay		Bailey	Cook	USA	1917	1919
Dan		Baker	PFC	USA	1917	1919
Ercil		Baker, Jr.	PFC	USA	1952	1954
Clarence	R.	Baldridge	PFC	AAF	1944	1945
Earnie		Baldridge	CW2	USA	1958	1979
Eddie		Baldridge	SGT	USA	1917	1919
Ezra	R.	Baldridge	Tech. 4	USA	1943	1945
Harold	Clayton	Baldridge	SGT	USAAF	1945	1948
Medford	Carl	Baldridge	CPL	USA	1952	1954
Wendell		Baldridge	SP4	USAR		1962
Wilburn		Baldridge	SGT	USA	1951	1953
Alan	Romans	Baldwin	LTC	USA	1968	1989
Earl	T.	Ball	SGT	USA	1945	1946
Jim	Wesley	Ball	SFC	USA	1978	1996
Brett	Charles	Ballard	CPT	USAF	1986	1991

Glenn	Ray	Ballinger	MM2	USN	1943	1947
Gabriel	C.	Banks	PVT	USA	1917	1919
Steven	Lafayette	Banks	SN1C	USN	1942	1945
Billy	Joe	Barber	AQ1	USN	1960	1966
George	Curtis	Barber	CPT	USA	1960	1968
Jack	Lee	Barber	PFC	USMC	1954	1955
Woodrow	W.	Barber	LCDR	USN	1944	1946
Hobart		Barbour, Jr.	SF2	USNR	1943	1946
Roger	W.	Barbour, Sr.	Tech 5	USA	1945	1946
Brian	Dean	Barker	SrA	USAF	1991	1995
Cledith	R.	Barker	SGT	USA	1942	1945
Clifford		Barker	SGT	USA	1942	1943
Devlyon	Scott	Barker	1LT	USA	1976	1980
Earcel	V.	Barker	PFC	USA	1944	1945
Elbert	Woodrow	Barker	PFC	USA	1959	1960
Elva	C.	Barker	CPL	AAF	1941	1945
Everett	R.	Barker	PFC	USA	1942	1946
Herbert	Donald	Barker	PFC	USA	1949	1952
John	D.	Barker	SSG	USA	1940	1945
John	Paul	Barker	Coxswain	USNR	1944	1946
Ollie	Winston	Barker	SGT	USMC	1942	1945
Oscar	J.	Barker	PFC	USA	1942	1945
Robert	L.	Barker	SP4	USA	1960	1966
Talmage	M.	Barker	PVT	USA	1942	1943
Troy	Ernest	Barker	SGT	USAF	1971	1975
Winford	Scot	Barker	A1C	USAF	1965	1969
Robert	E.	Barndollar	PFC	USA	1945	1946
Homer	Addison	Barnett	PVT	USA	1950	1950
Leslie		Barnett	PFC	USA	1918	1919
Sidney	L.	Barnette	PVT	AAF	1946	1947
Sidney	Lowell	Barnette	FN	USN	1947	1950
Joseph	Roe	Barrett	PCSN	USN	1987	1988
Molly		Barrett	LTJG	USN	1972	1975

Dennis	A.	Barricks	PVT	USAR		1965
Clark		Bascom	YN3	USNR	1918	1921
Will	H.	Basford	PVT	USA	1943	1943
William	Lawrence	Bate	SN1C	USNR		1945
Gardner		Bates, Jr.	PFC	USA	1954	1956
Donald	Hartley	Battson	SGM	USA	1951	1971
James	V.	Baumstark	PVT	SATC	1918	1918
Billy	R.	Bayes	ATN3	USNR	1958	1964
Duard	Ellsworth	Bayless	CPT	USA	1950	1952
Dennie	Lawrence	Bays	CPL	USMC	1943	1946
Donald	Frederich	Bays	2LT	USMC	1946	1949
Hazel	Christine	Bays	SPEC. 1 3C	USNR	1944	1946
Lee		Bays	PVT	USA	1944	1946
Robert	Logan	Bays, Jr.	Carpenter Mt. 1C	USN		1945
Donald	Lee	Beair	CMCA	USN	1971	1974
Dennis	Ray	Beamon	SP4	USA	1976	1979
William	R.	Becknell	SSG	USA	1942	1945
Sidney		Begley	GMC	USN	1940	1946
Harold	Larson	Bellamy	EM3	USN	1945	1947
Joe	Francis	Bendixen	SSGT	USAF	1950	1954
James	J.	Bendixon	LT	USCG	1990	1992
Robert	Edward	Bennett	AC3	USN	1955	1959
Harold	D.	Benteen	Cf. Pharm. Mt.	USN		1945
Earl	Joyner	Bentley	CPL	USAR	1950	1952
Larry	Xon	Besant	SSgt	USAF	1954	1957
Mary	Majorie	Besant	E-4	USN	1989	1998
Robert	John	Biegen	FTG2	USN	1970	1974
Harlon	M.	Binion	SN1C	USN	1942	1945
James	R.	Binion	PFC	USA	1942	1945
Leroy		Binion	Tech 5	USA	1942	1945
Miriam	C.	Binion	PFC	WAC	1943	1945
Raymon		Binion	MM2	USNR		1945
Asa	E.	Birchfield	PVT	USA	1942	1943

Charles	Edward	Bishop	SP4	USAR	1961	1962
Laverne	G.	Bishop	GM2	USN	1942	1945
Jan	Marlene	Biswas	SP5	USA	1976	1979
Jack	E.	Bizzell	SSGT	AAF	1944	1948
Arthur	Elmound	Black	FN2C	USNR	1944	1945
Bert	C.	Black	Tech 4	USA	1946	1947
Charles	Lydon	Black	CPL	USA	1952	1953
Christina	Rae	Black	PVT	USA	1999	2000
Clifford	A.	Black	PVT	USA	1942	1946
Dallas		Black	PVT	USA	1918	1919
Earl	Leo	Black	WT1	USN	1941	1947
Edward		Black	PVT	USA		1953
Grover	S.	Black	SSG	USA	1942	1946
James	Clay	Black	SP4	USA	1965	1967
John	M.	Black	PVT	USAF	1946	1947
John	W.	Black	PFC	USA	1944	1946
Milzia		Black	PFC	USA	1944	1946
Pete		Black	PVT	USA	1943	1945
Raymond	S.	Black	PFC	USA	1942	1945
Silas		Black	PFC	USA	1918	1919
Verlan		Black	PFC	USA	1951	1953
William		Black	SGT	USA	1942	1945
Allie	Jaye	Black, Jr.	PFC	USA	1961	1963
Ezra		Black, Jr.	Tech 5	USA	1947	1947
James	Gilbert	Black, Jr.	ET3	USNR	1944	1946
Charles	E.	Blair	PFC	USAAC	1943	1946
Denton	C.	Blair	SSG	USA	1944	1945
Denvil	Lee	Blair	A3C	USAF	1955	1955
Donald	Carl	Blair	PVT	USA	1957	1957
Earl		Blair	CPL	AAF	1942	1946
Franklin	P.	Blair	CPL	USA	1943	1945
Franklin	P.	Blair	CPL	USA	1944	1946
Fred	G.	Blair	PVT	USA	1918	1918

Galen	Loyan	Blair	A2C	USAF	1952	1956
Harold	F.	Blair	CPT	USA	1942	1945
Jackson		Blair	PVT	USA	1901	1904
Millard		Blair	PVT	USA	1917	1919
William	E.	Blair	Tech 5	USA	1942	1945
Kenneth	Earl	Bland	SP3	USA	1955	1958
Fred	William	Blanton	CPL	USA	1951	1953
Jack	Nelson	Blanton		USAF	1946	1952
Vernon	Everett	Blanton	PFC	USA	1942	1943
Joan	Phillys	Bledsoe	SGT	USAF	1965	1968
Oather	L.	Blevens	PVT	USA	1941	1945
Emory	J.	Blevins	PVT	USA	1948	1949
James	A.	Blevins	PFC	USA	1942	1945
Robert		Blevins, Jr.	BM2	USN	1941	1945
Junior		Blizzard	PFC	USA	1943	1945
Harvey	Owen	Blundell	PVT	USMC	1944	1946
Jimmie	Cleve	Blythe	SN2C	USN	1944	1946
Earl	L.	Boggess	SSGT	AAF	1941	1945
Burl		Boggs	SGT	USA	1945	1946
David	Allen	Bolm	PFC	USA	1959	1961
Glen	Owen	Boodry	PVT	USA	1951	1953
Thomas	Glen	Boodry	Lt.Col.	USMC	1979	2001
Francene	Laverne	Botts	CPT	USA	1986	1992
James	O.	Botts	SSGT	AAF	1945	1948
Charles	E.	Bowen	PFC	USA	1943	1945
Clauda	C.	Bowen	Tech 5	USA	1943	1946
Clayton	Lewis	Bowen	SN2C	USNR	1944	1945
George	Ewing	Bowen	SR	USN	1955	1955
Jack		Bowen	PVT	USA	1946	1947
Murvel	Glen	Bowen	SN1C	USNR	1944	1946
Samuel,		Bowen Jr.	YN3	USN	1952	1956
Harley	E.	Bowles	Tech 4	USA	1943	1946
Russell	H.	Bowles	SGT	USA	1944	1946

Arthur	E.	Bowling	CPL	USA		1953
Sneeden		Bowling	PFC	USA	1942	1944
Herbert		Bowman	PVT	USA	1918	1919
Lloyd	G.	Bowman	PVT	USA	1946	1947
Ward	W.	Bowman	Tech 4	USA	1943	1946
William	P.	Bowman	Tech 5	USA	1942	1945
Andre	B.	Bowne	PVT	USA	1943	1943
Andre	Bennett	Bowne	SN2C	USNR	1945	1946
Billy	Joe	Boyd	SP5	USA	1965	1967
Roy	U.	Boyd	SSG	USA	1943	1946
Thorton	P.	Boyd	PFC	USA	1917	1919
Willie	Albert	Boyd	PVT	USA	1918	1918
Earl	R.	Bradley	PFC	USA	1940	1942
Glendel	Rudolph	Bradley	CPL	USA	1952	1954
James	Glen	Bradley	EM2	USN	1981	1987
James	S.	Bradley	Tech 5	USA	1943	1945
John	Paul	Bradley	SGT	USAR	1967	1969
Orvill	Milford	Bradley	CPL	USA	1953	1954
Ova	C.	Bradley	MSG	USA	1941	1945
Philip	H.	Bradley	PVT	USA	1942	1946
Robert	Dale	Bradley	SSG	USA	1961	1962
Roscoe	T.	Bradley	Tech 5	USA	1942	1945
Sanford	Douglas	Bradley	PFC	USA	1951	1953
William	E.	Bradley	SSG	USA	1944	1946
William	Richard	Bradley	SSGT	USAF	1972	1976
Jason	Todd	Bradt	LCPL	USMC	1991	1995
James		Brammer	PVT	AAF	1943	1946
Ivan	E.	Branham	PVT	USA	1952	1953
Lloyd	A.	Branham	PVT	USA	1941	1941
Donald		Brewer	TSGT	USAF	1971	1973
Mitchell		Brewer	PVT	USA	1941	1943
William	Dewaine	Brewer	PFC	USA	1973	1977
William	Emerson	Brooks	SGT	USA	1951	1952

Aaron	William	Brown	SPC	USA	1995	1998
Arvil	J.	Brown	SP5	USAR		1972
Blayne		Brown	PVT	USA	1940	1945
Charles	G.	Brown	PVT	USA	1941	1947
Clarence		Brown	Tech 4	USA	1941	1945
Commodore		Brown	PVT	USA		1898
Courtney	O.	Brown	PFC	USA	1942	1945
Dennis		Brown	CPL	USA	1943	1945
Douglas	M.	Brown	PVT	USA	1918	1919
Dwayne	Michael	Brown	PFC	USA	1986	1986
Edward	Eugene	Brown	PVT	USA	1951	1951
Elkin		Brown		USA	1915	1937
Elmer	R.	Brown	PFC	USA	1945	1947
Ernest	Hobert	Brown	CPL	USA	1953	1955
Ernest		Brown	PVT	USA	1944	1945
Eugene		Brown	CPL	USMC	1951	1959
Harold	E.	Brown	SGT	USA	1946	1947
Harry	L.	Brown	PVT	USA	1924	1924
Henry	C.	Brown	PFC	USA	1942	1945
Herman	Clarence	Brown	CPL	USMC	1943	1946
James	A.	Brown	PVT	USA	1942	1943
James		Brown	PFC	USA	1942	1946
Jeffery	Thurman	Brown	PVT	USA	1972	1972
John	David	Brown	A1C	USAF	1972	1974
Larry	Gene	Brown	SP4	USA	1969	1971
Lloyd	J.	Brown	PFC	USA	1942	1945
Lloyd		Brown	PVT	USA	1917	1919
Logan		Brown	PVT	USA	1918	1918
Luster	J.	Brown	SGT	AAF	1941	1945
Maurice	S.	Brown	SGT	USA	1942	1946
Miles		Brown	PVT	USA	1944	1944
Omer	Lee	Brown	CPL	USA	1953	1955
Othie		Brown	PVT	USA	1942	1944

Reggie	Zane	Brown	A1C	USAF	1960	1963
Roger	R.	Brown	PFC	USA	1941	1946
Roy	Lee	Brown	PFC	USA	1950	1953
Wallace	Doris	Brown	SA	USN	1944	1944
Walter	S.	Brown	SSG	USA	1941	1945
Wilford	Wayne	Brown	SP4	USA	1977	1981
William	T.	Brown	Tech. 4	USA	1945	1946
Willis	Philmon	Brown	SN2C	USNR	1942	1946
Woodrow		Brown	SFC	USA	1942	1962
Hollie		Brown, Jr.	A1C	USAF	1952	1956
William	David	Brown, Jr.	SRA	USAF	1975	1979
Edmund	Karl	Buckner	SFC	USA	1976	1995
Ronnie	Carl	Buckner	PFC	USA	1966	1968
Rayford	Daniel	Bulloch	SN 2C	USN	1944	1945
James	E.	Bumgardner	PVT	USA	1944	1945
Vernon	Lambert	Bumgardner	Ship's Cook 3C	USNR	1944	1946
Bessie	Mae	Burchfield	PharmMt. 3C	USN		1945
Steve	Nathaniel	Burgan	SPC	USA	1988	1994
Charlie	E.	Burgess	PVT	USA	1918	1919
Jack	Bronson	Burgyo	CPL	USMC	1957	1959
Elton	L.	Burnett	PFC	USAAC	1943	1946
Franklin	C.	Burns	CPL	USA	1944	1946
James	Russell	Burrows	SP 4	USA	1959	1962
Andrew	Samuel	Burton	PVT	USA	1952	1955
Andy		Burton	PFC	USA	1946	1949
Andy		Burton	SP 4	USA	1958	1961
Coyle	V.	Burton	SGT	USA	1942	1945
Dee		Burton	SGT	USA	1941	1945
Donald	J.	Burton	SP 5	USA	1958	1961
John	Melvin	Burton	PFC	USA	1952	1954
Leonard	E.	Burton	PFC	USA	1942	1946
Ora	L.	Burton	PVT	USA	1945	1945
Victory	Vernard	Burton	PVT	USMC	1953	1954

William	Herbert	Bushong II	SP 4	USA	1968	1969
Charles	Homer	Butcher	SP 5	USA	1959	1962
David	Monroe	Butcher	SP 4	USA	1958	1961
James	A.	Butcher	1LT	USAAC	1942	1945
John	V.	Butcher	CPL	USA	1944	1948
Leonard		Butcher	PFC	USA	1916	1920
Vivian	Clycle	Butcher	SN 1C	USNR	1943	1946
Anna	Fae	Butler	MSGT	USAF	1973	1993
Elgan		Butler	PFC	USA	1941	1945
Emery	F.	Butler	PVT	USA	1918	1919
Homer	L.	Butler	Tech. 5	USA	1942	1946
James	W.	Butler	Tech. 5	USA	1942	1946
Jimmy	Charles	Butler	SP 4	USA	1972	1974
Johny	D.	Butler	PVT	USA	1944	1946
Mason	W.	Butler	PFC	USA	1942	1946
Ralph	Eugene	Butler	A1C	USAF	1950	1953
Vincent	Herman	Butler	SSG	USA	1977	1997
Tony	Wayne	Buttry	SP 4	USA	1987	1990
Allie	B.	Butts	PVT	USA	1943	1944
Herman	Chalmus	Butts	SP 4	USA	1958	1960
James	Ora	Butts	PVT	USA	1964	1965
Lawrence	L.	Butts	PVT	USA	1941	1943
Ray	Fortune	Butts	SN 2C	USNR	1944	1946
Roy	Edward	Butts	CCMM 3C	USN	1942	1948
Floyd	T.	Buza	PVT	USA	1943	1946
John	F.	Cabell, Jr.	Tech.3	USA	1942	1945
Stith	M.	Cain	SGT	USA	1942	1944
Harold	Wade	Cain, Jr.	Capt.	USAF	1964	1968
Tommy	Lee	Cains, Jr	PVT	USA	1997	1997
Wayne	Preston	Caldwell	TSgt	USAF	1968	1972
Marvin	Taylor	Cales	EM1	USNR	1944	1946
Billie	Wallace	Calhoun	Cpl	USMC	1943	1945
Willis	G.	Callahan	PVT	USA	1917	1919

Asa	E.	Calvert	SSG	USA	1943	1945
Chester	H.	Calvert	SGT	USA	1942	1945
George	W.	Calvert	CPL	USA	1944	1946
James	W.	Calvert	SGT	AAF	1941	1946
Oscar	L.	Calvert	PFC	USA	1942	1945
Walter	E.	Calvert	CPL	AAF	1943	1946
William	E.	Calvert	SSG	AAF	1942	1946
William	Orville	Calvert	RD3	USN	1951	1954
Frank		Calvert, Jr.	PFC	USA	1948	1951
John	B.	Calvert, Jr.	PFC	USA	1943	1946
Carl	T.	Campbell	PFC	USA	1942	1945
James	Edward	Campbell	PVT	USMC	1944	1945
Thomas	A.	Carew	SSG	USA	1942	1945
Cecil		Carey	PVT	USA	1918	1918
Hanson	C.	Carey	PFC	USA	1942	1945
Oval	A.	Carey	PVT	USA	1942	1944
Hayden	M.	Carmichael	T.SGT	USA	1942	1945
Jack		Carpenter	Tech. 5	USA	1944	1945
Paul		Carpenter	SN 1C	USNR	1945	1946
William	Harold	Carpenter	A1C	USAF	1951	1965
Helen	F.	Carr	Mailman 2C	USN	1944	1946
Walter	Winston	Carr	1LT	AAF	1942	1945
Thomas	Leland	Carroll	LCPL	USMC	1968	1974
Allie	B.	Carter	PFC	AAF	1942	1945
Carl	Jackson	Carter	CPL	USMC	1956	1958
Donald	Wayne	Carter	R2	USN	1955	1956
Jack	C.	Carter	Tech. 5	USA	1943	1945
Orville	John	Carter	PVT	USA	1918	1918
Ottis		Carter	PFC	AAF	1944	1945
Orville		Carter, Jr.	A1C	USAF	1950	1954
Willis		Carter, Jr.	SN 1C	USNR		1945
William	Van	Cartwright	SGT	USAF	1974	1978
Thomas	Allen	Caseman	SP 4	USA	1977	1981

Chalmer		Caskey	SKC	USN		1945
Delmar	L.	Caskey	PFC	USA	1942	1945
James	E.	Caskey	SP 4	USA	1953	1955
Van	R.	Caskey	PVT	USA	1944	1944
William		Caskey	PVT	USA	1901	1904
Gary	William	Caspar	CPL	USMC	1968	1969
Clifford	R.	Cassady	SGT	AAF	1942	1945
Charles	Edward	Cassidy	PFC	USA	1946	1952
Elijah		Cassity	SGT	USA	1950	1956
Fred	L.	Cassity	PFC	USA	1943	1945
Lloyd		Cassity	MSG	USA	1943	1946
Ralph	C.	Cassity	SSGT	AAF	1941	1945
Coy	J.	Castle	CPL	USA	1945	1946
Carl	Randall	Catron	SP 4	USA	1968	1969
Estill	L.	Catron	PVT	USA	1942	1945
Abel	L.	Caudill	PFC	USA	1942	1943
Carl	Edward	Caudill	SPC 4	USA ARNG	1966	1968
Cecil		Caudill	MSG	USA	1949	1951
Clarence	T.	Caudill	PFC	USA	1942	1945
Clarence	T.	Caudill	PFC	USA	1942	1945
Cleo	A.	Caudill	SGT	USA	1945	1946
Clinton		Caudill	FN 1C	USA	1918	1921
Clyde	Richard	Caudill	SP 4	USAR	1968	1969
Curnis	Rolland	Caudill	CPL	USMC	1943	1945
Delbert	A.	Caudill	SGT	USA	1942	1945
Donald	Thomas	Caudill	SP 4	USA	1967	1969
Edgar	C.	Caudill	PVT	USA	1943	1946
Ennis	Allen	Caudill	SN 1C	USNR	1943	1945
Estill		Caudill	PFC	USA	1942	1945
George	T.	Caudill	Tech. 5	USA	1943	1945
Glen		Caudill	Tech. 5	USA	1942	1945
Harry	H.	Caudill	PFC	USA	1940	1945
Harvey	A.	Caudill	PVT	USA	1942	1943

Jackie	Denver	Caudill	PFC	USA	1961	1963
James	C.	Caudill	PFC	USA	1942	1945
James	R.	Caudill	LT	USN	1942	1950
James	Roger	Caudill	A1C	USAF	1956	1960
James	T.	Caudill	Tech. 4	USA	1944	1946
John	H.	Caudill	PVT	USA	1918	1919
Murvel	C.	Caudill	CPL	AAF	1942	1945
Ora	V.	Caudill	FN 2C	USNR	1944	1945
Ora		Caudill	PVT	USA	1942	1945
Osborne	C.	Caudill	Tech. 4	USA	1945	1946
Oscar	Woodrow	Caudill	MotorMchMt. 3C	USNR	1945	1946
Ottis	Clayton	Caudill	SA	USN	1945	1945
Sam	Clinton	Caudill	Fireman 3C	USNR	1918	1921
Samuel	C.	Caudill	SA	USNR	1943	1943
Sara	Dea	Caudill	PFC	USA	1988	1989
Wayne	E.	Caudill	PFC	USA	1945	1946
Wilbur		Caudill	SSG	USA	1944	1946
William	Gregory	Caudill	SP 4	USA	1981	1984
Winfred	C.	Caudill	Tech. 4	USA	1942	1946
Arvel		Caudill, Jr.	PFC	USA	1952	1954
James	T.	Caudill, Jr.	SGT	USA	1968	1974
Hobart	Jack	Cecil	PVT	USA	1918	1918
Delbert	V.	Chadima	PFC	USA	1945	1946
Clyde	N.	Chadwell	PVT	USA	1942	1945
Donald	Reed	Chambers	SFC	USA	1972	1992
Marlin	Ray	Chapman	SP 4	USA	1959	1961
Michael	William	Chapman	SPC	USA	1996	1999
Jesse		Charles	SSG	USA	1939	1945
Hayes	J.	Choate	PFC	USA	1943	1946
Arthur		Christian	PVT	USA	1942	1948
Bobby	Erwin	Christian	SP 4	USA	1963	1965
Carl		Christian	SN 1C	USNR	1943	1946
Claude	O.	Christian	PFC	USA	1946	1948

Clilla	J.	Christian	CPL	USA	1917	1919
Earsel		Christian	T.SGT	USA	1939	1945
Henry	Albert	Christian	SN 1C	USNR		1945
Herbert		Christian	PFC	USA	1918	1919
Jimmy	Lansford	Christian	A1C	USAF	1952	1956
Ralph	W.	Christian	PVT	USA	1945	1945
Dennie		Christy	SN 2C	USN	1944	1946
Jimmy		Christy	PFC	USA	1942	1945
William	H.	Circle	PFC	USA	1918	1919
Clyde	B.	Clark	Tech. 5	USA	1942	1945
Gary	Lee	Clark	AC	USAF	1979	1983
Harry	Thomas	Clark	SMSgt	USAF	1973	1996
John	E.	Clark	Tech. 5	USA	1942	1946
John	Robert	Clark	CPL	USA	1948	1957
Lennie		Clark	PVT	USA	1918	1919
Luke		Clark	PVT	USA	1918	1918
Michael	Ray	Clark	SP 5	USA	1969	1971
Rusty	Lee	Clark	PVT	USA	1992	1993
Simon	P.	Clark	PFC	USA	1943	1946
James	Edwin	Clay	CPL	USMC	1942	1946
Don	R.	Claypool	T.SGT	AAF	1942	1946
Morgan		Clayton	CPL	USA	1917	1919
Clarence	G.	Clayton, Jr.	Tech. 4	USA	1943	1945
Earnest		Clevinger, Jr.	SSgt	USAF	1949	1952
Addie	Cecil	Click	SA	USNR	1943	1943
Billy	Joe	Click	CPL	USA	1952	1954
Chester		Click	SSG	USA	1943	1947
Ora	T.	Click	Tech. 5	USA	1946	1945
William	B.	Click	Tech. 4	USA	1944	1946
Jay		Clifford	CPL	USA	1953	1955
William	F.	Clifford	PVT	USA	1942	1942
Charles	Grover	Cline	A 1C	USAF	1956	1960
David		Cline	CPL	USA	1949	1953

Estel		Cline	PFC	USAAC	1942	1947
Joseph	Stewart	Cline	PVT	USARNG	1983	1983
Lowell		Cline	MSG	USA	1939	1961
Ralph		Cline	PFC	USA	1952	1954
Ray	M.	Cline	TSgt.	USMC	1941	1945
Riley	E.	Cline	Tech. 5	USA	1942	1946
Allen		Cline, Jr.	SSgt	USAF	1947	1952
Lindsey	Morton	Cloyd	AN 1C	USAF	1954	1954
Norma	Crager	Cloyd	AN 3C	USAF	1952	1954
Johnie	C.	Coffey	PFC	USA	1942	1945
Adron	Howard	Coldiron	PVT	USA	1949	1950
Albert	Lee	Coldiron	PFC	USA	1951	1953
Carl	Edward	Coldiron	SP 4	USA	1956	1958
David	Monroe	Coldiron	HMCS	USN		1981
Russel	C.	Coldiron	SSG	USA	1943	1945
Willie	Howard	Coldiron	CPL	USA	1952	1954
Gary	Lee	Collier	MS 1	USN	1985	1989
Fred	Sam	Collins	SN C1	USNR		1945
Fred		Collins	PFC	AAF	1946	1947
Garland	S.	Collins	SGT	USA	1942	1946
George	Earl	Collins	SP 4	USA	1968	1970
Haskel		Collins	PFC	USA	1940	1945
Ivel	B.	Collins	PVT	USA	1942	1945
Roger	Dale	Collins	PFC	USA	1984	1986
Virgil	L.	Collins	Tech. 5	USA	1942	1945
Wallace	Raymond	Collins	A1C	USAF	1951	1955
Dorothy	Cunyus	Collis	PFC	USMC	1944	1946
John	Ellsworth	Collis	ARM 2C	USN	1942	1946
Charles		Conley	PFC	USA	1940	1945
Chester	R.	Conley	Tech. 5	USA	1944	1946
George	L.	Conley	PVT	USA	1942	1945
Homer		Conley	Tech. 4	USA	1943	1945
Homer		Conley	CPL	USA	1949	1949

Robert	D.	Conley	PFC	USA	1942	1945
Sylvester		Conley	PFC	USA	1942	1946
Wiley	Frank	Conley	PVT	USMC	1953	1969
William	P.	Conley	PFC	USAR		1965
Charles	Elmer	Conn	SP 4	USA	1965	1967
Choncie		Conn	PFC	USA	1943	1945
Cyril	Cliffton	Conn	CPL	USA	1952	1954
Everett	B.	Conn	PFC	USA	1941	1946
Hollie		Conn	CPL	USA	1953	1955
James	L.	Conn	PVT	USA	1951	1952
Jerry	Russell	Conn	SGT	USA	1987	1991
Jesse	L.	Conn	PFC	USA	1942	1945
John	C.	Conn	PFC	USA	1944	1945
Marshall		Conn	SN 1C	USNR		1945
Maston		Conn	PVT	USA	1898	1899
Ora	A.	Conn	PFC	USA	1940	1945
Randolph	Lee	Conn	CarpenterMr. 3C	USNR	1945	1946
Randolph	R.	Conn	PVT	USA	1942	1945
Roy	Miller	Conn	PFC	USA	1951	1953
Virgil	J.	Conn	SSG	USA	1942	1945
Anthony		Cooley	SP 5	USA	1969	1971
James	Clyde	Cooley	SN 1C	USNR	1943	1946
Sherman	E.	Cooley	Tech 4	USA	1946	1947
Andy	M.	Cooper	PFC	USA	1946	1947
Blain		Cooper	PFC	USA	1951	1953
Charles	Ray	Cooper	SP 5	USA	1965	1967
Charlie	A.	Cooper	CPL	AAF	1942	1945
Fred		Cooper	PVT	USA	1918	1919
James	Paul	Cooper	SGT	USA	1975	1979
Otis	L.	Cooper	CPL	USA	1941	1945
Venton		Cooper	PFC	USA	1918	1919
Carl	Trent	Cornett	Elec.Mt. C1	USNR	1943	1945
Charles	Curtis	Cornett		USA		1956

Collie	B.	Cornett	PFC	USMC	1942	1945
James	Attis	Cornett	Fireman 1C	USN	1922	1946
Sammy	Frank	Cornett	SGT	USA	1978	1985
Willard	J.	Cornett	PVT	USA	1943	1946
William	E.	Cornett	PVT	USA	1943	1945
Ward		Cornette	SGT	USA	1917	1918
Anthony	Patrick	Costella	HTCS	USN	1975	1982
Arlie	Elvin	Cox	SSgt	USAF	1951	1955
Arnold	B.	Cox	SSG	USA	1942	1945
Arthur		Cox				
Charles	E.	Cox	SSG	USA	1942	1945
Charley		Cox	PFC	USA	1920	1921
David	Henry	Cox	Fireman 1st Cl	USNR	1944	1946
Eliza		Cox	TSgt	USAAC	1942	1945
Franklin	D.	Cox	Sgt	USMC	1952	1955
Gary	Charles	Cox	CPL	USA	1952	1954
George	Ewing	Cox	SP 4	USA	1958	1960
Henry	A.	Cox	PFC	USA	1942	1946
James	Ottis	Cox	SN 2C	USN	1920	1921
John	R.	Cox	CPT	USA	1968	1971
Johnny		Cox	PFC	USA	1945	1946
Johnny		Cox	PFC	USAR		1965
Kenneth	R.	Cox	Tech. 5	USA	1943	1945
Kenneth	Rudolph	Cox	CPT	USA	1958	1959
Leslie		Cox	Cpl	USAF	1946	1947
Lonnie		Cox	PFC	USMC	1956	1958
Milzie	F.	Cox	PVT	USA	1917	1919
Paul	Rayburn	Cox	A1C	USAF	1951	1955
Paul	W.	Cox	CPL	USA	1942	1954
Roy	Curtis	Cox	SA	USNR	1945	1945
Tobise		Cox	CPL	USA	1942	1945
Winfred	Randolph	Cox	SN First Class	USNR	1943	1946
James	W.	Coy	PVT	USA	1947	1947

James	Peter	Coyle	SGT	USAF	1966	1970
Fred	A.	Craft	PVT	USA	1942	1943
Henry	A.	Craft	PVT	USA	1942	1945
Fred	T.	Crager	BT 3	USNR		1963
Fred	Thomas	Crager	T 4	USN	1957	1960
Louie	Isadore	Crager	A1C	USAF	1954	1958
Wilbert	H.	Crager	SGT	USA	1946	1947
Danny	Wayne	Craig	Coxswain	USN	1941	1945
Early		Cranfill	PVT	USA	1917	1919
Allen	Ray	Crawford	SP 5	USA	1966	1968
Bernard	L.	Crawford	CPL	USA	1944	1948
Charles	David	Crawford	CPL	USA	1954	1957
Clarence		Crawford	SP 4	USA	1956	1959
Clifford	W.	Crawford	Tech.1	USA	1943	1945
Marland	David	Crawford	Cpl	USMC	1968	1969
Marland	L.	Crawford	T-4	USA	1943	1946
Murvil	R.	Crawford	A1C	USAF	1953	1957
Ray	E.	Crawford	T.Sgt	USMC	1939	1945
William	H.	Crawford	PFC	USA	1942	1945
Arthur		Creech	SN 2C	USNR	1945	1945
Arnold	L.	Crisp	PVT	USAAC	1942	1945
Elmer	Ray	Crisp	SN 1C	USN	1944	1946
Glenn	M.	Crisp	PVT	USA	1942	1946
Kenneth		Crisp	CPL	USA	1944	1946
Marvin		Crisp	SGT	USA	1948	1952
Willie		Crisp	PFC	USA	1942	1946
Denford		Crose	SP 4	USA	1966	1972
Murvel	Clay	Crosley	SGM	USA	1917	1919
Samuel	Lee	Cross	CW 3	USA	1983	1992
Holley		Crosthwait	PVT	USA	1918	1942
Edward	E.	Crosthwaite	Tech.5	USA	1943	1946
Harold	C.	Crosthwaite	PFC	USA	1942	1945
Jimmie	Ray	Crosthwaite	SGT	USAR	1958	1962

Russell	Byron	Crosthwaite	Signalman 3C	USN	1943	1946
Holly		Crostwait	PVT	USA	1918	1919
Ted	L.	Crostwait	LTC	USA	1943	1972
William	A.	Crowe	SGT	USA	1941	1945
Conrad		Crum	Fireman 1C	USN	1944	1946
Oscar	R.	Crum	CPL	USA	1943	1946
Windell	Herbert	Crumb	TMC	USN	1940	1960
Jeff	Scott	Crump	PFC	USA ARNG	1987	1987
Arnold		Cundiff	SA	USNR	1944	1944
Charles	David	Curtis	SN 3C	USN	1980	1984
Clayton		Curtis	PFC	USA	1942	1945
Delmore		Curtis	PVT	USA	1942	1942
Elbert		Curtis	CPL	USA	1951	1953
Glen		Curtis	PVT	AAF	1945	1947
Henry	R.	Curtis	PFC	USA	1912	1915
John	A.	Curtis	PFC	AAF	1941	1945
Wilford		Curtis	CPL	USA	1943	1946
William	H.	Curtis	CPL	USA	1946	1949
Frasher	F.	Dail	PFC	USA	1937	1941
Larry	Clifton	Dail	PFC	USA	1968	1970
Avery	Lawrence	Dailey	SGT	USA	1952	1954
Billy	Joe	Dailey	SP 5	USA	1966	1968
Ira		Dailey, Jr.	PFC	USA	1967	1969
Joyner	R.	Dameron	PFC	USA	1946	1948
James	N.	Dannar, Jr.	Tech. 3	USA	1942	1946
Forrest	L.	Danner	PVT	USA	1945	1945
Harold	J.	Danner	SSG	USA	1941	1945
Kenneth	Eugene	Darling	SP 4	USA	1973	1976
John	Thomas	Daugherty	Capt.	USMC	1942	1946
Chalmer		Davis	Tech. 5	USA	1942	1946
Charles	Thearl	Davis	PFC	USMC	1943	1946
Clifford	E.	Davis	PFC	USA	1943	1946
Frederick	Darrell	Davis	PFC	USA	1961	1964

W. Porter Daily, Jr., Lt. Army, 1969-71.

Henry	Lee	Davis	FAE-2	USN	1965	1965
Homer	L.	Davis	Tech. 5	USA	1943	1946
Jerrild		Davis	SFC	USA	1950	1953
Milton	P.	Davis	Tech. 4	USA	1924	1945
Russell	C.	Davis	PFC	USA	1941	1945
Russell		Davis	PVT	USA	1942	1945
William		Davis	PFC	USA	1942	1945
Lonnie		Davis, Jr.	A2C	USAF	1953	1957
Armstrong	Dawson	1st. SGT	USAAC	1901	1929	
Berlin		Day	PVT	USA	1942	1945
Chester	H.	Day	CPL	USA	1943	1946
Chiles	Okey	Day	BT 2	USN	1982	1986
Johnny	E.	Day	PFC	USA	1943	1947
Robert	Dolphia	Day	CPL	USMC	1965	1969
William	Clyde	Day	A3C	USAF	1951	1952
Dolphia		Day, Jr.	SGT	USA	1942	1945
Glennis	Carl	Dean	PFC	USA	1948	1952
Glennis	Carl	Dean	LTC	USA	1952	1970

Lloyd		Dean	A1C	USAF	1953	1957
Theodore		Dean	CPL	USA	1917	1919
Vernon	Lee	Dean	SSgt	USAF	1951	1955
Wayne	Lee	Dean	WaterTender 3C	USNR		1945
Ernest	Eugene	Debord	Sgt	USAF	1966	1969
Hurshel	Lee	Debord	SP 5	USA	1964	1967
Ivan	L.	Debord	Tech. 5	USA	1943	1945
Ronald	Owen	Debord	CPL	USMC	1968	1970
Lawrence	Karl	Decker	CPL	USA	1950	1953
Melba	C.	Decker	PFC	WAC	1943	1944
Robert	E.	Decker	Tech. 5	USA	1945	1946
Charlotte	Jean	Deem	PVT	USMC	1981	1981
Carl	E.	Dehart	SP 4	USAR	1966	1972
Charlie	B.	Dehart	SGT	USA	1942	1943
Claude	Clayton	Dehart	Sgt	USMC	1944	1946
Curtis	F.	Dehart	PVT	USA	1942	1942
Elmo	C.	Dehart	CPL	USA	1943	1944
Johnie	Estill	Dehart	PVT	USMC	1953	1953
Midford		Dehart	Tech. 4	USA	1943	1946
Phillip	Harrison	Dehart	SGT	USA	1969	1970
Roy	L.	Dehart	Tech. 5	USA	1943	1945
William	E.	Dehart	PVT	USA	1946	1948
William	O.	Dehart	PVT	USA	1943	1946
Arvetta	Kay	Delashmit	SP 5	WAC	1966	1969
Robert	Joseph	Delashmit	PVT	USA	1994	1995
Edward	C.	Detherage	PFC	USA	1918	1919
Jack	Duff	Dewey	WT 3C	USN	1944	1946
Henry	Thomas	Dewitt	SP 4	USA	1976	1979
Corbett		Dickerson	SN 1C	USN	1944	1945
Covey		Dickerson	PVT	USA	1917	1919
John	M.	Dickinson	PFC	USA	1942	1945
Seth		Dickinson	PFC	USA	1943	1945
Allie	Elwood	Dillon	Ship's Cook 2C	USNR	1942	1945

Charles	J.	Dillon	PVT	USA	1945	1945
Cletis	E.	Dillon	PFC	USA	1945	1947
Defford		Dillon	SFC	USA	1941	1948
Edward		Dillon	SFC	USA	1950	1953
Eldon	Ray	Dillon	SP 4	USA	1962	1965
Golfrey	C.	Dillon	PFC	USA	1945	1946
Homer	A.	Dillon	PFC	USA	1945	1946
Kenneth		Dillon	PVT	USA	1945	1947
Matthew	Cleveland	Dillon	HM 2	USNR		1973
Otto		Dillon	PVT	USA	1941	1947
Rudell	Royse	Dillon	SN	USN	1947	1949
Charles		Dillon, Jr.	Grade 4	USA	1945	1948
Arlie	B.	Donahue	PVT	USA	1944	1945
James	E.	Donnelly	1st Lt.	USAAC	1941	1946
Anthony	Glen	Dotson	SGT	USA	1982	1986
Joseph		Dowling	Sgt	USMC	1966	1970
Paul	T.	Dowling	T 4	USA	1945	1946
Paul	Thomas	Dowling, Jr.	MSG	USA	1977	1997
James	Leslie	Downing	Cpl	USMC	1954	1956
Robert	Glen	Drake	SP 4	USA	1971	1973
Teresa		Drogan	YN 1C	USN	1943	1946
Eric	Marque	Dulin	AO 3	USN	1973	1980
Freddie	Mitchell	Dulin	CPT	USA	1976	1985
James	Henry	Dulin	PFC	USA	1952	1955
Virgil	Wesley	Dulin	SP 3	USA	1953	1956
Clyde		Dunaway	PVT	USA	1942	1945
Johnson	Eugene	Duncan	AC	USAC	1942	1946
James	Casper	Durham	SP 5	USA	1966	1968
Marti	L.	Dye	Amn 2C	USAFR		1963
Elwood		Dyer	PVT	USA	1945	1945
Murvel		Dyer	PFC	USA	1942	1946
Robert		Dyer	PVT	USA	1942	1945
Edward	N.	Earley	Tech. 5	USA	1943	1946

Jackie	D.	Earley	CPL	USA	1953	1955
Delmar	L.	Earls	Tech. 5	USA	1942	1945
Johnny		Earls	PVT	USMC	1943	1945
Billy	Allen	Early	Ship'sCook SV 6	USNR	1943	1946
Ralph	Garland	Early	PFC	USMC	1945	1946
William	S.	Early	CPL	USA	1918	1919
Chester	L.	Easterling	Tech.4	USA	1940	1945
Earnest		Eden	SN 2C	USN	1942	1945
Frank		Eden	PVT	USA	1942	1945
James	Arthur	Edwards	AB	USAF	1960	1962
Richard	L.	Edwards	SSG	USA	1945	1947
Earl	R.	Egan	PVT	USA	1945	1946
Milford		Egan	CPL	USA	1943	1946
Avery	Loyd	Elam	BSM 1C	USN		1945
Elvis	N.	Elam	PFC	USA	1942	1944
Joseph	V.	Elam	SGT	USA	1943	1946
Normal		Elam	SGT	USA	1952	1955
Robert		Elam	SGT	USAAC	1942	1945
Wavel	P.	Elam	PFC	USA	1942	1946
Billy	Joe	Eldridge	SP 4	USA	1966	1968
Elva	E.	Eldridge	PFC	USA	1944	1945
Estill	Ray	Eldridge	SP 4	USA	1959	1961
Fred		Eldridge	CPL	USA	1951	1953
Henry	Thomas	Eldridge	ADRAN	USN	1960	1964
Hubert	H.	Eldridge	SGT	USA	1942	1945
James	Roger	Eldridge	SSgt	USMC	1953	1957
Jerry	Franklin	Eldridge	MSgt	USAF	1954	1974
Jess	Orville	Eldridge	SN 1C	USNR	1944	1946
Levi		Eldridge	SN	USN	1946	1954
Lloyd		Eldridge	Coxswain	USNR	1944	1946
Lowell		Eldridge	SP 4	USA	1966	1967
Roscoe		Eldridge	Tech 5	USA	1943	1945
Thomas	A.	Eldridge	PVT	USA	1945	1945

Harold G. Ellington, S/Sgt., Army Air Corps, 1943-1946

Troy		Eldridge	SA	USNR	1945	1945
William	Maurice	Eldridge	MSgt	USAF	1964	1984
David	Bryan	Elkins	PFC	USA	1983	1983
Audrey	F.	Ellington	PVT	USA	1918	1919
Chester	E.	Ellington	PFC	USA	1945	1946
Fred	C.	Ellington	CPL	USA	1917	1919
Harold	G.	Ellington	SSgt	AAF	1943	1946
Harold	Wendell	Ellington	CPL	USA	1963	1965
James	Lowell	Ellington	CPL	USA	1952	1954
Milford	B.	Ellington	SSG	USA	1944	1946
Phillip	S.	Ellington	PFC	USA	1942	1945
Reynold	C.	Ellington	PVT	USA	1920	1921
Harvey	J.	Elliott	PFC	USA	1944	1946
Alfred	M.	Ellis	Tech. 5	USA	1942	1945
Carlos	Leo Neal	Ellis	AN	USN	1950	1954
Davis		Ellis	SN 2C	USN	1944	1944

Hubert	Elwood	Ellis	SN	USN	1945	1949
Jack	D.	Ellis	CPL	AAF	1944	1947
Joe	R.	Ellis	PFC	USA	1942	1945
Hamm	C.	Elsworth	PFC	USA	1943	1943
Hiriam		Ely	Radioman 1C	USNR	1942	1945
Estill	Earl	Emmons	MotorMchMt 1C	USN	1941	1945
Boyd		Engle	PVT	USA	1963	1964
Robert	Lee	Eplee	SGT	USA		1961
Billy	Donald	Epperhart	MML3	USN	1954	1958
Chester		Epperhart	PFC	USA	1941	1945
Clarence	Elwood	Epperhart	PFC	USMC	1943	1945
James	Marion	Epperhart	SGT	USA	1967	1969
John	D.	Epperhart	GM1	USN	1942	1945
John	H.	Epperhart	PVT	KY Inf. Vol	1898	1899
Milford	H.	Epperhart	PVT	USA	1943	1944
Wheeler	P.	Epperheart	Cook	USA	1917	1919
Jordan		Ernest	PFC	USA	1944	1946

Ernest E. Epperhart, T/5, Army, 1940-KIA 1945.

Clayton		Ervin	SSG	USA	1943	1945
Clevie	L.	Estep	PFC	USA	1941	1945
Ernest		Estep	PFC	USA	1942	1946
Howard		Estep	PFC	USA	1944	1945
Lawrence	J.	Estep	Tech. 3	USA	1942	1946
Billy	Clarence	Evans	CW 2	USA	1951	1971
Eldon	T.	Evans	Col.	USAAC	1940	1946
George	B.	Evans	Tech. 5	USA	1941	1945
Guy	Hubert	Evans	SN 1C	USN	1946	1947
Jack		Evans	PVT	USA	1945	1947
James	R.	Evans	PVT	USA	1918	1919
James	T.	Evans		USA	1898	1899
John	F.	Evans	PFC	USA	1943	1945
Lester		Evans	CPL	USA	1951	1953
Ora	L.	Evans	PFC	USA	1944	1946
Warren	Mitchel	Evans	SSgt	USMCR	1942	1945
Russell	R.	Everman	PFC	USA	1943	1945
George	Warren	Eyster, Jr.	LT	USN	1951	1966
Daniel	Lewis	Fackler	LCpl	USMC	1959	1963
Chris	H.	Fannin	PVT	USA	1918	1919
Harold	Clell	Fannin	SP 5	USA	1967	1970
John	W.	Fannin	PFC	USA	1944	1945
Michael	Ora	Fannin	SP 5	USA	1968	1970
Michael	Maurice	Farrell	cpl	USMC	1990	1994
Elwood		Faulkner	CPL	USA	1940	1945
Dale	Alan Wheeler	Fay	PVT	USA	1975	1978
Phillip	Edward	Fay	SP 5	USA	1965	1968
Robert	L.	Fay	T-5	USA	1939	1945
Walter		Felty	PFC	USA	1946	1947
Arthur	W.	Ferguson	PVT	USA	1942	1943
Cecil	Delmas	Ferguson	SP 4	USA	1970	1971
Charles	Russell	Ferguson	Cpl	USMC	1982	1988
Edward	C.	Ferguson	Tech. 4	USA	1942	1945

Frankie	Lee	Ferguson	SP 4	USA	1964	1966
Gus		Ferguson	SN 1C	USNR	1942	1945
Guy	G.	Ferguson	PFC	USA	1942	1945
James	Lee	Ferguson	PVT	USA	1942	1943
Kermit	Eugene	Ferguson	SP 4	USA	1958	1961
Paris	Feral	Ferguson	A1C	USAF	1955	1959
Roy	R.	Ferguson	PFC	USA	1942	1945
William	C.	Ferguson	CPL	USA	1942	1946
John	Newton	Ferguson, Jr.	SP 4	USA	1961	1963
Arthur		Fielding	CPL	USA	1914	1920
George	D.	Fisher	PFC	USA	1942	1945
Paul	F.	Fisher	PFC	USA	1941	1945
Charles	Walton	Fitzpatrick	CSM	USA	1971	2001
Clarence	V.	Flanery	PFC	USA	1942	1945
John	L.	Flanery	PVT	USA	1917	1919
Johnie	W.	Flanery	PVT	USA	1942	1943
Ora	D.	Flanery	Cpl	AAF	1942	1946
Denver	Dean	Flannery	Av.Mch.Mt. 1C	USNR	1953	1964
Earnest	J.	Flannery	PVT	USA	1918	1919
Hubert	Moralen	Flannery	Cpl	USMCR	1943	1946
Isaac	Gary	Flannery	SP 5	USA	1966	1972
Jerry	Lee	Flannery	PVT	USAR	1970	1970
John	F.	Flannery	PFC	USA	1943	1943
Larry	David	Flannery	SP 4	USA	1961	1964
Lonnie	L.	Flannery	EMP2	USN	1954	1958
Richard		Flannery	PFC	USAR		1967
Rufus	H.	Flannery	PVT	USA	1946	1946
Russell	E.	Flannery	PVT	USA	1945	1945
Shirley	Thomas	Flannery	SN	USN	1954	1957
Warren		Flannery	T.SGT	USA	1943	1945
Wilford	Clyde	Flannery	CarpenterMt. 1C	USN	1941	1945
Woodrow	Wilson	Flannery	SN 1C	USNR	1944	1945
Anthony	Joseph	Flecha	HM2	USN	1968	1972

John C. Flannery, Sgt., Army, 1951-1954.

Francis	C.	Fogle	1st Lt.	USMC	1942	1956
Robert	Dale	Fordon	SFC	USA	1964	1970
Paul		Forman	PFC	USA	1942	1945
Ralph	Thomas	Fossett	CPT	USAR	1967	1969
Andrew		Foster	SA	USN	1944	1944
Gregory	Lee	Foster	HM3	USN	1982	1986
Jesse	Anderson	Foster	SGT	USA	1950	1953
Lee		Foster	PVT	KyInfVol US	1898	1899
John	Paul	Fouch	CMSgt	USAF	1952	1976
Paris	A.	Fouch	SSgt	USAAC	1941	1946
William	Hobert	Fouch	A1C	USAF	1952	1955
Rubye	Lee	Fowler	1st Lt.	USMC	1943	1945
Grover	C.	Fox, Jr.	SSG	USA	1943	1946
Benny		Fraley	SSG	USA	1967	1970

Carl	Vernon	Fraley	MotorMchMt 3C	USNR	1943	1946
Charles	E.	Fraley	Tech. 4	USA	1942	1946
Clester	Eugene	Fraley	SP 4	USA	1957	1959
David		Fraley	CPL	USA	1950	1952
Denzell	Ray	Fraley	E 4	USN	1962	1966
Earl	S.	Fraley	SSG	USA	1943	1946
Goble	D.	Fraley	CPL	USA	1941	1947
Granville	W.	Fraley	PVT	USA	1917	1919
Howard	Lee	Fraley	PFC	USA	1958	1960
James	C.	Fraley	CPL	USA	1942	1945
Jergie		Fraley	Tech. 5	USA	1943	1946
Lowell	E.	Fraley	PFC	USA	1942	1945
Luther	Franklin	Fraley	SSgt.	USAF	1950	1954
Robert	G.	Fraley	CPL	USAAC	1943	1945
Ronald		Fraley	SP 4	USA	1969	1971
Roy	E.	Fraley	PVT	USA	1942	1943
Roy	R.	Fraley	Cpl	AAF	1944	1946
Vaughn	Monroe	Fraley	SPC 4	USA	1969	1970
William	Decimal	Fraley	CPL	USA	1952	1954
William	L.	Fraley	PVT	USA	1944	1946
William	Lee	Fraley	T.Sgt	USAF	1950	1954
Scott	Earl	Fraley, Jr.	SMSgt	USAF	1971	1996
Paul	A.	France	SGT	USA	1946	1952
Carl	Clayton	Franklin	ChiefElecMt.	USN	1940	1948
Claude	R.	Franklin	Tech. 5	USA	1943	1946
Eldon	L.	Franklin	PFC	USA	1940	1941
Kent	Eugene	Freeland	SP 5	USA	1967	1969
Johnnie	Gaylord	Fryman	SP 3	USA	1956	1958
Calvin	H.	Fugate	Tech. 5	USA	1942	1945
Carl		Fugate	SSG	USA	1942	1945
Cathleen	Mae	Fugate	1LT	USAR	1977	1980
Charles	Alden	Fugate	T. SGT	USA	1949	1952
Earnest	R.	Fugate	PFC	USA	1941	1945

Lloyd	G.	Fugate	PVT	USA	1942	1945
Noah	E.	Fugate	CPL	USAF	1943	1946
Russell	G.	Fugate	SSG	USA	1940	1945
Ernest	Recel	Fugate, Jr.	SP 4	USA	1967	1970
Burnie		Fultz	PVT	USA	1941	1945
Charley		Fultz	Avia.MachMt 2C	USN	1942	1948
Charley		Fultz	SGT	USANG	1950	1956
Christopher	Van	Fultz	Cpl	USMC	1993	1997
Claude	Dwayne	Fultz	SP 4	USA	1975	1978
Clifford		Fultz	Av.MachMt. C2	USN	1942	1947
Curtis		Fultz	PVT	USA	1942	1945
Elijah	Moore	Fultz	SP 4	USA	1986	1989
Ervin		Fultz	PVT	USA	1949	1949
George	A.	Fultz	PFC	USA	1945	1946
Hubert	Thomas	Fultz	SP 2	USA	1952	1955
John		Fultz	T.SGT	USA	1941	1945
Paul	Edward	Fultz	SP 4	USA	1969	1971
Russell		Fultz	SP 3	USA	1954	1955
Samuel		Fultz	PFC	USA	1942	1945
Sollie	R.	Fultz	PVT	USA	1918	1918
Talmadge		Fultz	CPL	USA	1952	1954
Vernon	R.	Fultz	SP 4	USA	1968	1970
Adrian	A.	Fyffe	PFC	USA	1943	1944
Frederick	Sanford	Gais	LTJG	USN	1944	1947
John	Douglas	Galbraith	SP 4	USA	1976	1979
Terry	Clinton	Gallagher	SM 3	USN	1988	1991
Bobby		Gambill	A 1C	USAF	1954	1958
Clinton	Randy	Gardner	CPT O3	ARNUG	1985	1989
Watt		Gardner	PVT	USA	1942	1943
Robert	O.	Garries	PFC	USA	1945	1947
James		Garris	PFC	USA	1942	1945
John	P.	Gartin	SGT	USA	1948	1953
Harlan	W.	Gayheart	PVT	USA	1942	1946

Emmitt	F.	Gearhart	SGT	USAR	1951	1959
John	Maxwell	Gearhart	CarpenterMt. 1C	USN	1943	1945
William	L.	Gearhart	CPL	USA	1942	1946
Lloyd	H.	Gearheart	PVT	USA	1941	1945
James	W.	Gee	PVT	AAF	1942	1945
Arthur		Gee, Jr.	GM 1C	USN	1943	1945
James	Walter	George III	PVT	USA-ARNG	1996	1997
William	Kenneth	Ghee	1st LT. JG.4	USNR	1952	1955
Bert	Thomas	Gibson	RML	USN	1942	1948
Russell	Asa	Gibson	CPL	USA	1952	1954
Karen	Denise	Giles	Capt	USAF	1985	1992
Arlie	L.	Gilkison	PFC	USA	1943	1946
Billy	Grover	Gilkison	PFC	USA	1950	1952
Ora	H.	Gilkison	Tech. 5	USA	1943	1945
Ora	R.	Gilkison	PVT	USA	1918	1919
Otto	Hinton	Gilkison	SGT	USA	1962	1965
Robert	Dean	Gilkison	PN 2	USN	1952	1956
Simon	K.	Gillam	PVT	USA	1942	1943
Charles	Ray	Gilley	Sgt	USMC	1953	1956
Lonnie	J.	Gilliam	PVT	USA	1936	1947
Truly		Gilliam	SGT	USA	1942	1946
Walter	Scott	Gillock	SGT	USAF	1968	1972
Glenn		Ginter	SP 5	USA	1968	1971
Raymond	Edmond	Ginter	SGT	USA	1988	1991
John	Charles	Ginter	PFC	USA	1991	1992
Robert	Dan	Glahn	SP 4	USA	1985	1988
Ricky	Edward	Glover	SGT	USA	1983	1997
Willie		Glover	SGT	USA	1914	1920
Delmar	Paul	Goodman	SP 4	USA	1955	1958
Edward	N.	Goodman	PVT	USA	1918	1919
Homer	Nickel	Goodman	A2C	USAF	1955	1959
Russel		Goodman	PVT	USA	1918	1919
James	Robert	Gould	SK3	USN	1993	1997

Charles Gilley, Sgt., Marine Corps, 1953-56.

Robert	Barris	Gould	PVT	USAR	1960	1961
Robert	Barris	Gould	SP 4	USA	1960	1966
James	William	Gozzard	SP 4	USA	1966	1968
Donald	Rankin	Graham	SFC	USA	1948	1951
Wilma	Fay	Grant	A 2C	USAF	1952	1954
James	Waller	Gray	ER 3	USNR		1982
George	Thomas	Green	CPT	USA	1981	1991
Paul	Burton	Green	SSG	USA	1951	1975
Sam	Logan	Green	PFC	USA	1950	1952
Teddy	Franklin	Greene	SP 4	USA	1972	1976
Benjamin	Paul	Greenhill	Coxswain	USN	1941	1947
Clarence		Greenhill	T. SGT	USA	1945	1952
Bernard	Lee	Greer	PFC	USA	1951	1953
Arnold		Gregory	Tech. 5	USA	1944	1946

Charles	C.	Gregory	PFC	USA	1945	1946
Charles		Gregory	SFC	USA	1945	1977
Clella		Gregory	PVT	USA	1941	1943
Donald	G.	Gregory	PFC	USAR		1972
Ernest		Gregory	PFC	USA	1942	1945
Joseph	Medford	Gregory	A1C	USAF	1957	1961
Larry	D.	Gregory	PFC	USA	1968	1970
Lester	C.	Gregory	PFC	USA	1942	1945
Vincent		Gregory	Tech. 5	USA	1942	1945
Willis	B.	Gregory	PVT	USA		1919
Robert	Lee	Grey	SSgt.	USAF	1951	1954
Jim	H.	Gribbins	PVT	USA	1941	1941
Roger	Lee	Griffith	SP 5	USA	1968	1970
Danny	Dale	Griggs	SN	USN	1973	1976

Rodney Gordon, M/Sgt., Army, 1955-1979.

C. Nelson Grote, Pfc., Army, 1946-47.

John	Gerome	Grimaldi, Jr.	SN	USN	1965	1969
Vernon		Gross	SP 4	USA	1968	1970
Charles	N.	Grote	PFC	USA	1946	1947
Earl	T.	Grover	PFC	USA	1942	1945
Lester		Grubb	CPL	USMC		1945
Herston		Gullett	PFC	USA	1941	1945
William	D.	Gullett	SSG	USA	1942	1945
Alvie		Gulley	Tech. SGT	USA	1942	1945
Alvin		Gulley	CPL	AAF	1942	1945
Arnold	Alvin	Gulley	SFC	USA	1943	1969
Avery		Gulley	PVT	USAAC	1943	1946
Fred		Gulley	PFC	USA	1943	1946
Kenyon	D.	Hackney	PFC	USA	1943	1945

Lilburn	P.	Hackney	Cf. Carp. Mt.	USN		1945
Alvin	B.	Haines	PVT	USA	1914	1917
Charles	R.	Hall	PFC	USAF	1944	1948
Clifton		Hall	SP 4	USA	1960	1963
Daniel	B.	Hall	Tech. 5	USA	1946	1947
Denver	Pierce	Hall	Chief Specialist	USN	1942	1946
Deward		Hall	SSG	USA	1941	1949
Elmer		Hall	CW3	USA	1954	1977
Ernest	Gene	Hall	SSG	USA	1960	1963
George	William	Hall	LCpl	USMC	1960	1964
Howard	Corneiles	Hall	SN 2C	USN	1945	1945
Howard	Corneiles	Hall	S2C	USN	1945	1945
Jack	Vencil	Hall	SGT	USA	1948	1952
James	L.	Hall	PFC	USA	1943	1946
James	R.	Hall	Tech. 5	USA	1942	1946
Jessie	Fleming	Hall	SN	USNR	1944	1945
John	R.	Hall	SN	USN	1955	1957
LeRoy	C.	Hall	PVT	USA	1942	1945
Marion	M.	Hall	PFC	USA	1943	1945
Millard	C.	Hall	SN 2C	USN	1944	1944
Murvel	J.	Hall	SSgt	USAAC	1942	1945
Oliver		Hall	PVT	USA	1918	1919
Ollie	R.	Hall	Tech. 5	USA	1942	1945
Ralph	W.	Hall	CPL	USA	1951	1953
Randy	Lee	Hall	SP 4	USA	1971	1972
Samuel	Lee	Hall	SP 4	USA	1961	1964
Stewart		Hall	PFC	USA	1942	1944
Thelma	L.	Hall	Spec. 3C	USN		1945
Everett		Hall, Jr.	SGT	USAF	1965	1968
Terry	Lee	Hall, Jr.	1SG	USA	1974	1992
Everett	F.	Ham	PVT	USA	1918	1918
Jesse	R.	Ham	PVT	USA	1918	1919
LaVaughn	Lee	Hamblin	A1C	USAF	1963	1967

Andrew	Craig	Hamilton	PFC	USA	1917	1919
Elmer	T.	Hamilton	PFC	USA	1943	1945
Elwood		Hamilton	PFC	USA	1942	1945
Estill		Hamilton	PFC	USA	1947	1947
Freeman	J.	Hamilton	SP 4	USA	1960	1966
Isaac		Hamilton	PFC	USA		1945
James	Woody	Hamilton	MSgt	USAF	1950	1975
John	P.	Hamilton	PVT	USA	1918	1919
Marvin	Justin	Hamilton	SPC 3	USA	1955	1957
Stanley	C.	Hamilton	PFC	USA	1943	1946
Willis		Hamilton	PFC	USA	1943	1946
Taylor		Hamilton, Jr.	Tech. 5	USA	1944	1946
Ronald	Jennings	Hamlin	SN	USNR		1962
Arlie	B.	Hamm	PFC	AAF	1944	1945
Arthur	Harold	Hamm	Carpenters M 2C	USNR	1945	1945
Billy	Lee	Hamm	SGT	USAF	1971	1975
Earnest		Hamm	PFC	USA	1944	1945
Edmond	E.	Hamm	PFC	AAF	1942	1945
Gene	Sidney	Hamm	PFC (T)	USA	1950	1952
John	Billie	Hamm	TSgt	USAF	1968	1971
John	R.	Hamm	PVT	USA	1943	1944
Joseph	R.	Hamm	MSGT	USAF	1969	1992
Marvin	C.	Hamm	PVT	USA	1948	1948
Versie	A.	Hamm	PVT	USA	1943	1943
William	A.	Hamm	PVT	USA	1942	1945
Woodrow	Junior	Hamm	SP 4	USA	1967	1969
Timothy	Poland	Hammond	SPC 4	USA	1989	1992
David		Hamon	PVT	USA	1899	1905
Bennie	H.	Haney	T.SGT	USA	1943	1946
Elmo	L.	Haney	Tech. 5	USA	1943	1946
Michael	Jude	Hanrahan	PVT	USA	1970	1972
Alby	Ray	Hardin	SN 2C	USNR	1943	1946
Arlie		Hardin	PVT	USA	1942	1943

Austin	B.	Hardin	PVT	USA	1942	1943
Philemon	A.	Hardin	SSG	USA	1942	1945
Phillip	Michael	Hardin	SGT	USA	1970	1972
Vickie	Lee	Hardin	A 1C	USAF	1976	1980
Wilbur	C.	Hardin	PVT	USA	1944	1946
Jimmie	Ray	Hargett	SGT	USA	1952	1953
John	A.	Hargett	PFC	USAAC	1942	1945
William	R.	Hargett	PVT	USA	1939	1944
Bernard	P.	Hargis	Tech. 5	USA	1942	1945
Lloyd	Henry	Hargis	PVT	USA	1948	1950
Larry	Kenneth	Hargis	PFC	USA	1971	1971
Carlos	J.	Harmon	PFC	USAF	1951	1952
Clifford	Lee	Harmon	CPL	USA	1951	1953
Roger	Douglas	Harney	1LT	USAR	1973	1976
Daniel	Burk	Harr	SP 4	USA	1969	1970
Dennis	Skaggs	Harr	SP 5	USA	1968	1970
Harold	Edward	Harr	FN	USN	1955	1959
Paul	V.	Harr	PVT	USA	1958	1958
Vernon	Eugene	Harr	CPL	USA	1949	1953
William	Joseph	Harr	BMSN	USN	1962	1966
Avery	C.	Harris	PFC	USA	1946	1947
Harry	E.	Harris	PFC	USA	1943	1946
Michael	Ray	Harris	SGT	USAF	1969	1973
Paul	S.	Harris	Cpl	AAF	1941	1945
Woodrow	D.	Harris	1SG	USA	1939	1945
Walter	Samuel	Hart	PFC	USA	1961	1964
Will		Hart	Wagoner	USA	1918	1919
William	Lee	Hart	SN 1C	USNR	1943	1945
Maurits	John	Hartog	MMFN	USN	1973	1976
Chester	A.	Hatton	SSgt	USAAC	1942	1945
John	M.	Hatton	PVT	USA`	1942	1945
Kenneth	Alender	Hatton	SV 6	USN	1943	1945
Merrell		Hatton	PFC	USA	1942	1945

Fola	N.	Hayes	PFC	AAF	1942	1946
Lawrence		Hayes	SP 3	USA	1955	1958
Leon		Hayes	PVT	USA	1943	1945
Walton	E.	Hayes	SSgt.	AAF	1942	1945
George	Edward	Hays	MM3 PO 3	USN	1972	1976
John	Quintin	Hays	SGT	USA	1979	1993
Mark	Alan	Hays	TM 1	USN	1975	1980
Raymond		Hays	PVT	USA	1941	1945
Victor	Allen	Healey	SSG	USA	1978	1982
Michael	Clark	Hearn	SP 5	USA	1969	1971
Robert	Thomas	Heitz	FN 2C	USN	1945	1946
Donnie	Ray	Helterbrand	LCpl	USMC	1970	1972
Howard	Lee	Helterbrand	BM 3	USN	1966	1969
Mitchell	C.	Helterbrand	PVT	USA	1943	1945
Donald	Keith	Helwig	PVT	USA	1972	1972
William	Lee	Helwig	SP 4	USA	1968	1970
Jack	W.	Helwig, Jr.	Tech. 4	USA	1942	1946
Delbert		Henderson	PFC	USA	1944	1947
Franklin	Adam	Henderson	MMCS	USN	1956	1976
Earl	Allen	Henson	TM-3	USN	1952	1956
Robert		Henson	MSgt	USAF	1951	1971
Fant		Herrington	A1C	USAF	1950	1954
Benjamin	Franklin	Hicks	MMC	USN	1937	1958
David		Hicks	FN	USN	1972	1975
Jessie	N.	Hicks	PVT	USA	1941	1942
Warren	H.	Hicks	PFC	USA	1942	1945
George	C.	Hill	Tech. 4	USA	1942	1945
Leroy		Hill	Elec. Mt. 2C	USN		1945
Luther	Thomas	Hilliard	Sonarman 2C	USN	1943	1946
Alexander		Hilterbrand	SGT	USAF	1972	1975
Billy	Denver	Hinton	SN C1	USNR	1943	1946
Charles	L.	Hinton	PVT	AAF	1944	1945
Earsel	Leroy	Hinton	PVT	USA	1952	1954

Elmer		Hinton	PVT	USA		1942
Junior	A.	Hinton	Tech. 5	USA	1941	1945
Leroy	C.	Hinton	PFC	USA	1942	1945
Robert		Hinton	Tech 5	USA	1941	1945
James	Tilden	Hodge	LT 0-3	USNR	1971	1975
Herbert		Hogan	PVT	USA	1942	1943
Jeffery	Wayne	Hogan	AB	USAF	1972	1973
Buell		Hogge	SSG	USA	1942	1945
Charles	Allie	Hogge	A1C	USAF	1954	1957
Edmond		Hogge	PVT	USA	1957	1957
Elijah	Monroe	Hogge	LT	USN	1942	1946
Elson	A.	Hogge	CPL	USA	1941	1945
Ernest	D.	Hogge	Tech. 5	USA	1942	1946
Fred	M.	Hogge	Tech. 5	USA	1945	1947
Grover	C.	Hogge	PVT	USA	1918	1919
Irvin	Lester	Hogge	PFC	USMC		1962
Jack	Wilson	Hogge	PFC	USA	1950	1952
James	David	Hogge	MM3	USN	1956	1957
Kenneth	Burl	Hogge	SGT	USAF	1967	1970
Kenneth	Burn	Hogge	SGT	USAF	1967	1970
Leland	Harold	Hogge	SP 4	USA	1964	1966
Orville		Hogge	SN 2C	USN	1944	1960
Ray	E.	Hogge	PVt	USA	1945	1946
Anna	J.	Holbrook	Capt.	WAC	1943	1946
Harold	Edward	Holbrook	CPT	USA	1944	1945
Herman	Nelson	Holbrook	SGT	USA	1987	1994
Louie	E.	Holbrook	CPL	USA	1941	1948
Ralph	W.	Holbrook	FTM 2C	USN	1944	1946
Robert	Leroy	Holbrook	Pharmacists Mt.	USNR	1943	1946
Vallie	A.	Holbrook	PVT	USA	1942	1944
John	Will	Holbrook, Jr.	EN2	USN	1951	1954
James	Harold	Hollan	MMM 3C	USNR		1945
Clarence	Fredrick	Hollister	TSgt	USAF	1940	1960

Harold E. Holbrook, Ap. Seaman, Navy, 1944-45; Cpt., Army, 1951-53.

Robert	H.	Holt	SSG	USAAC	1941	1945
Lee	G.	Honaker	PVT	USA	1918	1918
Wayne	D.	Hood	1LT	USAR	1976	1979
Bert	M.	Hook	PFC	USA	1942	1945
Dan	Lee	Hopwood	SN 1C	USNR	1942	1945
Andrew	Floyd	Hornsby	Tech. 5	USA	1942	1943
Darius	H.	Horton	PFC	USA	1944	1945
James	Marty	Horton	PVT	USA	1976	1976
Roy	W.	Horton	PFC	USA	1943	1945
James	M.	Horton, Jr.	PFC	USA	1943	1945
Imogene		Hosack	PVT	USMC	1955	1956
Robert	D.	Hosack	PFC	USA	1942	1945
Leander		Hoskins	PVT	USA	1917	1919
Claude		Howard	SP 3	USA	1952	1955
James	Ballard	Howard	SP 3	USA	1953	1956

Steve	Allen	Howard	SP 4	USA	1982	1986
Steven	Edward	Howard	Cpl	USMC	1985	1993
Vernon		Howard	SGT	USA	1942	1946
Lan		Howard, Jr.	PVT	USA	1941	1941
Henderson	Howerton	PVT	USA	1917	1919	
Charles	Scottie	Hubbard	DC 3	USN	1957	1961
Herman		Hudson	PVT	USA	1935	1944
Herman	W.	Huffman	PVT	USA	1918	1919
Jesse	James	Humphries	CPL	AAF	1943	1945
Harold	T.	Hunt	CPL	USA	1942	1945
Reese	Thomas	Hunt	TSgt	USAF	1975	1976
Charles	E.	Hunter	Cpl	AAF	1945	1946
Tim		Hunter	SP 4	USA	1966	1969
Willard		Hunter	PFC	USA	1942	1945
Tandy		Hunter, Jr.	PVT	USA	1942	1943
Leslie	H.	Hurt	PFC	USA	1944	1945
Alpha	M.	Hutchinson	PFC	USA	1943	1945
Glenn		Hutchinson	SSG	USA	1942	1946
Samuel	Cecil	Hutchinson	PVT	USAR	1942	1944
David	R.	Hutchinson, Jr.	PVT	USA	1945	1945
George	Addison	Hyatt	PFC	USA	1951	1953
John	W.	Hyatt	PFC	USA	1945	1947
William	David	Hyatt	WaterTender 3C	USNR	1942	1946
William		Hyatt, Jr.	Tech. 5	USA	1945	1946
Roy	W.	Igo	Tech. 4	USA	1942	1945
Arthur	L.	Ingle	PVT	USA	1942	1943
Earl		Ingram	PVT	USA	1942	1943
Fred	G.	Ingram	PFC	USA	1942	1945
Glen	Allen	Ingram	SN 2C	USNR	1944	1945
Herbert	L.	Ingram	Tech. 4	USA	1941	1945
James	W.	Ingram, Jr.	PFC	USA	1943	1945
Archie	W	Ison	Tech. 5	USA	1942	1945
Arnold	J.	Ison	PFC	USA	1950	1952

Arnold	Lee	Ison	SGT	USAF	1971	1975
Cecil	R.	Ison	SP 4	USA	1970	1976
Donald	Claude	Ison	SPC	USA	1985	1989
Herman	Anthony	Ison	FR	USN	1979	1979
Ishmael	J.	Ison		USN	1958	1962
James	A.	Ison	SSgt	USAF	1966	1970
Phillip		Ison	OS 2	USN	1979	1983
Edwin	Earl	Jackson	DC 1C	USN	1944	1953
Fredrick	Carl	Jackson	BT 2	USN	1959	1968
George	O.	Jackson	Tech. 3	USA	1942	1946
James	Alfred	Jackson	SPC 4	USA	1959	1962
Lynden	C.	Jackson	PFC	USA	1944	1946
Marc	Dwayne	Jackson	PFC	USA	1983	1990
Phillip	Craig	Jackson	1LT	USA	1994	1998
Vernon	P.	Jackson	PFC	USA	1945	1947
William	Raymond	Jacobs	MotorMchMt. 1C	USNR	1943	1945
Chester	T.	James	PVT	USA	1942	1944
Cletis	Edgar	James	MSgt	AAF	1941	1945
Harlan	J.	James	SGT	USA	1942	1945
Timothy	Chenault	James	CPT	USA	1976	1981
Billie	Ray	James	SSgt	USAF	1951	1955
Leo		Jamison	PVT	USA	1942	1943
Ernest		Jayne	Sgt	AAF	1943	1945
Luther		Jayne	CPL	USA	1942	1944
Mason	H.	Jayne	SGT	USA	1942	1945
James	Ray	Jefferson	SP 4	USA	1972	1974
Benjamin	F.	Jenkins	PVT	USA	1939	1945
Charles	E.	Jennings	PFC	USANG	1921	1923
Charles	Edward	Jennings	CSP	USN	1944	1945
Clarence	William	Jennings	SGT	USA	1966	1968
Dorsie	C.	Jennings	SN 2C	USN		1945
Joseph	S.	Jennings	Tech. 5	USA	1944	1946
Marvin		Jennings	CPL	USA	1951	1953

Raymond		Jennings	SGT	USA	1948	1952
Rienzi	W.	Jennings	Tech.4	USA	1943	1945
Charles	T.	Jent	PVT	USA	1950	1956
Charles	Thomas	Jent	PVT	USA	1950	1952
Roy	V.	Jent	PFC	USA	1943	1946
Jerry	Lee	Jessie	SP 5	USA	1969	1971
Zack	Donald	Jessie	PVT-1	USA	1958	1958
Flanery	L.	John	PVT	USA		1919
Asa	Wayne	Johnson	SN	USN	1972	1975
Bruce	Delmore	Johnson	SP 4	USA	1960	1962
Carl	S.	Johnson	PVT	USA	1946	1947
Clinton	W.	Johnson	PFC	AAF	1942	1945
Corbie	S.	Johnson	Tech. 5	USA	1942	1945
Dale	Lee	Johnson	PFC	USA ARNG	1988	1989
Donald	Clintress	Johnson	SP 4	USA	1958	1961

Clinton W. Johnson, Pfc. Army Air Corps, 1942-45.

Douglas	Dale	Johnson	SGT	USA	1965	1968
Earl	G	Johnson	SP 4	USA	1957	1959
Eddie		Johnson	PVT	USA	1918	1919
Elbert	D.	Johnson	SGT	AAF	1942	1945
Ellis	L.	Johnson	AN 2C	USAF		1962
Floyd	Dean	Johnson	SSG	USA	1981	1985
George		Johnson	PVT	USA	1905	1908
George		Johnson	PFC	USA	1908	1911
George		Johnson	PFC	USA	1914	1920
George		Johnson	PVT	USA	1924	1925
Gerald	Eugene	Johnson	SPC	USA	1983	1999
Gregory	Darren	Johnson	PV 1	USA ARNG	1988	1996
Harold	Rudolph	Johnson	1st.SGT	USA	1949	1974
Hayward	A.	Johnson	PFC	USA	1941	1943
Homer	E.	Johnson	Tech. 4	USA	1945	1946
Ivo		Johnson	CarpenterMt. 3C	USN	1944	1946
Jack	Lowell	Johnson	Sgt	USMC	1953	1956
James	Darrell	Johnson	SGT	USA	1967	1970
Jesse	B.	Johnson	PVT	USA	1917	1919
Jesse	Thomas	Johnson	Baker 3C	USNR	1943	1946
Laban	Franklin	Johnson	CPL	USA	1951	1954
Larry	Dwain	Johnson	SP 4	USA	1977	1981
Lawrence	W.	Johnson	PVT	USA	1943	1944
Lonnie	Burl	Johnson	SGT	USA	1961	1962
Marion	J.	Johnson	PVT	USA	1946	1947
Marty	Ben	Johnson	SGT	USAF	1974	1978
Melvin		Johnson	PVT	USA	1942	1946
Michael	Darryl	Johnson	SP 4	USA & ANG	1983	1986
Morris	K.	Johnson	T-5	USA	1942	1946
Nikola	F.	Johnson	PFC	USA	1942	1945
Ora	Lee	Johnson	BT-1	USN	1955	1963
Pattie	Milton	Johnson	Carpenter Mt.3C	USNR	1945	1946
Ray	M.	Johnson	PVT	USA	1942	1944

Raymond	Junior	Johnson	PFC	USA	1963	1964
Rexford	Joe	Johnson	SP 4	USA	1956	1959
Russell	Delbert	Johnson	SGT	USA	1952	1954
Tony	Banford	Johnson	SP 4	USA	1958	1960
Virgil	Loverne	Johnson	SPC 3	USA	1954	1956
William	A.	Johnson		USA	1945	1948
William	A.	Johnson	PFC	USA	1944	1946
William	B.	Johnson	PFC	USA	1942	1945
William	Chalmer	Johnson	SP 4	USA	1967	1969
Zorie		Johnson	PVT	USA	1898	1901
Arthur	Dillard	Johnson, Jr.	PFC	USA	1957	1960
Linvell		Johnson, Jr.	PVT	USA	1953	1954
Dewey	L.	Johnston	CPL	USA	1942	1945
J.	C.	Jolley	PFC	USA	1955	1957
Adler	Stevenson	Jones	PVT	USA	1918	1919
Arno	Eldon	Jones	SP 5	USA	1978	1983
Brunell		Jones	CPL	USAR	1951	1959
Burnell		Jones	CPL	USA	1951	1953
Charles	Robert	Jones	SP-4	USA	1958	1960
Charles		Jones	CPL	USA	1918	1919
Charlie	Lemon	Jones	SSgt	USAF	1952	1956
Clinton		Jones	CPL	USA	1942	1945
Delno	Elmer	Jones	PFC	USA	1958	1960
Dile	R.	Jones	PFC	USA	1941	1946
Elmer	J.	Jones	PVT	USA	1941	1942
Ernest		Jones	BM 2	USN	1944	1955
Filmore	L.	Jones	CPL	USAAC	1942	1946
Gilbert		Jones	Tech. 4	USA	1942	1946
Gordon	L.	Jones	CPL	USA	1943	1946
John	David	Jones	SP 4	USA	1962	1964
John	Mattison	Jones	MM 3C	USN	1943	1946
Kenneth	E.	Jones	PFC	USAAC	1946	1947
Linden		Jones	SGT	USA	1952	1954

Lymon	B.	Jones	CPL	USA	1942	1946
Malcom	L.	Jones	Tech. 4	USA	1942	1945
Owen	E.	Jones	PFC	USA	1941	1945
Raymond	E.	Jones	PVT	USA	1939	1940
Roy	D.	Jones	SSG	USA	1939	1946
Roy	Edward	Jones	PVT	USA	1960	1963
Russell		Jones	PVT	USA	1918	1940
Samuel		Jones	FLC	USN	1916	1920
Walter	A.	Jones	PFC	USA	1918	1919
William	A.	Jones	PFC	USA	1945	1946
William	T.	Jones	Tech. 4	USA	1942	1947
Meredith		Jones, Jr.	SN 1C	USNR	1943	1945
James	T.	Jordan	PVT	USA	1943	1944
Jerome	D.	Judd	PFC	USMCR	1942	1944
Romie	Dustin	Judd	1LT	USA	1917	1919
Jefferson		Junior	PO2	USNR		1945
Francis	Marion	Justice	SN 1C	USN	1943	1945
Jerry	Reeves	Justice	ATN-3	USNR	1963	1969
John	A.	Justice	LCpl	USMC	1988	1990
Walter	Irvin	Karrick	MMFN	USN	1962	1964
Ronald	Wayne	Kautz	RM	USN	1980	1984
Aubrey		Kautz, Jr.	CPL	USA	1952	1953
Shawn	Eric	Kay	PFC	USMC	1994	1998
Hershell	Ray	Keeton	SrA	USAF	1975	1978
Larry	Junior	Keeton	PFC	USA	1966	1968
Lloyd		Keeton	PFC	USA	1942	1946
Ollie	J.	Keeton	PFC	USA	1948	1950
Robert	A.	Keeton	PFC	USA	1944	1946
Willard	F.	Keeton	Tech. 5	USA	1941	1945
William	P.	Keeys	SSG	USA	1944	1946
Ballard	J.	Kegley	PVT	USA	1918	1919
Chester	D.	Kegley	Tech. 5	USA	1942	1946
Delbert	C.	Kegley	CPL	USA	1946	1947

Jack	Junior	Kegley	MachMt. 2C	USNR	1942	1946
James	Harold	Kegley	BM2	USNR	1941	1945
John	Paul	Kegley	DCFN	USN	1951	1954
John	Rudolph	Kegley	SN 1C	USN	1946	1947
Lawrence	Edward	Kegley	SP 4	USA	1966	1968
Lovirdia		Kegley	PFC	USA	1943	1945
Marvin	Carol	Kegley	SN 2 C	USNR	1943	1945
Ora	V.	Kegley	CPL	USA	1939	1945
Raymond	H.	Kegley	LCpl	USMC	1981	1985
Thomas	E.	Kegley	PVT	USA	1918	1919
Thomas	Lee	Kegley	BT 1	USN	1977	1986
Chester	Talmadge	Kelley	LCDR	USN	1940	1954
Jack	Austin	Kelley	AviaMchMt C1	USN	1940	1946
Kelly	Freeman	Kellogg	Cpl	USMC	1994	1998
Charles	L.	Kelly	CPL	USA	1918	1919
John	F.	Kelly, Jr.	CPL	USMC	1961	1967
John	Frank	Kelsey	SP 4	USA	1958	1960
John	H.	Kelsey	PVT	KY INF VOL	1898	1899
John	S.	Kelsey	SGT	USAF	1967	1973
Willie	C.	Kelsey	PFC	USA	1944	1945
Frances	A.	Kendall	T 4	USA	1943	1945
Lester	V.	Kendall	PFC	USA	1943	1945
Willie	J.	Kendall	PVT	USA	1918	1918
Larry		Kennard	ETR 2	USNR		1966
Benjamin		Kerenza	S1C	USNR	1944	1946
Ligon	A.	Kesler	1st Lt.	AAF	1943	1945
Claude	Dillon	Kessler	PFC	USMC	1942	1946
Jerry	Lee	Kesterson, Jr.	SPC	USA	1992	1996
Adrian	L.	Kidd	PVT	USA	1943	1945
Alvin		Kidd	Tech. 5	USA	1942	1945
Berk		Kidd	PVT	USA	1918	1919
Clarence		Kidd	PVT	USA	1918	1918
Claude		Kidd	PVT	USA	1943	1943

Della		Kidd	PVT	USA	1942	1943
Earl	L.	Kidd	SSG	USA	1941	1945
Elvis	R.	Kidd	PFC	USA	1946	1947
James	L.	Kidd	SGT	USA	1944	1945
Kenneth	Berlin	Kidd	CPL	USA	1951	1953
Lawrence	M.	Kidd	CPL	USA	1951	1953
Lewra		Kidd	Tech 5	USA	1942	1944
Lois	Ruth	Kidd	Sgt	USAF	1966	1969
Marvin	A.	Kidd	PFC	USA	1952	1953
Ronnie	Michael	Kidd	SGT	USA	1968	1970
Russell	David	Kidd	EN 3	USN	1963	1966
Samuel	D.	Kidd	PFC	USA	1944	1945
Troy	J.	Kidd	Tech. 5	USA	1945	1946
Troy		Kidd	SP 4	USA	1968	1970
Mary	G.C.	Kincer	2nd LT	USA Nur.C	1943	1944
Shade	B.	Kincer	T.SGT	USA	1942	1945
Leo	Daniel	Kinder	Sgt.	USAF	1970	1974
Lloyd	L.	Kinder	PFC	USA	1942	1944
Paul	Eugene	Kinder	SP 3	USA	1954	1956
Gilbert	Leroy	King, Jr.	SP 4	USA	1971	1973
Charles	E.	Kiser	PFC	USA	1944	1946
Earl		Kiser	CPL	USA	1952	1954
Elbert	J.	Kiser	CPL	USA	1942	1945
George		Kiser	PVT	USA	1943	1944
Glenmore		Kiser	PFC	USA	1942	1945
John	W.	Kiser	PFC	USA	1944	1945
Joseph	Wayne	Kiser	SN	USN	1940	1949
Charley	C.	Kissick	PVT	USA	1942	1943
Harold	W	Kissick	SN	USN	1952	1955
William	L.	Kissick	Tech. 4	USA	1939	1945
James	Richard	Kissinger	CPL	USA	1949	1952
Johnie	L.	Kissinger	PVT	USA	1946	1946
Marvin		Kissinger	PVT	USA	1942	1943

Harold	W.	Kitchen	PFC	USA	1943	1946
Larry	Junior	Knipp	PFC	USA	1970	1970
Lawrence		Knipp	SSG	USA	1941	1945
Lewis	Edward	Kornman	Sgt	USMC	1968	1971
Ivan	Dale	Krow	Cpl	USMC	1967	1970
Lorenz		Lacy	PFC	USMCR	1943	1946
Robert	Ashley	Lacy	PVT	USAR	1986	1986
Wendell	Maye	Lacy	PFC	USMC	1952	1954
William	Anderson	Lacy	PVT	USA	1918	1919
Donald	Rudolph	Laferty	MSGT	USAF	1951	1971
Wayne	Martin	Lafferty	SP 4	USA	1966	1968
Allen	L.	Lake	CPL	AAF	1943	1945
Asa	William	Lamberet	CPL	USA	1953	1955
Arvil	G.	Lambert	SPC	USARNG	1965	1966
Benjamin	F.	Lambert	PVT	USA	1942	1944
Cecil	D.	Lambert	PFC	USA	1945	1946
Claude		Lambert	SN 2C	USNR	1945	1945
Glennis		Lambert	SN 1C	USN	1945	1946
Guy	Eddie	Lambert	SN 1C	USN	1942	1945
James	O.	Lambert	PFC	USA	1943	1945
Leo		Lambert	PVT	USA	1945	1945
Ollie	Ray	Lambert	CPL	USA	1952	1953
Ora	V.	Lambert	PVT	USA	1942	1943
Paul	Edward	Lambert	PVT	USA	1961	1964
Russell		Lambert	PFC	USA	1940	1944
Vernon	Raman	Lambert	A2C	USAF	1956	1960
Wardson	Stewart	Lambert	SN 1C	USNR	1943	1946
Warren	M.	Lambert	PVT	USA	1942	1943
Ollie	R.	Lambert, Jr.	PVT	USA	1946	1946
Michael	Wingate	Lambertson	SN	USCG	1973	1977
Asa	E.	Lame	PVT	USA	1942	1945
Jack	Jerome	Landreth	CPL	USA	1948	1952
Charles	O.	Lands	PVT	USA	1943	1947

John	Franklin	Lands	PVT	USA	1973	1973
Clark	Bascom	Lane	YN 3C	USNR	1918	1921
James		Lane	CPL	USA	1917	1919
William	C.	Lane, Jr.	CPL	USA	1942	1946
Robert	G.	Laughlin	CPL	USA	1942	1943
James	Cory	Laughner	SGT	USMC	1988	1996
Edward	M.	Law	PFC	USA	1942	1945
Keneth	Myrtle	Law	PFC	USA	1953	1954
Leslie	P.	Law	Tech. 5	USA	1944	1946
Mark	Dwayne	Law	MMFN	USN	1978	1984
Jackson	A.	Lawson	SGT	AAF	1942	1945
Charles		Layne	Tech. 5	USA	1942	1945
William	T.	Layne	PFC	USA	1942	1945
William	Tandy	Layne	CPL	USA	1953	1959
James	M.	Layne, Jr.	SGT	USA	1946	1947
Cornelius	O.	Leach	PFC	USA	1918	1919
Earl	Clark	Leach	CPL	USA	1949	1952
James	A.	Leach	SGT	USA	1947	1954
Alex	J.	Lemaster		USA	1943	1943
James	Cletus	LeMaster	LTC	ARNGUS	1968	1990
Audria	Clayton	Lewis	SP 4	USA	1959	1962
Burl	R.	Lewis	SGT	USA	1941	1945
Carl		Lewis	SN 2C	USN	1944	1946
Carlos	K.	Lewis	PFC	USA	1943	1947
Charles	O.	Lewis	Tech. 5	USA	1942	1946
Chester	C.	Lewis	Cpl	AAF	1944	1945
Danny	Elwood	Lewis	PVT	USAR	1969	1969
Darius	Dean	Lewis	SP 4	USA	1971	1972
Darrell	K.	Lewis	SP 5	USA	1969	1971
David	Ray	Lewis	SGT	USAF	1965	1969
Donald	R.	Lewis	SP 4	USAR	1971	1977
Dorris	I.	Lewis	CPL	USA	1942	1946
Earl		Lewis	PFC	USA	1942	1945

Earl		Lewis	T-5	USA	1947	1947
Emmet	Henry	Lewis	PFC	USA	1917	1918
Ernest	Earl	Lewis	SN 2C	USN	1944	1944
Jack	N.	Lewis	Tech. 4	USA	1942	1945
James	C.	Lewis	Tech. 5	USA	1944	1945
James	Richard	Lewis	TSgt	USAF	1968	1974
James	Sherman	Lewis	SP 5	USA	1965	1967
James	Vernon	Lewis	TSgt	USAF	1968	1971
Joseph	Dale	Lewis	PVT	USA	1973	1974
Lester	L.	Lewis	Tech. 5	USA	1942	1946
Marion		Lewis	PVT	USA	1918	1918
Mark	A.	Lewis	PFC	USMC		1980

Richard T. Lewis, Pfc., Army, 1917-1919.

Phillip	Randolph	Lewis	SSgt	USMC	1954	1958
Richard	T.	Lewis	PVT	USA		1919
Ronnie	C.	Lewis	SP 5	USA	1960	1965
Sam	L.	Lewis	Tech. 5	USA	1941	1945
Sidney	C.	Lewis	PVT	USA	1945	1945
Vaughn	L.	Lewis	Tech. 5	USA	1944	1945
Vaughn	Newton	Lewis	PVT	USA	1952	1955
Vincent	Elwood	Lewis	Spec.Artificer 3C	USNR	1945	1946
William	R.	Lewis	PFC	USA	1942	1945
William	R.	Lewis	CPL	AAF	1945	1946
Earl		Lewis, Jr.	LCpl	USMC	1969	1971
Clifford	E.	Lewman	CPL	USA	1944	1946
Casual		Linville	Tech. 5	USA	1944	1946
Larry	Darryl	Linville	SP 4	USA	1960	1963
Robert	P.	Lissal	PFC	USAAC	1943	1945
Frank	M.	Little	PVT	USA	1918	1918
Shelby	Luther	Little	SP 4	USA	1967	1969
Arch		Littleton	PVT	USA	1918	1919
Cephas	Tilden	Littleton	SP 4	USA	1959	1960
Garry	Dale	Littleton	SP 4	USA	1971	1973
Kenneth	Royce	Littleton	SP 4	USA	1971	1974
Clyde	M.	Litton	SSG	USA	1942	1946
Donald	E.	Litton	PFC	USA	1961	1962
Samuel	J.	Litton	Cook	USA	1918	1919
Irvin		Livingood	PFC	USA	1917	1919
Ralph		Livingood	Tech. 5	USA	1943	1946
Raz		Lofton	S.SGT	USA	1942	1945
Glen	C.	Logan	PFC	USA	1941	1945
Harlan	Ronnie	Logan	PFC	USA	1960	1963
Herman	Chester	Logan	SN 2C	USNR	1944	1945
Mark	H.	Logan	PVT	USA	1918	1919
Vinson		Long	CPL	USA	1914	1927
Richard	C.	Lovelace	PFC	USA	1942	1945

Bernard	F.	Lovely	SSG	USA	1944	1947
Ronnie	Darrell	Lovely	SP 4	USA	1966	1967
Warren		Lovely, Sr.	PVT	USA	1942	1942
Andy	W.	Lowe	Tech. 5	USA	1945	1946
Atlee		Lowe	MMR 2C	USN	1942	1945
Benjamin	F.	Lowe	SSG	USA	1941	1944
Charles	E.	Lowe	CPL	USA	1940	1945
Earnest		Lowe	PVT	USA	1918	1919
Eldon		Lowe	GM2	USN	1950	1954
Harlan		Lowe	A1C	USAF	1958	1964
Harlan		Lowe	SN 1C	USN		1945
John	E.	Lowe	CPL	USA	1942	1946
John	Edward	Lowe	SN 2C	USNR	1944	1945
Manuel	Elbert	Lowe	2LT	USAR	1976	1978
Marie	Ina	Lowe	SSgt	USAF	1955	1961
Roy	C.	Lowe	PFC	USA	1945	1946
Russell	Ora	Lowe	PFC	USA	1952	1954
Karen	Sue	Luman	SP 4	USA	1974	1977
James	William	Lunsford	SP 3	USA	1954	1956
Avery	W.	Lykins	PVT	USA	1942	1942
Chester	J.	Lykins	Tech. 5	USA	1941	1947
John	W.	Lykins	CPL	USA	1941	1945
Leonard		Lyon	PVT	USA	1918	1919
Ollie	M.	Lyon	PFC	USA	1942	1946
William	Franklin	Lyon	PFC	USA	1952	1954
Clyde	E.	Lyons	PVT	USA	1946	1947
Earl	Leroy	Lyons	CPL	USA	1952	1953
Jeffery	Nelson	Lyons	PFC E-3	USA-ARNG	1996	1996
Jesse	O.	Lyons	Chief Radioman	USNR	1945	1947
Jesse	Obel	Lyons		USN		
Robert	Gordon	Lyons	Cpl	USMC	1951	1953
Carl	Elwood	Lytle	SN 1C	USNR	1943	1946
Clarence	Nicholas	Lytle	SP 4	USA	1957	1959

Chalmer	E.	Mabry	Tech. 5	USA	1945	1946
David	W.	Mabry	PVT	USA	1944	1945
Everett	L.	Mabry	SP 4	USAR	1967	1968
Glenn	Martin	Mabry	SP 5	USA	1965	1967
James	E.	Mabry	PVT	USA	1943	1944
Lawrence	Elmo	Mabry	CPL	USA	1948	1952
Ora	L.	Mabry	PFC	USA	1944	1946
William		Mabry	Tech. 4	USA	1942	1945
William	James	Mack	Chf. Spec. (A)(T)	USN	1942	1963
James	Ralph	Madden	Cpl	USMC	1951	1953
Rufus	Earl	Madden	PFC	USA	1954	1956
Acle		Maddox	PVT	USAR	1914	1920
George		Maddox	PVT	USA	1918	1919
Paul	Franklin	Maddox	SN 1C	USNR	1944	1945
Alton	Hodge	Malone	SP 4	USA	1956	1959
John	William	Manley	PFC	USMCR	1943	1945
Grace	F.	Mann	Auxiliary	USA AuxCr	1942	1943
Joseph	Spencer	Mann	SGT	USAF	1966	1970
Earnest	C.	Manning	Tech. 5	USA	1945	1946
Lowell	D.	Manning	S.SGT	USAR	1961	1967
Bert	Robert	Markwell	SN 1C	USN		1945
Carl		Markwell	Tech. 5	USA	1941	1945
Deloris		Markwell	PVT	USA	1947	1951
Harold		Markwell	CPL	USA	1953	1955
James	Rhondell	Markwell	SP 4	USA	1976	1979
Burley		Markwell, Jr.	PVT	USA	1948	1953
Michael	Steven	Marriner	CPL	USA	1990	1992
Dof		Marshall	PFC	USA	1943	1946
James	E.	Marshall	SGT	USA	1945	1946
Elmer	Estell	Mart	PFC	USMC	1944	1946
Alvin	E.	Martin	SGT	USA	1945	1946
Andrew	Jackson	Martin	SP 5	USA	1961	1964
Chris		Martin	SN 1C	USN	1944	1946

Eugene		Martin	SSG	USA	1942	1951
George	C.	Martin	SGT	USA	1943	1945
Johnson	L.	Martin	PFC	USA	1917	1919
Lee	C.	Martin	SGT	AAF	1942	1945
Merle		Martin	SKC	USN	1940	1946
Michael	Scott	Martin	SGT	USAF	1968	1971
Olan		Martin	SN 1C	USN	1942	1946
Ronald	Barry	Martin	SGT	USA	1959	1962
Steve	Arnold	Martin	SP 4	USA	1972	1974
Alvin	E.	Martin, Jr.	PVT	USA	1945	1945
Robert	Carey	Martin, Jr.	MT 1	USN	1978	1985
Sam	McKinley	Martin, Jr.	SN 2C	USN		1945
Earl	W.	Martindale	PharmMt. 1C	USN	1942	1945
Edward	T.	Martt	PVT	USA	1941	1945
Joseph		Martt	PVT	USA	1898	1899
Stanley	Earl	Martt	SP 2	USA	1953	1956
Victoria	M.	Martt	Tech 5	WAC	1945	1946
John	W.	Masters	PFC	USA	1945	1946
Marion		Masters	PVT	USA	1917	1919
Mervin	A.	Masters	Tech. 4	USA	1942	1945
Edgar	S.	Mauk	CPL	USAAC	1941	1945
Joe	J.	Mauk	CarpenterMt. 2C	USN	1945	1945
Reason	G.	Mauk	PVT	USA	1918	1918
Frank	R.	Maxey	CPL	USA	1917	1919
John	O.	Maxey	CPL	USA	1949	1951
Richard		Maxey	PFC	USA	1946	1948
Arlie	Sherman	May	SP 4	USA	1960	1962
Forest	L.	May	PVT	USA	1947	1948
Hershal	B.	May	PFC	USA	1941	1944
Morton	C.	May	SFC	USA	1910	1919
Vernon		May	CPL	USA	1953	1955
Warren	W.	May	SN 1C	USN	1942	1945
Thomas	Lansford	May, Jr.	ICCS (SW)	USN	1987	1993

Charles	H.	Mayhall	Tech. 5	USA	1944	1946
Charles	M.	Mayhall	CPL	USAR	1950	1951
Creston	C.	Mayhall	1LT	USA	1918	1919
Creston	C.	Mayhall, Jr.	SSG	USA	1943	1946
William	Robert	Maynard	PVT	USA	1975	1977
Claude	H.	Mays	PVT	USA	1945	1945
Clyde		Mays	PVT	USA	1943	1945
Millard		Mays	PVT	USA	1918	1918
Roma	W.	Mays	Tech. 4	USA	1944	1946
Donald	J.	McBrayer	SP 4	USAR		1968
Herbert	J.	McBrayer	Cpl	AAF	1942	1946
Homer	W.	McBrayer	SSG	USA	1943	1945
James	E.	McBrayer	SGT	AAF	1944	1945
Paul	V.	McBrayer	PVT	USA	1943	1945
William	H.	McBrayer	PFC	USA	1942	1945

J. Earl McBrayer, Sgt., Army Air Corps, 1944-45.

Jack	Carrington	McCarty	PFC	USMC	1945	1946
Winifred	Vaughn	McCarty	EM3	USNR	1943	1946
Lewis		McClain	PVT	USA	1942	1943
Medford		McClain	CPL	USA	1941	1944
William	L.	McClain	SGT	USA	1943	1947
Murvel	Eugene	McClure	SN 2C	USN	1942	1946
Arthur	J.	McClurg	PFC	USA	1943	1945
Forest	Glenn	McClurg	CPL	USA	1951	1955
James	Wilbur	McClurg	PVT	USA	1957	1957
Joseph	F.	McClurg	PVT	USA	1945	1945
Monroe	Winston	McClurg	CPL	USA	1952	1954
Ralph	F.	McClurg	PVT	USA	1944	1944
Rollie	W.	McClurg	PFC	USA	1942	1945
Roy		McClurg	PVT	USA	1917	1919
Jame	William	McCoy	SPC	USA	1989	1993
Emil	C.	McDaniel	Tech. 3	USA	1945	1947
Gerald	Marlin	McDaniel	SGM	USA	1949	1974
Hezia	Allen	McDaniel	MR 3	USN	1951	1956
Hubert	F.	McDonald	PVT	USA	1917	1919
Carl	Arthur	McDowell	PFC	USMC	1943	1945
Margaret	Anne	McDuffie	CPT	USAF	1988	1991
George	W.	McEldowey	PVT	USA	1917	1919
Ezra	C.	McFarland	CPL	USA	1942	1945
Raymond	P.	McGarey	T-5	USA	1942	1945
Alvin		McGary	Lt.Col.	USAF	1941	1961
Dan		McGill	PFC	USA	1917	1919
Oscar		McGlothin	PVT	USA	1939	1941
William	D.	McGlothin	PFC	AAF	1942	1946
Leon		McGlothlin	CPL	USA	1946	1950
Gale	Hayword	McGuire	PFC	USA	1951	1953
Charles	E.	McIntosh	SP 5	USA	1967	1970
Acy	C.	McKenzie	PFC	USA	1942	1945
Charles	F.	McKenzie	PFC	AAF	1943	1945

Guy McKenzie, S/1, Navy, 1943-1946.

Coleman	A.	McKenzie	CPL	USAAC	1941	1945
Earl	Roger	McKenzie	PFC	USMC	1956	1958
Eugene		McKenzie	PFC	USA	1943	1945
Fant		McKenzie	PFC	USA	1942	1945
Gary	Dean	McKenzie	SP5	USA	1966	1978
Guy	Snyder	McKenzie	SN 1C	USNR	1943	1946
Haskell	B.	McKenzie	PFC	USA	1945	1946
James	Gary	McKenzie	SP 3	USA	1953	1955
Lester	C.	McKenzie	PFC	USA	1943	1946
Paul	E.	McKenzie	Tech. 5	USA	1944	1946
Robert	S.	McKenzie	PFC	USA	1943	1946
William	Andrew	McKenzie	MSgt	USAF	1942	1963
Charles	Elbert	McKinney	A2C	USAF	1949	1953
Conrad	P.	McKinney	SN 2C	USN		1945
Danny	Joe	McKinney	SP 4	USA	1970	1971
Edison	Lee	McKinney	PVT	USA	1952	1953
Joseph	L.	McKinney	PVT	USA	1943	1943
Wilbour	Dixon	McKinney	Cpl	USMC	1943	1946

Sylvan		McKinney, Jr.	MotorMchMt. 3C	USN	1943	1946
Krista	Leigh	McManus	PFC	USAR	1999	2000
Shelt		McQuinn	PVT	AAF	1943	1945
Everett	L.	McRoberts	PVT	USA	1943	1944
Larry	Earl	McRoberts	SP 4	USA	1973	1977
Ora		McRoberts	PVT	USA	1918	1918
Randy	Wayne	McVet	QMSA	USN	1973	1975
James	B.	McVey	PVT	USA	1942	1943
Randy	Wayne	McVey	QMSA	USNR	1973	1975
Charles	Edward	Meade	SPC 4	USA	1989	1992
Claude	Edward	Meade	CSM	USA	1961	1991
Claude	Wesley	Meade	SPC	USA	1990	1994
Herbert		Meade	CPL	USA	1951	1953
William	M.	Meade	PVT	USA	1917	1918
Robert	Eugene	Meadows	1LT	USA	1955	1957
Hughes		Medaris	PFC	USA	1943	1945
Carlos	Anthony	Meredith	MM1	USN	1974	1980
Carl		Messer	SGT	USA	1942	1945
Jack		Messer	PFC	AAF	1944	1946
James	L.	Messer	CPL	USA	1951	1953
James	Madison	Messer	Coxswain SV	USN	1944	1946
John	B.	Messer	PVT	USA	1918	1919
John	Paul	Messer	Radio Man 1C	USNR		1945
Joseph		Messer	Tech. SGT	USA	1944	1945
Oval	F.	Messer	PVT	USA	1940	1945
Thomas	P.	Messer	PVT	USA	1942	1942
William	H.	Messer	PFC	USA	1943	1946
Ivan	F.	Middleton	SGT	USA	1945	1947
James	Delmo	Middleton	SP 4	USA	1967	1969
Jeffery	Lee	Middleton	HM 3	USN	1973	1976
Troy	Thomas	Middleton	PFC	USA	1954	1956
Guy	S.	Miles	1 LT	USA	1942	1946
Malcom	Tracy	Miles	ETN2	USN	1970	1976

Charles	T.	Miller	PFC	USA	1942	1945
Fred	C.	Miller	CPL	USA	1943	1946
Harold	Frank	Miller	Elec. Mt. 1C	USN	1942	1948
Herbert	Alfred	Miller	PFC	USMC	1944	1946
Leo	Martin	Miller	Elec.Mt. C3	USN	1942	1945
Marcus	J.	Miller	Tech. 3	USA	1944	1946
Vernon	Leo	Miller	PFC	USMC	1944	1946
Walter	Joseph	Miller	Ship's Cook 3C	USN	1943	1945
William	J.	Miller	PFC	USA	1918	1919
Stephen	Douglas	Mills	PVT	USA	1979	1981
Susan	Lynn	Mills	SGT	USA	1979	1986
James		Mit	SGT	USA	1943	1945
James	W.	Mitchell	PVT	USA	1946	1947
Thomas	C.	Mobley	PVT	AAF	1945	1946
Thomas	Clark	Mobley	SN 2C	USNR	1946	1946
Harve	W.	Mobley, Jr.	PFC	USA	1946	1948
Edward		Mocabee	Tech. 4	USA	1942	1946
Max	Edgar	Molihan	SSgt	USMC	1957	1970
George	Harry	Molton	RCT	USA	1958	1960
Alan	Thomas	Mong	LCDR	USNR	1990	1994
Odus		Montgomery	TSgt	AAF	1941	1945
Allie	Ray	Moore	SN 1C	USNR	1945	1946
Bobby	Carrol	Moore	SP 5	USA	1957	1966
Charles	Raymond	Moore	SP 4	USA	1970	1971
Clyde	Powell	Moore	Radioman 2C	USNR	1943	1946
Earl		Moore	Tech. 5	USA	1943	1946
Granville		Moore	CPL	USA	1952	1954
James	Ray	Moore		USN	1955	1959
James	Ray	Moore	CW 3	USA	1968	1988
Luther	S.V.	Moore	PFC	USA	1942	1945
Robert	Bobby	Moore	SP 4	USA	1958	1961
William	Wade	Moore	PFC	USA	1942	1943
Willis		Moore	SGT	USA	1942	1945

Hurshal		Moore, Jr.	PFC	USA	1950	1952
Thomas	Leland	Moore, Jr.	SP 5	USA	1967	1970
John	Joseph	Morehouse	SPC	USA	1991	1993
Martin	L.	Morehouse	PVT	USA	1942	1944
David	Brian	Morris	SPC	USA	1986	1989
Fenton	L.	Morris, Jr.	CPL	USA	1944	1946
Claude	E.	Morrison	SSG	USA	1941	1945
David	Lee	Morrison	CPL	USA	1950	1952
Gary	Richard	Morrison	SGT	USA	1983	1989
Paul	Joseph	Mulcahy, Jr.	MSG	USA	1953	1979
Billy		Mullen	SGT	USA	1947	1949
Lonnie	M.	Mullen	CPL	USA	1951	1953
Bennett	E.	Mullins	Tech. 5	USA	1940	1945
Donald	Richard	Murphy	PVT	USA	1960	1961
Kelia	Ann	Murphy	1LT	USA	1967	1969
Lowell	V.	Murray	PVT	USA	1951	1952
Lowell	Vernon	Murray	CPL	USA	1951	1952
Timothy	Gene	Musgrove	HM 3	USN	1980	1984
Charles	E.	Mutters	SGT	USA	1942	1945
Robert		Mutters	1SG	USA		1935
Monte	B.	Mutters, Jr.	PVT	USA	1942	1945
William	H.	Myers	PVT	USA	1898	1898
Clarence		Myers, Jr.	Painter 1C	USNR	1942	1946
Cecil	R.	Mynhier	PFC	USAAC	1943	1946
Harold	E.	Mynhier	PFC	USAR	1953	1961
Levi	J.	Mynhier	PVT	USA	1943	1943
Meredith	H.	Mynhier	Col	USAF	1944	1980
Roy	V.	Mynhier	CPL	USA	1941	1946
Olen		Nantz	SFC	USA	1950	1972
Robert	Tyler	Needham	PVT	USA	1971	1971
Don		Nesbitt	CPL	USA	1943	1951
Joe		Nesbitt	CPL	USA	1940	1945
Ernest		Netherly	PVT	USA	1941	1945

Fred		Netherly	PFC	USA	1945	1945
Rickie	Lee	Netherly	SGT	USA	1968	1970
Roy		Netherly	PVT	USA	1927	1933
Roy		Netherly	PFC	USA	1942	1943
Roy		Netherly	Baker 1C	USNR	1943	1945
Samuel	Vernal	Netherly	PVT	USA	1950	1952
Howard	Eugene	Newell	PFC	USA	1952	1954
Jerry	Layne	Newman	CW-3	ARNGUS	1982	1998
Joseph		Nice	PVT	USA	1917	1918
David	Allen	Nickell	AB	USAF	1964	1966
George	Russell	Nickell	PFC	USA	1966	1968
Grover	L.	Nickell	PFC	USA	1944	1946
James	David	Nickell	SP 4	USA	1969	1972
Robert	Jackson	Nickell	Cf. Mach. Mt.	USN	1939	1945
Walter	R.	Nickell	PVT	USA	1918	1919
William	A.	Nickell	CPL	USA	1940	1946
Kenneth		Nickells	PVT	USA	1942	1945
Cooksey		Noranelle	1st Lt.	USA	1942	1946
Ted	Harper	Ockerman	PFC	USA	1949	1952
Merilee	Suzanne	Olson	PFC	USA	1979	1980
Earl	Edward	Oney	SN 1C	USNR	1945	1946
Earnest		Oney	PFC	USA	1944	1946
Eugene	R.	Oney	CPL	USA	1939	1945
Phillip	Charles	Oney	EM3	USN	1976	1980
Leo	D.	Oppenheimer, Jr.	Tech. 3	USA	1942	1946
Kenneth	Martin	Orciere	Elec. 1C	USNR	1950	1951
James	Wesley	Osborne	SP 4	USA	1981	1985
Ruth	B.	Osborne	SP 4	USA	1982	1985
Gee		Oscar	PFC	USA	1942	1945
Jessie	Carl	Ouderkirk	PFC	USA	1954	1958
John	Lindsey	Owen	PFC	ARNG Ky.	1986	1987
Billy	Ray	Owens	CPL	USMC	1952	1954
Frank		Owens	Tech. 5	USA	1943	1946

Jesse		Owens	Fireman 2C	USNR	1944	1946
Victor	G.	Owens	PFC	USA	1945	1946
Walter		Owens	Shipfitter 3C	USNR	1944	1945
William	C.	Padgett	PFC	USA	1941	1945
Allie	H.	Parker	CPL	USA	1918	1919
Denver	G.	Parker	PFC	USA	1941	1945
Elmer	Elwood	Parker	SN 2C	USN	1944	1946
Jack		Parker	Tech. 4	USA	1944	1946
Jimmy	Dean	Parker	SPC 4	USA	1994	1998
Lonnie	Steven	Parker	SP 4	USA	1966	1968
Richard	Allen	Parker	SSG	USA	1957	1977
Willie	Elmer	Parker	CarpenterMt. 1C	USNR	1943	1945
Herman		Parson	CPL	USA	1942	1946
Kenneth	Lee	Parsons	PVT	USA	1953	1954
Franklin	Delano Rossevelt	Patrick	PVT	USA	1954	1956
Kenneth	C.	Patrick	PFC	AAF	1942	1946
Albert		Patton	Tech. 5	USA	1944	1946
Hank		Patton	CPT	USA	1985	1996
William	Ashley	Payne	SP 4	USA	1983	1985
Alfred	M.	Peed	Tech. 4	USA	1944	1946
Billy	J.	Peed	PFC	USA	1943	1946
George	W.	Pelfrey	SN 1C	USN		1945
Lloyd	H.	Pelfrey	SSG	USA	1942	1945
Robert	M.	Pelfrey	CPL	USA	1951	1956
Samuel		Pence	BoatswnMt. 1C	USN	1940	1946
Elizabeth	Ann	Penix	PharmMt.3C	USCG		1945
Coy	Ronald	Pennington	SP 4	USA	1964	1967
Gary	Michael	Pennington	SP 5	USA	1967	1968
Glenn	N.	Pennington	SP 4	USAR		1965
Harvey	T.	Pennington	SP 4	USAR		1975
Harvey	Thomas	Pennington	SP 4	USA	1969	1971
Hubert	Wilson	Pennington	Cpl	USMCR	1944	1946
Ishmel	R.	Pennington	Tech. 5	USA	1944	1946

Phillip		Pennington	PVT	USAAF	1946	1947
Vanzel	Nelson	Pennington	SGT	USA	1952	1955
Vasel		Pennington	PVT	USA	1942	1942
Wendell		Pennington	SP 5	USA	1969	1972
Wilford		Pennington	SP 4	USA	1963	1965
William	C.	Pennington	Tech. 5	USA	1943	1945
Lowell		Pennington, Jr.	LCpl	USMC	1970	1972
Lionel		Perdue, Jr.	SFC	USA	1947	1969
Clayton	M.	Perkins	CPL	USA	1946	1949
Cleo	V.	Perkins	Tech. 5	USA	1943	1946
James	R.	Perkins	PFC	USA	1944	1946
Jerry	L.	Perkins	SP 5	USA	1972	1973
Jesse	Charles	Perkins	TSgt	USAF	1961	1975
Millard		Perkins	PFC	USA	1942	1945
Robert	Lee	Perkins	SPC 5	USA	1956	1962
William	C.	Perkins	PFC	USA	1943	1946
William	M.	Perkins	CPL	USA	1941	1945
Frank	L.	Pernell	PFC	USA	1942	1945
Jeff	D.	Pernell	PVT	USA	1942	1945
Arnold	O.	Perry	PFC	USA	1943	1946
Calvin	Clay	Perry	SN 2C	USNR	1943	1946
Calvin	E.	Perry	PVT	USA	1945	1947
Charlie	E.	Perry	PVT	USA	1942	1943
Edward	L.	Perry	PFC	USA	1943	1945
Eugene	L.	Perry	PVT	USA	1942	1944
Howard	J.	Perry	PFC	USA	1943	1945
Jackie	Lee	Perry	A03	USN	1957	1961
Marvin	Powers	Perry	Coxswain	USNR	1943	1945
Monta	Woodford	Perry	SN 1C	USN		1945
Ollen	B.	Perry	CPL	AAF	1942	1945
Ollie		Perry	PVT	USA	1918	1919
Orvil	C.	Perry	PVT	USA	1943	1944
Thomas	A.	Perry	PVT	USA	1943	1944

Clayton Perkins, T/5, Army, 1946-49.

Howard	G.	Peters	T.SGT	USA	1948	1952
Wayne	P.	Pettie	SP 4	USAR		1963
Gary	Lee	Pettit	SP 4	USA	1971	1972
Harrison		Pettit	PVT	USA	1944	1945
Ewing		Pettitt	SN	USN	1956	1945
Leonard		Pettitt	A2C	USAF	1952	1956
James	Junior	Phillips	Avia.Ordman 3C	USN	1942	1946
Richard	Allen	Phillips	SGT	USA	1986	1991
Toney	C.	Phillips	1LT	USA	1944	1945
Curtis		Phipps	YN 2C	USNR	1942	1943
Lester	K.	Phipps	PVT	USA	1942	1944
Leo		Pictor	MSGT	USA	1930	1950
Homer	Otis	Pittit	CS2	USN	1941	1945
Arthur		Plack	PVT	USA	1942	1945
Elma		Plank	Tech. 4	USA	1942	1945
Farell	Lynn	Plank	SP 4	USA	1977	1980
Gary	Lee	Plank	SP 4	USA	1969	1971

Homer	Lee	Plank	A/TC	USAF	1949	1953
J.	D.	Plank	A1C	USAF	1952	1956
Jackie	Keith	Plank	SGT	USA	1969	1971
Ralph	H.	Plank	CPL	USA	1943	1945
Raymond		Plank	PVT	AAF	1942	1946
Robert		Plank	PFC	USA	1944	1946
William	G.	Plank	PVT	USA	1943	1946
Donald	Lee	Plunkett	SP 3	USA	1956	1958
Charles	Christopher	Poarch	SPC 4	USA	1985	1989
Charles	Deward	Porter	CPL	USA	1950	1952
Daniel	Louis	Porter	SGT	USA	1983	1984
Eugene	T.	Porter	PFC	USA	1942	1945
James	R.	Porter	AMR 3	USN	1960	1964
Jim	W.	Porter	PFC	USA		1946
Kenneth	R.	Porter	PFC	USA	1944	1946
Kenneth	Ronald	Porter	SSgt	USAF	1968	1962
Larry	Wilson	Porter	SGT	USA	1966	1969
Lloyd		Porter	PFC	USA	1944	1946
Rodney	R. B.	Porter	PVT	USA	1943	1943
Roy	W.	Porter	PVT	USA	1942	1943
Ruth	Christine	Porter	CPL	WAC	1950	1953
Wayne	T.	Porter	PFC	USA	1943	1949
Wickliff	H.	Porter	SP 4	USA	1957	1962
William	Roy	Porter	CPT	USA	1967	1970
Herman		Posten	PVT	USA	1914	1920
Bernie		Poston	PVT	USA	1917	1918
Donald	Claud Lou	Poston	SN	USN	1950	1953
Glenn	Buren	Poston	PharmMt.3C	USNR	1943	1946
James	Eugene	Poston	SOG	USN	1960	1964
Lunda		Potter	SSGT	USA	1940	1945
Donald	G.	Powell	RCT	USA	1960	1960
James	H.	Powell	T-4	USA	1942	1945
George	T.	Powers	T.SGT	USA	1944	1946

Douglas	Jim	Prather	MSgt	USAF	1971	1991
Grover	C.	Prather	SSG	USA	1941	1945
Perry	M.	Prather	PVT	USA	1917	1919
Perry		Prather	SP 4	USA	1973	1974
Rebecca	Lynn	Prather	SPC	USA	1991	1991
Wess		Prather	Fireman 3C	USNR	1918	1921
Benjamin	Thomas	Prewitt, Jr.	GM 3	USNR	1942	1945
Edgar	Poe	Price	A1C	USAF	1951	1955
Johnny	Carl	Price	SP 5	USA	1970	1972
William	L.	Price	PVT	USA	1942	1943
Roy	R.	Prince	PVT	USA	1944	1946
Thomas	Wilburn	Prince	CPL	USA	1952	1953
Charles	B.	Proctor	PVT	USA	1918	1919
Carl	Albert	Prust, Jr.	SGT	USA	1979	1984
James	H.	Puckett	CPL	USA	1945	1948
Clifford	Ray	Purvis	SMSgt	UAAF	1955	1982
Gilbie	A.	Purvis	PFC	USA	1942	1945
Hobart		Purvis	PFC	USA	1917	1919
Marvin	Elwood	Purvis	SN	USN	1952	1956
Milburn	O.	Purvis	PFC	USMC	1952	1954
Willard	Herman	Purvis	SSgt	USMC	1952	1962
Marvin	Bryan		PVT	USA	1996	2000
Lee		Quesenberry	PVT	USA	1918	1919
David	Edward	Quesinberry	SP 4	USA	1960	1962
Elgie		Quesinberry	Tech. 5	USA	1944	1946
Millard		Quesinberry	PFC	USA	1941	1945
John	W.	Quesinberry, Jr.	CPL	USAF	1949	1959
Frederick	L.	Quinton	AB	USAF	1956	1960
Earl		Quisenberry	SGT	USA	1945	1951
Oscar		Quisenberry	SGT	USA	1941	1945
Clifford	Christian	Quisgard	SFC	USA	1953	1974
Clifford	R.	Radar	SGT	USA	1942	1945
Bridget		Ramey	PFC	USA	1943	1945

Ernest	Delbert	Ramey	PFC	USA	1954	1956
Gilbert	Neal	Ramey	SP 5	USA	1966	1972
Glenn	Robinson	Ramey	MM 1	USN	1978	1984
Hobert	L.	Ramey	PFC	USA	1941	1945
Jeff		Ramey	PVT	USA	1918	1919
Kenneth	P.	Ramey	PFC	USA	1959	1961
Larry	L.	Ramey	PVT	USA	1942	1945
Sardil	L.	Ramey	PVT	USA	1942	1943
Taylor		Ramey	PVT	USA	1918	1919
Jose	Luis	Ramos	SP 4	USA	1969	1970
Clyde		Ramsey	PFC	USA	1943	1946
Everett		Randal	PVT	USA	1917	1919
William	H.T.	Ratliff	PFC	USA	1943	1945
Frazer	Allen	Ravenscraft	Coxswain	USN	1942	1945
Charles	C.	Rayburn	CPT	USA	1942	1946
Adrian	M.	Razor	Tech 3	USA	1942	1945

Frazier A. "Bud" Ravenscraft, Petty Of. (3rd), Navy, 1942-45.

Allie	E.	Razor	Tech. 5	USA	1943	1946
Ewell	C.	Razor	T 5	USA	1943	1946
John	Michael	Reed	SP 4	USA	1971	1973
Raymond	Samuel	Reed	A1C	USAF	1971	1974
George	B.	Reeder	Tech. 4	USA	1942	1945
Harold	E.	Reeder	PFC	USA	1943	1946
John	P.	Reeder	Tech. 5	USA	1943	1946
Lewis	W.	Reeder	PFC	USA	1917	1919
Mitchell	Guy	Reeder	PFC	USA	1972	1972
Vernon	Dewey	Reeder	T.SGT	USMC	1942	1945
Charles	W.	Reeves	PFC	USA	1945	1946
Bennie	Junor	Reffett	PFC	USA	1951	1953
Ernest	F.	Reynolds	CPL	USA	1943	1946
Ivan	Lee	Reynolds	SSgt	USAF	1952	1956
James	R.	Reynolds	CPL	AAF	1943	1946
John	H.	Reynolds	CPL	USA	1917	1919
Paul	J.	Reynolds	1st Lt.	AAF	1942	1945
Paul		Reynolds	SGT	USA	1941	1945
Samuel	Edwards	Reynolds	LT	USN	1944	1953
Sealey	Edward	Reynolds	CPL	USA	1953	1955
Virgil	Louis	Reynolds	MachMt C3	USN	1948	1952
Ray		Reynolds, Jr.	PFC	USA	1946	1947
Ross	Christopher	Rhodes	CPL	USMC	1996	2000
John	Witzal	Rice	Coxswain	USNR	1943	1946
Joseph	B.	Rice	PFC	USA	1946	1947
Joseph		Rice	PVT	USA	1917	1918
Lucien	Harvey	Rice	SP 5	USA	1956	1959
Michael	Wade	Rice	SP 4	USA	1969	1971
Ward		Rice	PVT	USA	1944	1944
Wayburn	Joseph	Rice	SN 1C	USN	1943	1946
Burrell		Richardson	PVT	USA	1918	1919
Clayton		Richardson	PFC	USA	1946	1948
Clifford	Carl	Richardson	PFC	USA	1952	1960

Lucien H. Rice, Sp. 5, Army, 1956-59.

Glen		Richardson	PFC	USA	1949	1953
Leonard	E.	Richardson	Tech. 5	USA	1944	1946
Vernard	Arvil	Richardson	PVT	USMCR	1943	1943
William	L.	Richardson	PFC	USA	1945	1946
Clester	E.	Riddle	T.SGT	USA	1940	1945
Earnest		Riddle	Fireman 2C	USNR	1945	1945
Elam	Glenwood	Riddle	SN 2C	USNR	1943	1946
Ernest	Karl	Riddle	SP 4	USA	1966	1968
John	Ray	Riddle	SP 4	USA	1981	1985
Charlie	I.	Riggs	CPL	USA	1951	1953
Harry	F.	Riggs	SGT	USAAC	1942	1946
Ronnie	William	Riggs	SP 5	USA	1974	1978
James		Riggsby	PFC	USA	1918	1919
Talmadge	C.	Riggsby	SP 7	USA	1958	1970
Vernon	R.	Riggsby	SGT	USA	1959	1964
Jessie`	C.	Rigsby	PVT	USA	1942	1945

Boyd	William	Riley	PVT	USA	1951	1952
Donald	S.	Riley	PFC	USA	1943	1946
Homer	E.	Riley	PVT	USAAC	1942	1946
John	Joseph	Riley	TSgt	USAF	1966	1970
William	Joseph	Riley	SP 3	USA	1954	1956
Donnie	L.	Rivers	PFC	USA		1969
Forest	Edgar	Rivers	PFC	USA	1951	1953
Allie	D.	Roberts	PFC	USA	1942	1945
Elbert	E.	Roberts	PFC	USA	1942	1946
Emmett		Roberts	PVT	USA	1917	1919
Garry	Ray	Roberts	PFC	USAR	1961	1962
Harlan	E.	Roberts	PVT	USA	1941	1945
Jack		Roberts	Tech. 4	USA	1943	1945
Morton	H.	Roberts	PVT	USA	1918	1919
Norman	N.	Roberts	SGT	USA	1942	1946
Ollie	K.	Roberts	SA	USNR		1945
Paul	Garred	Roberts	LCpl	USMC	1982	1985
Pinkard		Roberts	PVT	USA	1918	1919
Quentin		Roberts	SN 1C	USNR	1944	1946
Ralph		Roberts	Sgt	USAF	1945	1948
Ray		Roberts	SSgt	AAF	1943	1945
Willie	C.	Roberts	CPL	USA	1945	1946
Charles	Clifton	Robinson	Sgt	USAF	1967	1971
Joe		Robinson	PFC	USA	1941	1946
John	Edward	Robinson	Coxswain	USNR	1943	1946
Kenneth		Robinson	Tech. 5	USA	1942	1945
Kevin	Ray	Robinson	SGT	USR	1997	2001
Rexford		Robinson	SSG	USA	1942	1946
James	Dewitt	Robinson, Jr.	TSgt	USAF	1976	1996
Kenneth	Douglas	Robinson, Jr.	SPC 4	USA	1989	1992
Edgar	Lee	Roe	CPL	USA	1952	1954
Enoch		Roe	PVT	USA	1946	1947
Gary	Edward	Roe	SPC 4	USA	1983	1991

Luther	A.	Rogers	Tech. 5	USA	1942	1946
William	W.	Rogers	PFC	USA	1941	1945
William	T.	Romans	PFC	USA	1942	1945
Charlie	D.	Rose	PVT	USA	1942	1945
Harold	Seitz	Rose	SGT	USMC	1950	1956
James	Brady Clifford	Rose	SN 1C	USNR	1944	1946
James	B.	Rose	PVT	USA	1917	1927
William	R.	Rouse	PFC	USA	1942	1945
Grover	Cleveland	Row	SSgt	USAF	1950	1953
Christopher	Ryan	Rowley	PV1	USA	1991	1991
Donald	Buryl	Royce	AB	USAF	1953	1958
George	E.	Royce	T.SGT	USA	1941	1946
Raymond	Eugene	Royce	SGM	USA	1939	1970
Ronald	E.	Royce	SGT	USAF	1971	1974
Acy		Royse	PFC	USA	1917	1919
Allie	Winford	Royse	SGT	USA	1952	1954

Roger D. Russell, E-4, Army, 1971-1973.

Denney	Everett	Royse	CPL	USA	1953	1955
Donald	Burchase	Royse	SSG	USA	1965	1968
James	Arthur	Royse	SN 1C	USN	1944	1945
Lisa	Carole	Royse	PVT	USA	1980	1981
Oval	E.	Royse	PFC	USA	1942	1945
Zora	F.	Royse	Tech. 5	USA	1942	1945
Robert	Ray	Russell	FR	USN	1972	1973
Roger	Dale	Russell	SP 4	USA	1971	1973
Walden	L.	Sagraves	Tech. 5	USA	1945	1946
Anthony	V.	Salvato	2nd Lt.	AAF	1943	1945
John	C.	Salyers	PFC	USA	1942	1945
Laverne	Newton	Sargent	AB 2	USN	1951	1955
Paul		Sargent	CPL	USA	1942	1946
Grover	G.	Saunders	Tech. 4	USA	1942	1946
James	C.	Saunders	PFC	USA	1943	1945
Hubert	E.	Saylor	PFC	USA	1940	1945
Bernard		Scaggs	PFC	USA	1944	1945
Charlie		Scaggs	SSG	USA	1941	1945
Markham	Bernt	Schack	SGT	USAF	1961	1968
Andrew	Christopher	Schenck	IS 3	USN	1986	1989
James	Leon	Scott	Cpl	USMC	1956	1961
Frankie		Seagraves	PFC	USA	1940	1945
Adrian		Sergent	AN	USN	1952	1958
Elmon		Sesco, Jr.	Coxswain	USNR	1944	1946
David	Lee	Setser	Maj.	USAF	1986	2000
Howard	Lee	Setser	PFC	USA	1958	1960
Estell		Sexton	PVT	USA	1942	1943
Ray	T.	Sexton	PFC	USA	1942	1945
Winefred	Eugene	Sexton	SN	USN	1943	1945
Howard	Kincaid	Shackelford	SP 5	USA	1960	1962
Phillip	David	Sharp	SPC	USA	1998	2001
Michael	Terry	Shay	SP 4	USA	1963	1966
Thomas	Sherwood	Shay	PFC	USMC	1954	1957

Edwin	C.	Shelton	PVC	USA	1943	1945
Jesse	H.	Shelton	SGT	USA	1942	1945
Ralph	Edward	Shoaf	MAJ	USA	1979	1996
John	Robert	Shotwell	SP 5	USA	1967	1970
Howell	D.	Shouse	PVT	USA	1943	1943
Edward	Robert	Sies	PFC	USMC	1954	1957
Terry	Lynn	Silcox	PVT	USA	1974	1976
James		Simmons	SFC	USA	1977	1983
Michael	S.	Sims	SP4	USA	1973	1976
Carl	R.	Sizemore	SGT	USA	1961	1967
Arthur	Dallas	Skaggs	SP 4	USA	1969	1971
Carl		Skaggs	PVT	USA	1943	1944
Clayton	Zerl	Skaggs	CPL	USA	1951	1953
Earl	J.	Skaggs	PVT	USA	1943	1943
Harlin		Skaggs	PVT	USA	1909	1912
Ira		Skaggs	PFC	USA	1942	1943
Jewell	Juanita	Skaggs	PN 3	USN	1962	1966
Larry	Don	Skaggs	SP 4	USA	1977	1980
Orville		Skaggs	PFC	USA	1942	1945
Sanford		Skaggs	PFC	USA	1918	1919
Volney	L.	Skaggs	Tech. 4	USA	1936	1945
William	Humphrey	Skaggs	SGT	USA	1952	1954
Frederick	Brian	Skaggs	PFC	USA	1966	1966
Elden	Stirl	Skeens	CPL	USA	1948	1951
Owen		Skeens	Tech. 4	USA	1943	1945
Billy	E.	Sloan	CPL	USAR		1961
Billy	R.	Sloan	CPL	USA	1953	1955
George		Sloan	PVT	USA	1942	1944
John		Sloan	PFC	USAAF	1942	1945
Milton		Sloan	PFC	USA	1941	1945
Robert		Sloan	Radioman 3C	USNR	1943	1946
William	B.	Sloan, Jr.	Tech. 4	USA	1943	1946
Curtis		Slone	SP 3	USA	1954	1957

Henry		Slone	PVT	USA	1917	1919
John	Henry	Slone	Tech.3	USN		1945
Lurvile	J.	Slone	SN 1C	USN	1944	1945
Clarence		Slusher	Tech. 5	USA	1942	1945
Frank	B.	Slusher	PVT	AAF	1941	1945
Henry	M.	Slusher	PVT	USA	1919	1920
Joe	Tom	Slusher	MM3	USN	1951	1955
Carl	B.	Sluss	2nd LT	USA	1942	1943
Lonnie	Clyde	Sluss	PFC	USA	1952	1954
Morton	F.	Sluss	PVT	USA	1942	1943
James	Gray	Smalley	SN 1C	USNR	1945	1946
Clellie	R.	Smedley	SGT	USAR	1952	1960
Joseph	Clinton	Smedley	PFC	USA	1957	1959
Murlin	C.	Smedley	Tech. 5	USA	1942	1945
Oscar	V.	Smedley	PFC	USA	1936	1947
Ronald	Ray	Smedley	GMGC	USN	1974	1980
William	D.	Smedley	Tech. 5	USA	1941	1944
Billy	L.	Smith	SGT	USA	1942	1945
Charles	Cleveland	Smith	SN	USN	1942	1945
Charles	R.	Smith	CPL	USA	1943	1946
Clifford	S.	Smith	CPL	USAAC	1940	1945
David	Lloyd	Smith	SP 4	USA	1985	1988
Earl		Smith	PFC	USA	1942	1945
Jack	Claborn Lee	Smith	SGT	USA	1949	1952
Jack		Smith	PFC	USA	1941	1945
James	D.	Smith	PVT	USA	1943	1945
James	R.	Smith	SP 4	ANG-Mich.	1968	1974
John	Edward	Smith	CPL	USA	1950	1953
Kevin	Rex	Smith	CPL	USA	1986	1989
Mary		Smith	MAJ	USA	1982	1990
Robert	Talmadge	Smith	CPL	USA	1949	1952
Russell		Smith	PVT	USA	1918	1919
Serl	R.	Smith	PVT	USA	1944	1944

Thomas		Smith	PFC	USA	1942	1945
Edward		Smith, Jr.	SP 5	USA	1964	1967
Johnny	Edward	Snipes	SP 4	USA	1958	1960
Alvin	M.	Sorrell	PFC	USA	1948	1949
Deward	R.	Sorrell	Tech. SGT	USA	1941	1945
Eugene		Sorrell	Cpl	USMC	1951	1959
Herbert	O.	Sorrell	PVT	AAF	1944	1945
Joseph	W.	Sorrell	Tech. 5	USA	1945	1946
Ottis	R.	Sorrell	PVT	USA	1941	1941
Eddie	Dean	Sorrell, Jr.	SGT	USA	1997	2001
Johnny	Mack	Souder	AT 2	USN	1975	1979
Carl	C.	Sparkman	CPL	USA	1945	1947
Clellie	O.	Sparkman	PVT	USA	1942	1943
Garred	Francis	Sparkman	Cpl	USMC	1954	1957
Gerald	Clinton	Sparkman	SGT	USAF	1972	1976
Roy	C.	Sparkman	Tech. 5	USA	1942	1945
Russell		Sparkman	Tech. 5	USA	1941	1945
Charles	E.	Sparks	PFC	USA	1941	1945
Curtis	Eugene	Sparks	SP 4	USA	1980	1984
Edgar		Sparks	Tech. 4	USA	1941	1945
Elbert	G.	Sparks	SSG	USA	1941	1945
Elmer	C"	Sparks	SN 1C	USNR	1945	1946
Franklin	David	Sparks	PVT	USA	1952	1952
Hazel	H.	Sparks	PFC	WAC	1944	1945
Ivan	Denis	Sparks	SN 1C	USNR		1945
Virgil		Sparks	Tech. 4	USA	1942	1945
Willie		Sparks	Tech 5	USA	1941	1945
Levi		Sparks, Jr.	PFC	USA	1946	1949
Norman	David	Spencer	PFC	USMCR	1944	1946
Stanley	Vaughn	Spencer	PFC	USA	1979	1982
James	Douglas	Spencer, Jr.	LCpl	USMC	1992	1995
Gary	Bruce	Spicer	STGSA	USN	1976	1978
John		Spillman	PVT	USA	1917	1920

Steven	August	Sposa	SP 4	USA	1982	1984
Billy	W.	Spurlock	SP 4	USAR		1963
Bobby	Gene	Spurlock	PFC	USA	1957	1959
Larry	Verner	Spurlock	SSG	USA	1964	1968
Avery		Stacy	PVT	USA	1942	1943
Claude	J.	Stacy	PFC	USA	1950	1956
Elmer	P.	Stacy	PFC	USA	1942	1945
Walter	C.	Stacy	PFC	USA	1944	1946
Jessie	E.	Staggs	PVT	USA	1942	1945
Joseph	L.	Staggs	T.SGT	USA	1940	1945
Richard	Sparks	Staggs	A1C	USAF	1952	1954
Charles		Stamm, Jr.	SP 4	USA	1972	1974
Asa	C.	Stamper	SGT	USA	1943	1945
Bennie	H.	Stamper	PFC	AAF	1942	1946
Bennie	W.	Stamper	A1C	USAF	1954	1955
Charles	C.	Stamper	PFC	USA	1946	1947
Claude	Earl	Stamper	SN 1C	USNR	1944	1945
Clayton		Stamper	PVT	USA	1943	1945
Clifford		Stamper	PVT	USA	1918	1918
Harry		Stamper	PFC	USA	1917	1919
James	R.	Stamper	PFC	USA	1946	1947
John	V.	Stamper	SP 5	USA	1956	1962
Kenneth	F.	Stamper	PVT	USA	1943	1945
Lloyd	Dillon	Stamper	TSGT	USAF	1956	1977
Robert	H.	Stamper	PFC	USA	1942	1945
Troy	W.	Stamper	Tech. 5	USA	1943	1945
Van	R.	Stamper	PVT	USA	1942	1945
William	T.	Stamper	PVT	USA	1942	1943
Thomas	Allen	Stanforth	spc	USA	1991	1994
Charles 1969	Franklin	Stansbury	SGT	USA/ARNG		1968
Frank		Stapleton	PFC	USA	1944	1945
Arnold	B.	Staton	PVT	USA	1942	1947

Silas	V.	Staton	PVT	USA	1942	1943
Jesse		Steagall	PVT	USA	1917	1918
Cecil	R.	Stegall	PFC	USA	1942	1944
Curtis	W.	Stegall	PFC	USA	1942	1945
Glenmore		Stegall	Tech. 5	USA	1944	1946
Glen	Elwood	Stephens	SGT	USA	1967	1969
Thomas	W.	Stern	PVT	USA	1972	1973
John	Stephen	Stetler	AB	USAF	1975	1975
Bobbie	Thorman	Stevens	PVT	USA	1951	1954
Charles	Lloyd	Stevens	Field Music 1C	USMC	1943	1946
Delbert		Stevens	PFC	USA	1942	1943
Donald	Barrett	Stevens	SMSgt	USAF	1953	1975
Gary	Wayne	Stevens	SP 4	USA	1965	1967
Harry	L.	Stevens	Cook	USA	1917	1919
James	H.	Stevens	PFC	USA	1941	1943
Jeffery	Andrew	Stevens	CPL	USMC	1984	1988
Jerry	Daniel	Stevens	PFC	USA	1959	1960
Jerry	M.	Stevens	PFC	USA	1941	1945
Jerry	Wayne	Stevens	SGT	USAF	1971	1975
Larry	Joe	Stevens	PVT	USA	1975	1975
Larry		Stevens	PVT	USMCR	1956	1956
Larry	Joe	Stevens	SGT	USAR		1986
Lynden	Morris	Stevens	PFC	USA	1951	1953
Mark	Scott	Stevens	CPT	USA	1994	1997
Murvil		Stevens	SP 4	USA	1968	1969
Norman		Stevens	SGT	USA	1951	1954
Oscar	Wayne	Stevens	SP 5	USA	1967	1969
Phillip	Ray	Stevens	LCpl	USMC	1986	1990
Stanley	Franklin	Stevens	CPL	USA	1952	1954
Stearial		Stevens	T-5	USA	1941	1945
Sterial		Stevens	Tech. 5	USA	1941	1945
Thearl	Denvil	Stevens	SN 1C	USNR	1944	1945
Roger	Logan	Stevens	SPC 5	USA	1968	1969

Thomas		Stevens, Jr.	PFC	USA	1950	1952
Rodney	Joe	Steward	RM 2	USN	1952	1956
Chalmer	H.	Stewart	PFC	USA	1942	1945
Corby		Stewart	PFC	USA	1942	1945
James	M.	Stewart	Tech 5	USA	1943	1946
Jason		Stewart	PVT	USA	1918	1930
Katherine	Anne	Stewart	SGT	USA	1978	1991
Orville		Stewart	PVT	USA	1943	1945
Richard	Wayne	Stewart	PFC	USA	1951	1954
Samuel	Critten	Stewart	SN 1C	USNR	1943	1946
William	Edwin	Stewart	HMC	USN	1942	1971
Elmo		Stigall	PFC	USA	1951	1952
James		Still	TSgt	USAAF	1942	1945
Chester	H.	Stinson	CPL	USA	1918	1919
Harry	L.	Stinson	Tech 4	USA	1943	1945
Howard	Kenneth	Stinson	Fireman 1C	USNR	1944	1946
James	E.	Stinson	SSgt	USAAC	1942	1946
Jessie		Stinson, Jr.	SGT	USA	1958	1964
Robert	W.	Stokes	PFC	USA	1943	1946
Grant	Matthew	Stokley	PFC	USA	1988	1990
Hubert	E.	Stoll	SGT	USAFR	1946	1950
Carl		Stone	Tech. 4	USA	1943	1946
David		Stone	A1C	USAF	1961	1965
Richard	T.	Stone	PFC	USA	1944	1949
Walden	Lee	Stone	SP 4	USA	1971	1973
John		Story	PVT	USA		1973
Claude	Allie	Strange	SP 5	USA	1968	1970
Grant		Strange	PFC	USA	1940	1965
Bradley		Stump	PVT	USA	1939	1942
Vincent		Sturfill	PVT	USA	1941	1941
Andy		Sturgill	PVT	USA	1918	1919
James	P.	Sturgill	PFC	USA	1939	1945
Paul	W.	Sturgill	MSG	USA	1949	1975

Vincent		Sturgill	PVT	USA	1942	1943
W.	E.	Sturgill	PFC	USA	1943	1945
Wayne	L.	Sturgill	Tech. 5	USA	1941	1945
Woodrow		Sturgill	SSG	USA	1970	1975
Dallas	Thurman	Swetnam	MSgt	USAF	1953	1973
Ben	F.	Swim	Mech.	USA	1918	1919
Clinton	Carl	Swim	SN 1C	USN	1946	1948
Lee	R.	Swim	SGT	USA	1942	1946
Manzel	Clayton	Swim	Coxswain	USNR	1943	1946
Ralph	R.	Swim	SGT	USA	1942	1945
Steve	Loren	Swim	SGT	USA	1971	1977
William	Thomas	Swim	LCpl	USMC	1956	1959
Burley	Thomas Cecil	Switzer	SPC 4	USA	1966	1968
Charles	W.	Switzer	PFC	USA	1942	1945
Chester	R.	Switzer	PFC	AAC	1942	1945
John	R.	Switzer	PFC	USA	1942	1945
Aaron	N.	Tackett	PFC	USAAC	1942	1946
Abner	C.	Tackett	PFC	USA	1918	1918
Bucky	Roger	Tackett	TSgt.	USAF	1957	1977
Charles	R.	Tackett	Tech. 5	USA	1942	1945
De	Forest	Tackett	PVT	USA	1949	1949
Elvis	C.	Tackett	PFC	USAR		1967
Ernest	A.	Tackett	SGT	USA	1943	1945
Ernie	J.	Tackett	SGT	USA	1943	1949
Harlen	B.	Tackett	PFC	USA	1942	1945
Harvey	S.	Tackett	MSG	USA	1944	1946
Heraldon	L.	Tackett	SSG	USA	1942	1945
James	Robert	Tackett	SN 1C	USNR	1942	1945
Lillian		Tackett	AviaStoreKp. 3C	USN	1944	1946
Vernon	Webster	Tackett	SMSgt	USAF/ANG	1956	1986
William	Clinton	Tackitt	CPT	USAR	1974	1977
David	Willard	Tandy	SP 4	USA	1975	1978
David	Lynn	Taylor	SGT	USAF	1974	1980

Ronnie	Estill	Taylor	SGT	USA	1978	1985
Roscoe		Taylor	CPL	USAAF	1941	1945
Willis	L.	Taylor	CPL	USA	1950	1954
Arthur		Templeman	PVT	USA	1918	1919
Billy	E.	Templeman	A 2C	USAF	1956	1960
Cletis	E.	Templeman	PFC	USA	1945	1946
Ivan	Clayton	Templeman	SN 1C	USNR	1943	1946
Paul	Edward	Templeman		USAF	1943	1960
Glendon		Terrell	PFC	USA	1945	1946
Paul	H.	Terry	Tech. 5	USA	1941	1946
Jon	Scott	Thatcher	MS 2	USN	1984	1989
Albert	K.	Thomas	Tech 5	USA	1944	1947
Arthur	S.	Thomas	PVT	AAF	1945	1946
Carl	E.	Thomas	PFC	USA	1942	1945
Earl	Clinton	Thomas	MSG	USA	1952	1958
Earnest	Eugene	Thomas	PFC	USA	1957	1959
Eugene	G.	Thomas	PFC	USA	1918	1918
Gilbert		Thomas	T 5	USA	1940	1945
James	B.	Thomas	PFC	USA	1939	1945
James	C.	Thomas	PFC	USMC	1951	1952
James	E.	Thomas	PFC	USA	1941	1945
James	H.	Thomas	PVT	USA	1941	1945
John	Carl	Thomas	Soundman 2C	USN	1940	1945
John	Paul	Thomas	PVT	USAF	1951	1952
John		Thomas	SN	USNR		1975
Leslie	Carl	Thomas	CM 2	USN	1968	1970
Norman	E.	Thomas	TSgt.	AAF	1941	1945
Raymond		Thomas	SSG	USA	1943	1946
Ruben	Franklin Delano	Thomas	MSC	USN	1967	1989
Scott	H.	Thomas	PVT	USA	1898	1899
Sigmon	Alan	Thomas	SPC	USA	1989	1993
Willard	R.	Thomas	CPL	USA	1941	1942
Willie	Alen	Thomas	PFC	USA	1950	1952

Clyde	A.	Thomas, Jr.	AN	USAF	1980	1984
Bill	E.	Thompson	CPL	USA	1942	1946
Charles	B.	Thompson	1st Lt.	USAF	1954	1956
Clarence	H.	Thompson	F 3	USN	WW I	
Dan	R.	Thompson	PFC	USA	1946	1947
Dexter	Darrell	Thompson	SP 5	USA	1972	1975
Donald		Thompson	SPC 4	USA	1958	1961
Earnest	V.	Thompson	PVT	USA	1944	1944
Frank		Thompson	CPL	USA	1918	1919
Fred	Ervin	Thompson	SN 2C	USNR	1944	1944
Harvey		Thompson		4 KY INF	1898	1898
James	Rae	Thompson	ElectMt. 2C	USN		1945
James	V.	Thompson	SGT	USA	1941	1945
James	H.	Thompson	PVT	USA	1917	1919
Jesse	C.	Thompson	CPL	USA	1903	1911
John	R.D.	Thompson	PVT	USA	1945	1948
Johnie	R.	Thompson	SSG	USA	1943	1945
Lowell	DeWayne	Thompson	LCpl	USMC	1983	1987
Melvin	D.	Thompson	PFC	USA	1942	1946
Olive	P.	Thompson	PVT	USA	1942	1945
Paul	David	Thompson	A1C	USAF	1955	1959
Richard	Glennis	Thompson	Sgt	USAF	1969	1971
Richard	Perry	Thompson	2nd Lt.	USMC	1967	1974
Verless	P.	Thompson	PFC	USA	1944	1945
Virgil	A.	Thompson	PFC	USA	1947	1948
William	C.	Thompson	PFC	USA	1943	1945
William	Allen	Thompson	CPL	USA	1952	1954
James	Virgil	Thompson, Jr.	SP 4	USA	1969	1971
Homer	R.	Thurman	PFC	USA	1944	1947
Homer	Russell	Thurman	SFC	USA	1949	1969
William	H.	Thurman	Tech. 5	USA	1942	1945
Melissa	Nadine	Tierney	PFC	USA	1990	1993
Albert		Todd, Jr.	AN	USN	1951	1955

Charles	E.	Toler	PFC	USA	1946	1948
Charles	Edward	Toler	PFC	USA	1960	1967
Danny	Edward	Toler	SP 4	USA	1969	1975
Gary	Lee	Toler	SP 4	USA	1971	1974
Clinton	H.	Tolliver	PVT	USA	1901	1903
Joseph	Harlan	Tolliver	Cpl	USMC	1941	1945
Hendrix		Tolliver, Jr.	A1C	USAF	1950	1954
William	B.	Tomlinson	PFC	USA	1942	1946
Elden	K.	Tracy	PFC	USA	1941	1945
Beauford		Trent	PFC	USA	1945	
Cecil		Trent	CPL	USA	1953	1955
Corbia		Trent	PFC	USA	1945	1947
Denville	Ray	Trent	A1C	USAF	1952	1956
Earsel		Trent	PVT	USA	1942	1943
Henry	H.	Trent	PVT	USA	1942	1944
Hobert		Trent	PFC	USA	1942	1947
Hubert	Ernest	Trent	1st Lt.	USAF	1942	1962
Lenard	L.	Trent	PFC	AAF	1943	1945
Leonard		Trent	SPC	USA	1962	1964
Omer	L.	Trent	Tech. 4	USA	1942	1945
Wyatt		Trent	Tech 5	USA	1945	1946
Herbert	C.	Triplett	1st LT	USA	1945	1946
David	A.	Trumbo	PVT	USA	1941	1942
Grover		Trumbo	SGT	USA	1941	1944
Henry	C.	Trumbo	SGT	USA	1939	1943
John	P.	Trumbo	SSG	USA	1942	1945
William	Randall	Tufts	SP 5	USA	1963	1965
Audrey	K.	Turner	PVT	USA	1941	1944
Bert		Turner	PVt	USA	1942	1943
Carl		Turner	CPL	USA	1942	1945
Charles	E.	Turner	TSgt.	AAF	1942	1945
Clarence	E.	Turner	CPL	USA	1940	1943
Clayton	Ray	Turner	Av. Mach.Mt.	USN	1942	1943

Eugene	A.	Turner	Tech. 4	USA	1946	1947
Michael	Elwood	Turner	Capt.	USMC	1968	1974
Raymond	C.	Turner	Tech. 4	USA	1942	1945
Roy	M.	Turner	Tech. 5	USA	1942	1946
Leroy	Joseph	Ulrey	LTC	ARNGUS	1933	1964
Harold	Levant	Utterback	QM 1C	USN	1942	1945
Phillip	William	Van Kersen	HM 2	USN	1967	1970
William	Roger	Varney II	A1C	USAF	1989	1992
Sandra	L.	Vaughn	SPC	USA	1988	1992
Glenn	Wells	Vencill	PNC	USN	1938	1958
Kenneth	McKee	Vencill II	ETCM(SW)	USN	1961	1991
Victor	A.	Venetozzi	SSG	USA	1939	1945
Lois	Lee	Vice	PFC	USA	1981	1982

Kenneth M. Vencill II, ETCM (SW), Navy, 1961-91.

David	Wickliffe	Victor, Jr.	MAJ	USAFR	1979	1983
Elwood	T.	Waddell	CPL	USA	1945	1950
Roger	Allen	Waddell	SP 4	USA	1969	1970
Ronnie	Gayle	Waddell	SP 4	USA	1984	1988
Talmadge	Elwayne	Waddell	SP 4	USA	1957	1959
Bennie	Harold	Wages	SP 4	USA	1960	1963
Charlie		Wages	PVT	USA	1917	1919
Eugene	H.	Wages	PVT	USA	1939	1940
Leonard	Roy	Wages	SN 2C	USN	1944	1945
Ralph	Eugene	Wagoner	PFC	USA	1952	1954
Ronald	Lee	Walke	1LT	USA	1966	1968
Robert	K.	Walker	PFC	USA	1943	1945
Austin		Wallace	PVT	USA	1943	1946
Clifton	H.	Wallace	SP 4	USAR	1959	1965
David	Frank	Wallace	SN 1C	USNR	1944	1946
Ernest	C.	Wallace	PVT	USA	1943	1944
Everett	Russell	Wallace	SPC	USA	1987	1989
James	Edward	Wallace	PFC	USA	1952	1954
Junior		Wallace	PVT	USA	1950	1952
Kenneth	Norman	Wallace	PVT	USA	1962	1962
Linvill	Ray	Wallace	SPC 4	USAE	1966	1972
Ora	Vernon	Wallace	Fireman 1C	USNR	1943	1945
Watha		Wallace	PVT	USA	1942	1942
Ray	M.	Walters	CPL	USA	1946	1947
Henry		Walton	PVT	USA	1918	1919
Johnny	H.	Walton	PVT	USN	1952	1954
Roy	Gaines	Walton	SA	USN	1951	1951
George	Edward	Waltz	SN 1C	USNR	1944	1946
Luster	V.	Waltz	PFC	USA	1942	1945
Don	Madison	Ward	SP 3	USA	1953	1955
Edward		Ward	Tech. 4	USA	1927	1945
Elisha	F.	Ward	PFC	USA	1957	1959
Leo	W.	Ward	Tech. 5	USA	1946	1947

Les		Ward	PFC	USA	1918	1919
Arnold	E.	Warren	SGT	USA	1943	1946
David	S.	Warren	CPL	USMC	1987	1993
Harold	L.	Warren	Tech. 4	USA	1945	1946
Raliegh		Warren	Tech. 5	USA	1942	1945
William	Chester	Warren	SN 1C	USNR	1943	1946
Clarence	O.	Watson	PFC	USA	1943	1946
Ishmail		Watson	PFC	AAF	1942	1945
John		Watson	Water Tender 3C	USNR	1943	1946
Lawrence		Watson	SN 2C	USNR		1945
Proctor	V.	Watson	PFC	USA	1945	1946
Vinson	Alan	Watts	PFC	USA	1953	1955
Dorsey	Lawrence	Weddington	Mach.Mt. 1C	USN	1942	1945
Felix	D.	Wellman	SGT	USA	1917	1919
Robert	S	Wellman	PVT	USAAC	1943	1946
Felix	D.	Wellman, Jr.	1st LT	AAF	1942	1945
Feliz	Dennis	Wellman, Jr.	Capt.	USAF	1951	1958
Bobby	Lee	Wells	CPL	USA	1950	1951
Charles	L.	Wells	PFC	USA	1945	1946
Drexal	R.	Wells	SSG	USA	1941	1945
Forest	Eli	Wells	MotorMchMt. 3C	USN	1944	1945
James	Clay	Wells	SPC 5	USA	1958	1962
James	Milford	Wells	CPL	USA	1945	1946
Lonzo	Lee	Wells	Cpl	USMC	1972	1976
Manning		Wells	MotorMchMt 3C	USN	1941	1944
Paul	M.	Wells	PFC	USA	1945	1946
Walter	S.	Wells	SFC	USA	1918	1919
Byron	E.	Wentz	1st Lt.	USAAF	1944	1945
James	Patrick	Wesley	PFC	USMC	1943	1946
Robert	P.	Wesley	Sgt	AAF	1943	1946
Redwine		West	PVT	USA	1942	1943
Robert	Lennard	Wetherbee	TSgt	USAF	1955	1975
Milburn	R.	Wheeler	Sgt	USAAC	1942	1945

Harold White, Pfc., Army, 1951-53.

Reginald	Kenneth	Wheeler	SGT	USAF	1971	1976
Samuel	E.	Wheeler	PFC	USA	1942	1945
Charley	F.	White	PFC	USA	1942	1945
Charlie	B.	White	SFC	USA	1949	1952
Chester	A.	White	PVT	USA	1942	1945
Chester	R.	White	AA	USN	1955	1959
Claude	Jessie	White	T.SGT	USMC	1942	1945
David	T.	White	SP 4	USAR		1975
Donald	Leo	White	A1C	USAF	1954	1958
Forest	Wayne	White	SN 2C	USNR	1944	1945
George	E.	White	TSgt	AAF	1942	1945
Harold	Lee	White	PFC	USA	1951	1953
James	D.	White	PFC	USA	1943	1945
James	H.	White	SFC	USA	1951	1953
John	E.	White	PVT	USAAC	1939	1946

Lloyd	Dewitt	White	DFC	USN	1957	1980
Michael	Todd	White	Cpl	USMC	1973	1976
Paul	J.	White	PVT	USA	1941	1942
Raymond	Edward	White	CPL	USA	1951	1953
Ryan	Scott	White	Cpl	USMC	1992	1996
T.D.		White	CPL	USA	1940	1945
Watt		White	SM 3C	USN	1943	1945
Wendill	Scottie	White	SP 4	USA	1971	1977
William	D.	White	Tech. 5	USA Sig.C.	1943	1946
Edward		Whitt	PVT	USA	1917	1920
James	Robert	Whitt	SP 4	USA	1965	1967
Louied	Ernest	Whitt	SSgt	USAF	1969	1973
Minton	Edward	Whitt	CPL	USA	1951	1953
Richard	M.	Whitt	A2C	USAF	1955	1960
Rodney	Wayne	Whitt	PVT	USA	1992	1993
Benjamin		Whittingham	PVT	USA	1945	1945
Kendel		Wierman	Fireman 2C	USN	1918	1921
Vernon	L.	Wierman	PVT	USA	1942	1944
George	W.	Wiggins, Jr.	SSG	USA	1942	1945
Allie	Wilburn	Williams	GM 2C	USN	1944	1946
Angela	Dawn	Williams	SGT	USAF	1978	1982
Audrey	Lee	Williams	PFC	USMC	1944	1946
Clayton	C.	Williams	PFC	USA	1947	1948
Cleo	Cottle	Williams	MMM3C	USNR	1943	1945
Ernest		Williams	Cpl	USMC	1943	1946
Hobart	R.	Williams	Tech. 4	USA	1942	1945
James	Albert	Williams	PFC	USA	1950	1952
James	Harrison	Williams	A2C	USAF	1959	1961
James	L.	Williams	PVT	USA	1942	1942
Kenneth	D.	Williams	PFC	USA	1942	1945
Leonard	L.	Williams	PFC	USA	1944	1946
Morris	Garner	Williams	A2C	USAF	1953	1959
Murvell	Ray	Williams	SP 4	USA	1962	1965

Oakie		Williams	PFC	USA	1944	1946
Oscar	Clayton	Williams	SP 4	USA	1958	1964
Raleigh	E.	Williams	SGT			1946
Randolph	T.	Williams	BoatswainsMate	USNR	1942	1945
Rufus		Williams	SFC	USA	1971	1991
Samuel	L. D.	Williams	QM 2C	USN	1941	1945
Troy	W.	Williams	Tech. 4	USA	1942	1945
Ward		Williams	Tech. 5	USA	1942	1945
Will	E.	Williams	PVT	USA	1943	1943
Richard	Ward	Williams, Jr.	SGT	USAF	1971	1976
Paul	Mackie	Williamson	CPT	USA	1943	1968
Bennie	J.	Wilson	SP 5	USAR	1971	1972
Burnice	R.	Wilson	PVT	USA	1944	1945

Lester Lee Lewis, T/5, USA, 1942-1945.

Cheryl	Lynn	Wilson	A 1C	USAF	1985	1988
John	W.	Wilson	PFC	USA	1942	1946
Marvin	L.	Wilson	PVT	USA	1947	1947
Mary	Ann	Wilson	SP 4	USA	1958	1962
Oliver		Wilson	PFC	USA	1941	1941
Marvin		Wilson, Jr.	Mailman 3C	USNR	1944	1946
Dennie	Leon	Winburn	MSgt	USAF	1963	1983
Tammie	Denise	Winburn	AB	USAF	1984	1986
Roy	J.	Winkleman	PFC	USA	1943	1946
Eva	Marie	Winkler	SN 2C	USN	1943	1944
George	Gammon	Witcher	PFC	USAR	1958	1962
Delmer	Ray	Withrow	SFC	USA	1973	1978
Herbert		Withrow	PVT	USA	1918	1919
Jack	Allen	Withrow	PVT	USA	1972	1972
Roy	E.	Witt	1st Lt.	USMCR	1945	1949
William	L.	Wolfenbarger	Cpl	USMC		1979
Virgil	H.	Wolfford	PVT	USA	1918	1919
Earl	Clinton	Wood III	MAJ	USA	1981	1991
Donald	Redmond	Woodall	Cpl	USMC	1960	1964
Clifford	Denver	Wootan	PFC	USA	1953	1955
Clyde		Workman	PFC	USA	1943	1946
Denzill		Workman	SP 4	USA	1959	1962
Omar	Michael	Workman	SP 4	USA	1967	1968
Robert	W.	Workman	Ap. SN	USN		1945
Virgil		Workman	PFC	USMC	1945	1945
Curtis	R.	Worthington	SSG	USA	1945	1947
Calvin	F.	Wright	Tech. 5	USA	1943	1946
Carl		Wright	PFC	AAF	1942	1945
George	T.	Wright	PVT	USA	1941	1945
Sam		Wright	PFC	USA	1942	1945
Wade		Wright	PFC	USA	1917	1919
Cecil	K.	Younce	SP 5	USAR	1964	1970
Don	Bruce	Young	A2C	USAF	1955	1958

Jack Kegley, AM/2, USN, 1942-1946.

Addendun to Appendix 2/21/03

Earl	R	Alexander	SP4	USA	1959	1961
Stefan		Armstrong	AW2	USN	1979	1983
Thomas	L	Armstrong	SP4	USA	1970	1973
William	G	Bailey	FN	USN	1952	1956
Benjamin	E	Baldridge	PVT	USA	1944	1945
Elijah		Bentley	SP4	USA	1957	1960
Ernest		Bentley	CPL	USA	1952	1953
Junior	L	Bentley	PFC	USAR	1951	1960
Herschel	N	Brown	PFC	USA	1943	1945

Filmore L. Jones, CPL, AAC, 1942-1946.

Dellmer	T	Buckner	PFC	USAR	1958	1959
John	P	Burton	SPC	USA	1971	1991
Elmer		Burton, Jr.	SP4	USA	1965	1967
Ronald	W	Buttry	PFC	USA	1956	1962
James	M	Carpenter	SP5	USA	1966	1968
Thomas	L	Carroll	LCPL	USMC	1968	1970
Gary	W	Casper	CPL	USMC	1968	1969
Lee	N	Casper	PVT	USMC	1945	1946
Lonnie		Castle	SP4	USA	1962	1965
Robert	C	Caudill	SMSGT	USAF	1979	1992
Henry	A	Caudill, Jr.	SP4	USA	1970	1971
Woody	V	Clark	MSGT	USAF	1967	1988
Donald		Click	SP4	USA	1965	1967
Glenn	E	Cline	LTJG	USN	1971	1973
Fred	S	Collins, Jr.	PFC	USAF	1946	1947

Charles	R	Conn	MAJ	USA	1976	1991
Charles	C	Cornett	SP2	USA	1953	1956
Arthur		Cox	SP5	USAR	1964	
Clyde		Cox	CPL	USA	1943	1951
Eliga		Cox	TSGT	USAAC	1942	1945
Charles	D	Crawford	CPL	USA	1962	
Marland	L	Crawford	T4	USA	1943	1946
Gary	W	Crisp	CSM	USA	1968	1995
Vernon	R	Cundiff	A1C	USAF	1956	1960
Claude	P	Day	SP4	USA	1968	1969
Robert	J	Delashmit	PVT	USA	1994	1995
Eldon	R	Dillon	SP4	USAR	1958	
Dewey	J	Duff	WT3	USN	1944	1946
Sunny	C	Dulin	SP4	USA	1959	1962
Joseph	R	Evans	T4	USA	1942	1946
Ronald	L	Evans	EMFN	USN	1949	1953
Lawrence	D	Fannin	SN	USN	1943	1945
Francis	G	Fogle	1LT	USMC	1942	1956
Philip	W	Fraley	SP4	USAR	1966	1972
James	G	Fultz	SSG	USA	1974	1994
Kenneth	A	Fultz	SP4	USAR	1968	1972
Charles		Ginter	PVT	USA	1964	1965
Ricky	E	Glover	SGT	USA	1983	1997
James	A	Gray	SFC	USA		
Michael	A	Gulley	SP4	USAR	1968	1974
Floyd	E	Hall	CPL	USA	1953	1955
Palmer	L	Hall	PFC	USA	1943	1945
Thomas	R	Hamilton	SP4	USA	1968	1970
William	T	Hamilton	2LT	USAR	1976	1978
Lonnie	D	Hamlin	SSG	USA	1977	1993
Harlan	T	Hamm	MNC	USN	1937	1953
Willie	I	Hamm	CPO	USN	1936	1960
Clyde	E	Hayes	SP4	USA	1975	1978

Benjamin	E	Hays	QM3	USN	1988	1992
Jack	W	Helwig	PFC	USMC	1917	1919
Jack	W	Helwig, Jr.	T4	USA	1942	1943
Leroy		Hill	EM2	USN	1942	1945
Arthur	W	Hogge	CMS	USAF	1944	1971
Marvin		Howard	SGT	USA	1969	1970
Everett		Isaac	PFC	USA	1943	1945
Marvin	J	Jackson	SP3	USA	1955	1957
Harvey	L	Jent	Cook	USA	1917	1918
Harvey	L	Jent, Jr.	CPL	USMC	1963	
Carl	I	Johnson	SP5	USA	1968	1974
Ellis	R	Johnson	GMG3	USN	1983	1987
Ernie	L	Johnson	PVT	USA	1969	1969
Kenneth	C	Johnson	AA	USN	1955	1959
Ernest		Jordan	PFC	USA	1944	1946
Dale	E	Kelsey	SP4	USA	1969	1971
Donna	J	Kirkwood	SP4	USA	1988	1990
Jared	D	Kissick		USA	1996	1998
Chester	V	Kitchen	PVT	USA	1942	1943
Andy		Lambert, Jr.	PVT	USA	1944	1945
James	V	Lewis	TSGT	USA	1951	1971
Elmer	E	Long	SP4	USA	1962	1965
Billy	R	Lowe	SP4	USA	1965	1967
Dempsey	E	Lowe	SP5	USAR		1974
Joseph	E	Macke	PFC	USMCR	1955	1963
Tilman		McBrayer	A3C	USAF	1955	1959
Marlin	B	McDaniel	PFC	USA	1986	1986
Patrick	R	McDaniel	SRA	USAF	1973	1977
Horace	D	McKinzie	PFC	USMCR	1956	1958
Charles	E	Meade	SGT	USMC	1965	1969
Billy	R	Messer	SP4	USA	1961	1963
Claudie	A	Messer	MSGT	USA	1976	1997
Max	A	Middleton	CPL	USA	1951	1953

Green	R	Miller	PFC	USA	1957	1959
Wayne	E	Moore	SSG	USAR	1961	1966
Wayne	E	Moore	SP4	USA	1960	1962
Clifford	H	Muse	SP4	USAR		1964
Michael	A	Ockerman	2LT	USA	1989	1989
Billy	J	Oney	SP4	USAR		1967
Bobby	R	Oney	A1C	USAF	1954	1957
Brandin	K	Perkins	EC2	USN	1996	2001
Dwight	R	Pierce	PFC	USA	1944	1945
Arthur		Plank	PVT	USA	1942	1945
William	R	Poston	SR	USNR	1962	1963
Johnny		Primeau, Jr.	CPT	USA	1980	1986
Timmy		Puckett	PVT	USA	1988	1988

Ted L. Crosthwait, CPT, AAC, 1942-1946.

Carrel	E	Reynolds	MSGT	USAF	1975	1992
Ottis		Roark	SSGT	USA	1942	1945
J	L	Ryan	LtCol	USA		
Brian	W	Skaggs	PFC	USAR	1991	1991
Murlin	C	Smedley	T4	USA	1942	1945
Lester		Smith	SP5	USA	1968	1970
Timmy	D.	Smith, Jr.	SPC	USAR	1992	1996
Billy	L	Sorrell	SN	USN	1952	1954
Howard	A	Spurlock	CPL	USA	1918	1919
Norman	S	Stamper	USN	1943	1946	
Glenn	E	Stephens	SGT	USA	1967	1969
David	A	Stevens	SGT	USAF	1965	1969
Donald	L	Stevens	PFC	USA	1957	1959
Gregory	D	Stevens	PFC	USMC	1968	1969
James	L	Stevens	COL	USA	1968	2002
Mark	S	Stevens	MAJ	USA	1994	1997
Cecil	H	Stewart	PFC	USA	1943	1945
Donnie	H	Stewart	A1C	USAF	1963	1967
Roy	E	Stewart		USA	1957	1963
Arthur	L	Stewart, Jr.	T5	USA	1942	1946
Adam	B	Surface	SP4	USA	1994	1998
Eugene	G	Thomas	PFC	USAF	1946	1949
Willis	D	Tiller	SP5	USA	1966	1972
Wendall	L	Trent	SSG	USA	1989	1999
Larry	G	Turner	SGT	USAR	1971	
Clifton	H	Wallace	SP4	USA	1959	1961
Glenvill		Wallace	PVT	USA	1945	1946
Robert	I	Wallace	PVT	USA	1945	1947
Wendell	L	Watson	IC3	USNR	1961	1967
Norman	L	Wells	PVT	USA	1898	1899
David	T	White	SP4	USA	1969	1971

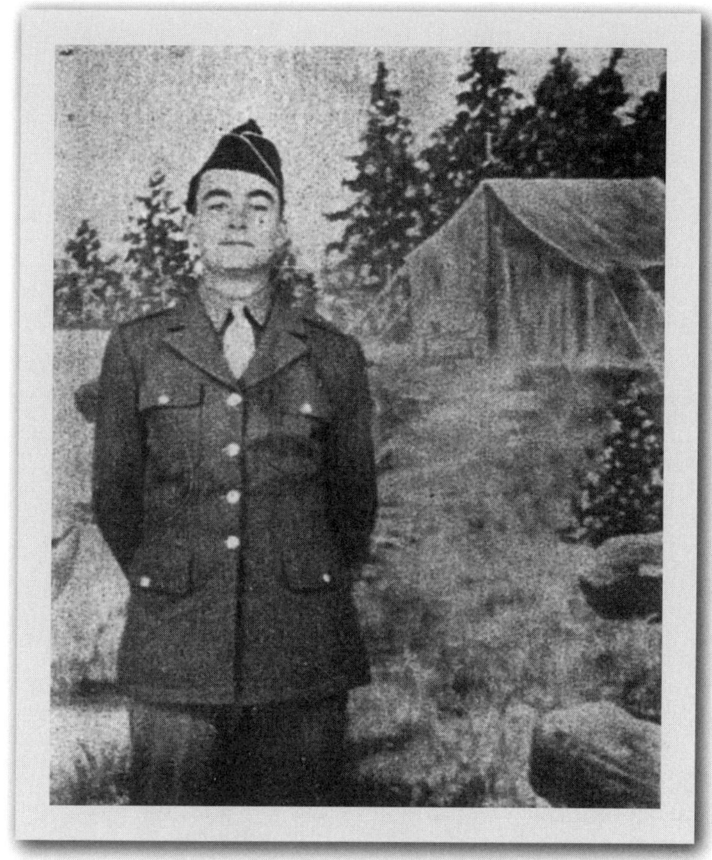

Kenneth Crisp, CPL, USA, 1944-1946.

Roy	A	White	A1C	USAF		1976
Lanny	J	Williams	SSGT	USAF	1968	1972
Bennie	J	Wilson	SP5	USAR	1966	1968
M	L	Withrow	AD3	USN	1951	1955
Barbara	A	Wood	DPSN	USN	1979	1985
Clifford	D	Wooten	PFC	USA	1953	1955
Herman		Workman	CPL	USAR	1953	1961

James D. White, PFC, USA, 1943-1945.

George Burgess, FL/O,
Army Air Corp., 1944-1946.

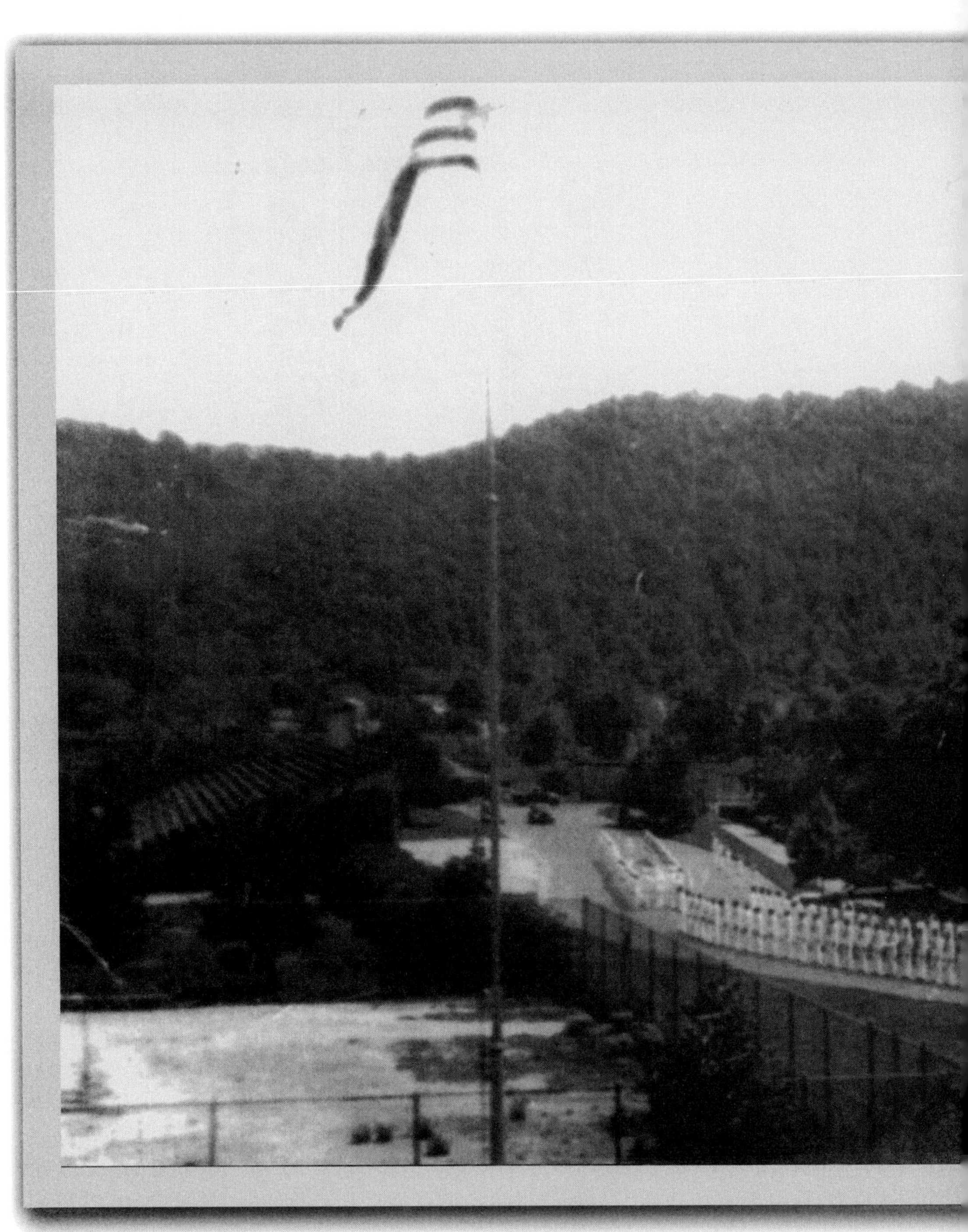

Revelie at Morehead State College in 1944. Up to 600 sailors were enrolled in a Navy electricity course each quarter during WWII.

Jack Ellis, Cpl., Army Air Corps, 1944-1947.